OPPOSITES: SIDE BY SIDE

OPPOSITES: SIDE BY SIDE

THE RED
by ŞANAR YURDATAPAN

THE GREEN
by ABDURRAHMAN DİLİPAK

Foreword by ARON AJI
Afterword by JONATHAN SUGDEN
Translated from the Turkish by İSFENDIYAR ERALP

GEORGE BRAZILLER PUBLISHER
New York

Originally published in Turkey under the title
Kırmızı İle Yeşil/Yeşil İle Kırmızı by Aykırı

First published in the United States of America in 2003 by George Braziller, Inc.

For information, please address the publisher:

GEORGE BRAZILLER, INC.
171 Madison Avenue
New York, NY 10016

LIBRARY OF CONGRESS CATALOGING-IN-PUBLICATION DATA:
Yurdatapan, Sanar.
    [Kırmızı İle Yeşil, Yeşil İle Kırmızı. English]
    Opposites : side by side / The red by Sanar Yurdatapan, The green by
Abdurrahman Dilipak ; foreword by Aron Aji ; afterword by Jonathan Sugden ;
translated from the Turkish by Isfendiyar Eralp.
        p. cm.
    ISBN 0-8076-1520-X
    1. Islam—Turkey. 2. Atheism—Turkey. 3. Freedom of religion—Turkey.
4. Freedom of speech—Turkey. 5. Human rights—Turkey. I. Dilipak, Abdurrahman,
1949- II. Title.
    BP63.T8Y8713 2003
    306.6'97'09561—dc21

                                                            2003052423

Design by Sara E. Stemen

Printed and bound in the United States of America.

FIRST EDITION

CONTENTS

FOREWORD

"Difference of opinion in the community is a token of divine mercy."
—7th Article of the *Fiqh Akbar*, by Abu Hanifa[1]

I recently attended an interfaith peace gathering at which clergy from various faith traditions took turns stressing the beliefs that bond us together. Moved by the hopeful and elegant messages that echoed one another, I still couldn't resist noting to myself that the map of common ground delineated by the speakers appeared discouragingly small, set as it was against the diligently underplayed yet no less deeply felt geography of tormenting differences that awaited us outside the chapel doors. Our peaceable island rejoiced in the same glow of mercy, the same loving smile evident on the myriad faces of our one same god, and it allowed no room for the real, obstinate—even often valid—disagreements in the way we, the diverse peoples made in one divine image, have tended to perceive, speak of, and treat one another. Our peace demanded assent, acquiescence. True, it promised calm, healing, a fellowship of kindness and civility, but I also felt impoverished in the process. Human—and divine—richness depends on difference, superabundant difference. We argue, hurt, fight but also seek to make peace, heal, and love on account of our differences. Differences make dissent possible, and dissent is the means by which we test, temper, and attune our respective truths, which otherwise lose their timbre in the damp air of unqualified assent. To imagine the elusive outlines of comprehensive peace—not just an island but a world entire—we need to brave the difficult realm of our differences, learn to face and understand them, learn to listen at least as much as we want to be heard.

The task has often been difficult and unsettling, and made all the more so for us—the inhabitants of the largest self-professed peaceable island

---

1. The *Fiqh Akbar* means "the greatest fiqh" and is generally used in reference to several collections of canononical creeds, the most famous of which is by Abu Hanifa (d.767 C.E.).

called America—since 9/11, when our truths were grimly challenged, and we have grown weary of differences. "Why do they hate us?" The question has reverberated often, but the answers offered have just as often been self-defensive, self-affirming, falling short of the honest accuracy and understanding possible only when we listen deeply to voices of opposition. Difficult and unsettling, yes, but also indispensable.

Opposites: Side by Side, by Şanar Yurdatapan and Abdurrahman Dilipak, is an invitation to such listening. A side-by-side presentation of the views of a staunch, secularist atheist and a devout Muslim, the book is a formidable defense of freedom of expression—which, without deep listening and regard for difference, tends to yield little other than noisy dissonance. *Opposites: Side by Side* is about Turkey and its less-than-consistent history of secularism, but it is more than a local critique and call for reform in a particular country, since the authors' strikingly divergent intellectual orientations are at the forefront of their project. In two sets of corresponding essays, Yurdatapan and Dilipak articulate their positions on topics of wide-ranging existential and political relevance: human origin (evolution/creation), existence vs. afterlife, ethics vs. religion, scholasticism vs. theology, reason and free will, faith and politics, holy war, gender roles, ethnic conflict, East/West, human rights, freedom of thought and of conscience, and so on. Unburdened by the need to change the other's mind or to prove himself right, each author writes with equal measures of candor and conviction.

Yurdatapan's atheism is clearly the result of patient and deep introspection, and his language is free of arrogance or mockery. Especially poignant are his descriptions of his conversations about life and God with his children; in these passages, Yurdatapan is touchingly human and lyrical. His political views bear the credibility of experience, his long struggle for human rights in Turkey. Yurdatapan demonstrates a keen sense of the republic's history, weighing its laudable original libertarian aspirations against its failures in practice, in order to accentuate in that history not the intractable causes of defeat but the certain potential for reform. A 'devout patriot' true to the literal meaning of his name, Yurdatapan speaks with justified reproach about the state of civil liberties in Turkey, but he also speaks with unflinching passion and urgency about what his country can be.

In his turn, the theologian Abdurrahman Dilipak also embraces the secular principles of the republic and advocates human rights without compromise. Dilipak stresses the reformist origins of Islam and the central-ity of reason, individual confession, education, and, yes, democracy regarding Islam. In his set of essays, Islam comes across as clearly compati-ble with the structures and principles of a modern state. His knowledge of the Qur'an is deep and nuanced, and he reads the key precepts of the faith compellingly, progressively, and by steadfastly resisting the self-serving, reductive orthodoxist claims of self-appointed religious leaders. His com-mentary on Islam should definitely serve as an antidote to the mispercep-tions that have sadly come to define Islam in the West.

Neither of the authors a stranger to persecution, and both recognized by Human Rights Watch for their activism, Yurdatapan and Dilipak offer a compelling panorama of the contradictions that permeate modern Turkey's secular history. Their accounts challenge the fear-born political expedience of depersonalizing categories—i.e., religious, ideological, ethnic—and rationing individual freedoms according to affiliation. (Growing up Jewish in Turkey, I had at times thought that the secular republic protected my freedoms more than it did those of devout Muslims like Dilipak, or leftist radicals like Yurdatapan.) The two authors speak instead as *individuals* and for *individual* freedoms, insisting on a vision of society that fearlessly accommodates difference as a matter of its respect for the dignity of the individual. As Yurdatapan puts it: "On the face of this earth, many nations, and in each, millions of people. Let us allow each one to cultivate freely his or her own identity, his or her own individuality. Our world is like a flower garden of many cultures, many colors. Let us preserve it so we can live in this garden the way we want and the way we believe."

Opposites: Side by Side is a powerful testament to friendship culti-vated in civil disagreement based on mature intellectual positions rather than on bargained-down, diluted personal values. We may quarrel with some of the claims of either author, but therein lies the book's achievement: *Opposites: Side by Side* envisages—and invites us to participate in—the kind of peace that is possible through listening to and understanding our adversaries. What good is freedom of expression otherwise?

Aron Aji
Butler University, Indianapolis

ACKNOWLEDGMENTS

Turning *Kırmızı İle Yeşil/Yeşil İle Kırmızı*—the original Turkish version of this book—into *Opposites: Side by Side* would not have been possible without the supreme efforts of several people. Aron Aji's constant advice and knowledge were invaluable from acquisition to publication, and this sensitivity is reflected in his beautiful foreword. Unfailingly responding to never-ending queries about Turkey with thoughtful and thorough answers, Jonathan Sugden of Human Rights Watch provided editorial assistance that was integral to *Opposites*. It is thanks to his intense familiarity with both the East and the West that this book is richly footnoted for both those familiar with Turkey as well as those who are just beginning to learn about it. In addition, we are grateful for his impeccable afterword. Thanks are also due to our translator İsfendiyar Eralp, as well as to our copyeditor, Madeline Gutin-Perri, the book's designer, Sara Stemen, our proofreader, Diana Drew, and Caroline Green, all of whom worked with incredible accuracy, speed, and patience.

NOTES

Kırmızı İle Yeşil/Yeşil İle Kırmızı means *Red and Green/Green and Red* in Turkish. In Turkey, the color red represents the left and the color green represents Islam. *Opposites: Side by Side* retains this distinction in the form of section titles: *The Red* by Şanar Yurdatapan and *The Green* by Abdurrahman Dilipak.

Şanar is pronounced "Shanar." Turkish is pronounced exactly as it is written. Ş= sh; C = j; J is a soft j, as in French "bonjour"; Ç = ch; ğ is silent; undotted i (ı) is a normal "i" pronounced at the back of the mouth.

THE RED

BY ŞANAR YURDATAPAN

CONTENTS

1. THINK, THINK, COMMIT A "CRIME"!

Preface to the Unpublished First Edition (1995)

Dear Readers,

Perhaps the fact that Abdurrahman Dilipak and I have decided to write a book together will surprise you. Well, that's understandable. One of us comes from the secular world, the other from Islamic circles. Why are two individuals with such different worldviews getting together, and what are they trying to do?

Are they trying to find some middle way to reconcile their views?

Some people might even feel cross with us...doesn't reconciliation mean compromising your views? If we are going to come to terms, won't one of us have to sacrifice a little of his Islamic beliefs, and won't the other have to sacrifice a little of his secular worldview?

Let us say right from the start: That is not our intention.

Our aim is not to reach an understanding by discussion or argument. Instead, we start out by reminding each other of the famous words of the great French thinker Voltaire:

—I do not share your beliefs.

—Nor do I share yours! But I'll struggle to the last to defend your freedom to express your views.

—And I yours.

These days, conversations about differences in views often end with an exchange of insults and sometimes a punch in the nose, so we believe the first steps toward peaceful coexistence are to learn to show each other tolerance and to set an example for others.

Our sincere wish is that people who have different ways of thinking and views of the world will try to listen to and understand each other and get used to doing so. After all, we do not have to accept every opinion we hear and understand. But unless we listen to and understand the opposing viewpoints voiced by those who defend them, dialogue is impossible. All we will get is cacophony, with everyone talking at once. And isn't that exactly what we have today?

We know that it will not be easy to break down hardened views and prejudice, but even if it is difficult, we have to start somewhere.

People have often asked, and still ask me today, "What do you think you are doing? The Sheriat supporters[2] are just using naïve people like you. If they seize power one day, do you think they will give you a chance to even open your mouth? They are all practicing *takiyye*."[3] Lying is not a problem for them because in Islam telling lies is permitted if it is done for the sake of the religion and the lie is told on the path to Allah.

How can we refuse to believe what a person clearly and openly declares, in front of everyone's eyes, on the grounds that, "We can't be sure that he is not lying"?

The disgust provoked by self-styled Sheriat supporters, religious bigots who do not recognize nonbelievers' right to live and breathe, should not be laid at the door of other Muslims who are not like that. How can I put Ali Bulaç, Altan Tan, and Mustafa İslamoğlu, whom I wish I had met earlier in my life, in the same category as a bunch of bloodthirsty fanatics?

As you might expect, Dilipak is the target of much the same criticism—even of attacks.

So these are the thoughts and feelings with which we put together this book. These days, nearly all facts are subject to deliberate distortion. We wanted our readers—especially those from the younger generation—to see how the contemporary questions that preoccupy them are viewed from two widely differing viewpoints. And especially how, when they are presented side by side, our readers can weigh these viewpoints using their own intellect and conscience as they make up their own minds and settle on their own opinions.

---

2. Muslims who say they want to establish an Islamic form of government.

3. Deceitfulness, particularly as practiced by someone pretending not to be a devout Muslim. Takiyye, Turkish form of the Arabic *taqiya*: "fear, caution, prudence; (in Shi'itic Islam) dissimulation of one's religion (under duress or in the face of threatening damage)." (*The Hans Wehr Dictionary of Modern Written Arabic*, Ed. J. M. Cowan [Ithaca, NY: Spoken Language Services, Inc., 1976]).

We will be satisfied if our efforts contribute to creating a society in which we can all live together in peace and friendship, "together, side by side, with all our differences."

With my most sincere affection,
Şanar Yurdatapan
İstanbul, May 1995

2. THINK, THINK, COMMIT A "CRIME"!

Six Years Later, an Addition to the Preface (2001)

This book was actually supposed to be published six and a half years ago. A newspaper publishing house was initially enthusiastic about our idea. We selected this particular publishing house because it was publishing books as well as newspapers and selling them cheaply at newsstands. We thought this would help us reach a bigger audience. But when we handed over our manuscript, the publisher began to squirm. (Who knows? Perhaps "those who work in the interests of national security" played some role in this.)

Anyway, one thing followed another. Dilipak and I returned to our normal daily business, and the manuscript was shelved.

In the intervening six years, a lot of water flowed under the bridge. In 1995, our Civil Disobedience for Freedom of Thought[4] started as an elite movement, but it soon began to attract masses of people from many different circles with widely differing beliefs. In our book *Freedom of Thought 2000*, we collected and republished every text and speech the courts had prosecuted and "found guilty" since 1995. Before the ink on that book (and the four indictments drawn up against it) had dried, we, along with 77,663 others, published *Freedom of Thought for Everyone*. And just as the trial of the 77,663 guilty authors is getting under way (I wonder what stadium they are planning to use as a courtroom for that trial!), our next book, *Freedom of Thought 2001*, will hit the stands under the signature of 200,000 publishers.

We did not satisfy ourselves with publishing these books, though. One day writers, another day artists, another day lawyers in their gowns, and even members of parliament were taking turns lining up at the doors of the public prosecutor's office with their confessions: "Please don't forget me. If expressing my opinion is an offense, then I too have committed this offense, Mr. Prosecutor."

---

4. A detailed history of the civil disobedience campaign is given in chapter 17.

It was then that Dilipak and I returned to our book project. At first, I thought we should update what we wrote six years previously, but on rereading the text, I changed my mind and felt that we should leave it as it was to show the reader how we have failed to progress as a society, how we even seem to have drifted backward. (In what is to come, I may mention developments that occurred in the intervening years since I originally wrote the text, and these additions I will indicate.)

In reality, though, neither life nor society nor history goes backward. Turkey's forward momentum is unstoppable. The internal dynamics of our society demand it.

We are not going back; we are just being stretched under tension.

İstanbul, August 2001

3. THINK, THINK, BUT FOR GOD'S SAKE DON'T OPEN YOUR MOUTH!

Recently, a government official who shall remain nameless treated me to the following beauty of an observation:

"In Turkey, thinking is not forbidden. Everyone is free to write and speak as they wish. But if what they write contains an offense, obviously, prosecutors and courts will act swiftly and do whatever is necessary!"

This is madness.

If prosecutors and courts are going to act swiftly when you say what you think, then what has become of freedom of thought?

If, on the one hand, they tell you that you are free, but on the other, they show you the stick, how are you supposed to speak or write? At best, all you can do is think and think, like a cow chewing her cud. Cows think and think all day long, from morning until night, but they cannot open their mouths and tell us what they have been thinking. Have these officials got so used to treating us like cattle that they believe we actually are cattle?

IS FREEDOM OF THOUGHT A LUXURY?

Domestic and international pressures have placed freedom of thought on the Turkish agenda to such an extent that no one can now ignore this problem. No day seems to pass without television news or newspaper pictures of our best-known writers and artists at the courtroom door.

At the same time, we hear the echoes of the terrible war that is pitting our children against one another and claiming their lives every day.[5] Screaming for war is allowed, but calling for peace is tantamount to treason. During Peace Week, we held a demonstration in which we poured our Peace Starter Mix into the Bosporus, like the legendary Nasreddin Hodja,[6]

---

5. The conflict between the illegal armed Kurdistan Workers' Party (PKK) and Turkish government security forces between 1984 and 1999 claimed more than thirty thousand lives.

6. See note 49 on Nasreddin Hodja.

who put a spoonful of curd into a lake, hoping to turn it all into yogurt. We knew our efforts were as unlikely to be successful as his, and, sure enough, the leading participants ended up at the police station. Our government halfheartedly talks the talk about fundamental freedoms—because it feels the pressure of Europe—but simultaneously it does all it can to obstruct the path to freedom. In TV discussions, in newspaper news and opinion columns, freedom of thought is always on the agenda.

That is all very well, but to the ordinary citizen on the street, this freedom of thought must seem like mere intellectuals' business, an ongoing tug-of-war between them and the state. And the politicians and the media, who are resolved not to do anything that might provoke people to take any meaningful action, are doing their best to make it seem like that.

But everyone needs freedom of thought. Why? We need it to protect our lives, our daily bread, our rights. We need it so we can unite to protect our rights.

Look, here are two incidents from the newspapers of April 18, 1995:

In the first one there is a mother in great sorrow, the mother of Hasan Ocak.[7] The security forces took her son away, she says. Seven witnesses testify to having seen him at police headquarters, yet the police chief denies it. The woman is going out of her mind. Unable to bear the injustice she is faced with, in court she calls out something like, "What kind of justice is this?" No sooner does she open her mouth than she is indicted under Article 159 of the criminal code (questioning the integrity of the judiciary) and imprisoned for a month. Thus the wretched mother learns what happens if she protests injustice.

EVERYONE NEEDS FREEDOM OF THOUGHT!

They need it to defend their rights against injustice.

The second item, from the same day's newspapers: Police arrest six trade unionists.

---

7. After the "disappearance" of Hasan Ocak in İstanbul in January 1995, his parents began a vigil on Saturday mornings on İstikal Street in the center of the city. They were soon joined by the mothers of other victims of "disappearance." For two years, the "Saturday Mothers" were a highly embarrassing fixture. The police persistently harassed, detained, ill-treated, and prosecuted the mothers, but all this happened in the full glare of the media. The mothers' action effectively stopped the proliferation of "disappearances" in Turkey.

Why? Because they distributed leaflets without permission.

The constitution and the law on meetings and demonstrations may clearly say "prior permission not necessary," but, in practice, to distribute leaflets, to put up posters, to hold a protest march, or to organize a public meeting is to put yourself at the mercy of the police. If he does not like it, he can say, "This is illegal," and you can no longer distribute your leaflets, put up your posters, or gather for speeches.

In September of 1994, Peace Week posters were banned in just this way. Yet all the posters showed was a picture of doves and the word *peace* in five languages. Yes, the little word *peace* in Turkish, English, French, German, and Kurdish. What are you smirking about? Isn't everybody in the state apparatus telling us that Kurdish is not forbidden?[8] Perhaps the governor's office did not like one of the doves. We haven't yet gotten to the bottom of the mystery—but we won our counteraction in the courts, and our posters and our doves won their freedom. We'll put them up on the walls in September of 1995.

To return to the trade unionists...what did their leaflet say? It went something like this: "It makes no sense at all! Last year, inflation was over 150 percent, but they are planning to give us a 25 percent raise. Are we crazy? We are getting poorer by the day. We cannot accept this. Let's get together through the union, strike, and protect our daily bread."

Could such a leaflet ever get official permission? Of course not! "How dare you talk about strikes?" the state would say. "Especially now, when we need national unity and togetherness more than ever." And supposing they try to do the impossible and go on strike? Well, the National Security Council would meet, give one of their "advisory decisions" beginning with

---

8. There has been considerable liberalization in the area of language during the past decade. In 1991 the law that prohibited Kurdish in speech and writing was abolished, and several newspapers and magazines are now published in minority languages (though those produced in Kurdish are frequently the object of confiscation or police raids for suspected separatism). In March 2000, the Supreme Court ruled in a test case concerning a child who had been given a Kurdish name that children could legally be given names of non-Turkish origin. In August 2002, some obstacles to broadcasting and education in Kurdish were lifted. However, any poster in Kurdish would very likely be banned by the local governor as "separatist" or subject to prohibitions still in force concerning the use of languages other than Turkish in politics.

the words *For reasons of national security*, and the government would prohibit the strike.

And where did you get the idea that civil servants have the right to join
a trade union? How could official business get done if state officials were to
have a falling out with the government? Wherever in the world could such a
thing happen? What? Did you say everywhere in Europe? You say we
signed the International Labour Organization agreement? And it was
approved by our parliament? Good heavens, I must have been ill that day!
And you say it is in the Coalition Government Protocols? For shame! This
must be something the Social Democrats sneaked through. Anyway, it is out
of the question. No such law could ever pass the Turkish Grand National
Assembly![9] If I say it won't pass, it won't pass, so that's the end of it.

This is why we need freedom of thought. We need it in every home.
Every wife needs it so she can say what she wants without fear of her husband beating her. Schoolchildren need it so they can learn to express their
views without fear of their teachers and have the civilized courage to
speak, listen, and have respect for views that are opposed to theirs. So they
can be brought up in such a way that if one day they become members of
parliament, they do not try to break each other's heads. So the shameful
scenes of brawls in parliament we have recently seen on television can be
packed away to the Museum of Thought Crimes that the Turkish
Journalists' Association is about to open.

2001 Note: The association disappointed its president Nail Güreli on the
matter of the museum. The museum was eventually opened in 1997 in the
city of İzmir on the initiative of a young lawyer named Murat Alpaslan, but
it failed for lack of financial support, and the project is now stuck in the
deep freeze.

For Abdurrahman Dilipak's views on this subject, see Green *chapters 2, 3, and 11.*

---

9. Turkish parliament.

4. WHAT "THOUGHT" IS AND WHAT "THOUGHT" ISN'T

Members of parliament and highly placed state officials who talk about how thought and expression can be criminal are either mixed up in their heads or expert at mixing up other people's heads. The matter is straightforward enough.

Is there any limit to freedom of expression? Of course there is!

You cannot insult another person—that would clearly be an offense.

And it would be an offense to say to someone, "Go and give that man a good beating."

It would also be an offense to say, "Such and such a man is a traitor; it's okay to kill him."

Of course these would be criminal acts. Nobody is denying that.

Obviously, where insult is an attack on an individual's personal rights, as in the first example, it should be considered an offense.

The second example is incitement to commit an offense, which should be considered an offense.

The third example is praising an action deemed an offense under the law. None of the three are covered by freedom of thought. Each is already an offense under the Turkish criminal code, and has no connection with the Anti-Terror Law[10] or the other legal articles that outlaw thought and that deserve to be abolished.

Surely the members of parliament must know all this perfectly well, right?

Of course they do!

Well, why do they carry on the way they do, then?

Because they think ordinary people neither know these things nor understand them. They say to themselves that ordinary folk neither read nor think and would never raise their voices. If two or three individuals do

---

10. Turkey's Anti-Terror Law of 1991 draws an extremely broad definition of terror that criminalizes many nonviolent forms of expression.

speak up, they are declared "traitors to the motherland" and are stuffed in jail. It is as simple as that!

Well, the game is up.

Before I move on to another topic, I must emphasize that *as long as thought itself remains an offense,* other offenses like "praising an action deemed an offense under the law" and "incitement to commit an offense" are meaningless.

For example, if you heard that an absurd law had been passed that forbid wandering along the seashore, what would you say? Your first reaction might be, "That's crazy! How could they try to criminalize such a thing? There's nothing nicer than wandering along the beach on a nice day filling your lungs with ozone."

Now you've done it! You committed the offense of "praising an action deemed an offense under the law." And that's not all. Perhaps your second reaction would be, "Someone's pulling our leg. Let's go to the café at the seaside and have a nice cup of tea." And you're in trouble again! This time you committed the crime of "incitement to commit an offense."

Yes, this is what happens. Once *thought* is outlawed, actions such as "praising an offense" and "incitement to commit an offense" become meaningless and ridiculous. And let me remind everyone that if you forget yourself and say, "How can you have a law like this? To hell with your justice!" then Article 159 of the Turkish criminal code ("Questioning the integrity of the judiciary") is lying in wait for you.

—I'll just put the lot of you under lock and key.

—Fine. Put us away if you like, but aren't you going to have to build an awful lot of prisons?

WE SHOULD BE FREE TO THINK THIS AND THAT, YOU SAY, BUT WHAT ABOUT ISLAMIC FUNDAMENTALISM?

Here come the really dangerous questions!

Should people be free to get up and say, "Sheriat is good. Turkey should be governed by Sheriat laws?" Should they be free to make that sort of propaganda?

Yes, let them say it!

Yes, they should be free to make their propaganda!

Living in a secular world is the only guarantee for our freedoms. Yes, I am against the Sheriat because it defends all sorts of inequalities and constantly conflicts with the needs of contemporary life. But I must first defend the right of others to explain those things that I am against, and it is my right to hear those things directly from the mouths of the people who support them. I must hear Dilipak's views from Dilipak, Toktamış Ateş's views from Toktamış,[11] and not from indictments written by Ankara State Security Court prosecutor Nusret Demiral.

Second, when passing on my secular views to my children, should I gag the opposing idea and only speak myself? Should I act like General Kenan Evren[12] before the referendum for the 1982 constitution?

And third, why should anyone who has confidence in his views be worried if the opposing idea gets an airing? I have no doubts about my worldview (dialectical materialism) aside from the scientific skepticism that I hope I never lose. I believe my worldview provides a holistic vision that I have frequently put to the test, and I see it as the only belief system that gives a coherent and consistent explanation of the world and its societies. I must, however, continue to test that system whenever a new situation arises. If I find that some aspects are deficient in explaining the world, I must review my beliefs. And in order to do this, I need to hear views that oppose mine. If I am so terrified of them that I have to gag them, who is to show me where I am going wrong?

2001 Addition: The Higher Education Council (YÖK)[13] forced final-year students of the Theology Faculty of Marmara University to choose between their moral beliefs and their right to education. Female students

---

11. Professor Toktamış Ateş, columnist in the daily *Cumhuriyet (Republic)*, strong defender of secularism, and author of *Laiklik (Secularism)*, (Ankara: Ümit Publications, 1996).

12. Kenan Evren, the general who led the military coup in 1980 and later appointed himself president of Turkey. He manipulated a referendum to secure approval of a military-designed constitution by a reluctant public.

13. The YÖK was established by the military following the 1980 coup. It includes a military representative and has wide-ranging powers to control the university system in ways that conflict with academic freedom.

were not allowed to sit for end-of-year exams if they were wearing a headscarf, a covering for hair and neck favored by some Muslim women. Those who were not willing to uncover their heads were not permitted to take the exams and lost the right to earn their diploma. They resisted, and rightly so. Regardless of bitter winter conditions, they stood at the university gate, waiting to be admitted. I was one of those who went to offer them support.

Do not forget, though, that this is an issue with at least two sides. If I, as an atheist, oppose a threat to a fundamental freedom by standing by young women who refuse to stop covering their heads—something very much contrary to my beliefs—then they should stand by their fellow students when these students are targeted because they wear miniskirts or because they do not fast in the holy month of Ramadan.

Although I think it is wrong for young women to deny daylight and sunshine to their hair and their heads, this opinion is mine, but the head is not. It is up to the individual whether or not to cover her head, and no one else should force her to dress one way or another.

While we are on the subject of headcovering, I would like to pose a parallel question to fathers who are devout Muslims.

I have two daughters. One is twenty-three, the other sixteen years old. Both of them know full well that if they decided to cover themselves up, rather than bringing material or moral pressure to bear, I would only be sad and wonder where I had gone wrong. Covered or not, they are my children, pieces of my soul. Of course, this would provoke a lot of talk in my milieu. To my face and behind my back, people would say, "Şanar Yurdatapan's daughter has taken the veil," and I would be the butt of anger and ridicule. Yet, I would give all the gossips the same reply:

"My responsibility was to give my children the information they will need in their lives, and I fulfilled that responsibility. I must respect whatever decision they make on the basis of that knowledge. I am different from my father, and there's no reason why I should have to be the same as he was. My daughters do not have to turn out as I want them to. They must live their own lives as they wish."

Are you, Muslim men, prepared to say the same thing?

When the word goes around in your circle, "Have you heard? Ahmet's daughter has taken off her scarf and bared her head!" will you give the same response as I have, or will you beat your daughter and tell her she has stained your family honor (*namus*)?[14]

I am responsible for my own honor and reputation. I believe my honor and reputation will be measured according to whether I am a decent, honest, and respectable person, and that I will be granted respect provided I do not hurt, harm, or infringe on the rights of others.

Unfortunately, I look around and see that most males are so idle and apathetic that they prefer to let their honor and reputation be carried by their mothers, sisters, wives, and daughters. For some reason, and at the same time, the behavior of their female relatives, or even all the womenfolk of their district, threaten to stain the honor and reputation of the men. Doesn't this strike you as a bit twisted?

Let us return to our young daughters. Like every other child, right from when they were babies, they tried to copy what we did. By imitating us, they tried to win the approval of their elders. So it is hardly surprising that a young girl who grew up in an environment where headcovering is the norm should cover her own head. What worries me is what happens if she does not want to cover her head. What then? We all know that the intense psychological pressure directed at her alone will be unbearable, not to mention the possibility of real bullying. If even grown-ups cannot

---

14. *Namus* is an extremely powerful idea in Turkish society, and probably at its strongest among poor, devout families in the eastern half of the country. "Honor killings—the killing by immediate family members of women suspected of being unchaste—continued in rural areas and among new immigrants to cities; according to media reports, there may be dozens of such killings every year. Under the law, persons convicted of killings that were "provoked" (such as honor killings) may receive a lighter sentence than for other types of killings. Because of further sentence reductions for juvenile offenders, observers note that young male relatives often are designated to perform the killing. Recently, three brothers were convicted of murdering their fifteen-year-old sister after she ran away from an arranged marriage to an older man. The court imposed sentences between four and twelve years; however, the court stated that they would only have to serve approximately one-third of their sentences because of their young age and because the boys were provoked. In May in Adana, a fourteen-year-old boy was arrested for stabbing his mother to death. "Government authorities have tried to send a clear message of intolerance for this practice through the prosecution of those responsible for the killings." U.S. Department of State, *Country Reports on Human Rights Practices*: Turkey, March 4, 2002.

resist social pressures, where does that leave our young daughters? How can we be sure they have exercised free choice in their decision to cover themselves up?

There are complaints that in Turkey, religion is under pressure. It is true that people do not encounter problems as long as religious organization is under state control, but all support and tolerance is removed when people try to practice their religion according to their own wishes.

Yes, in the early days of the republic, the state subjected religion to forms of repression we now consider unacceptable. This was understandable. They wanted to restructure society completely and to make science paramount. You can establish a strong modern society only with properly educated citizens who are equal in the eyes of the law. But the existing order was completely infused with religion and wanted everything to continue unchanged. It was meaningless to ask people what they wanted. They were still not liberated from the sense of being *kul*—servants or slaves, that is, of Allah, but also of authority in general. People who have not achieved the status of independent individual are inevitably going to bow down in servitude before the taboos of a restrictive society. We see heavy-handedness in the republic's approach to many issues when it exercises its power to break down the tyranny of conservative social rules. Coercion against coercion. This is the law of revolutions!

But is it possible to say the same thing is going on seventy-odd years later? Just twenty-five years after the founding of the republic, the new classes who were challenging authority wove popular resentment together with religious motifs and got themselves elected to Ankara to form a government. Initially called the Democratic Party (DP), this group later became the Justice Party (AP). For many years they got along with Islam very well, provided they could use religion to serve their own political purposes. They opposed the left, which was critical of the economic order, by parading their religious beliefs as part of the "fight against communism." In their struggle to suppress the left, they resorted to the cudgel, and then the knife, and, finally, the gun.

The Islamists' big "mistake" was to decide to organize themselves rather than let powerful interests set the agenda for them. From that day on, they have been branded as dangerous.

2001 Addition: But the biggest assault on politically organized devout Muslims came shortly after the Susurluk[15] scandal hit the headlines. The lid of Pandora's box was lifted for a moment, and out crept snakes, centipedes, crimes, murders, arms trafficking, drug smuggling, narcotics, feudal landlords, members of parliament, police chiefs, mafiosi, extreme right-wing groups, village guards, and JITEM.[16] More and more connections came to light, and the clues led toward the topmost echelons of government. What is more, the public, who had hitherto been passive onlookers, began mass protests every evening by switching their lights on

---

15. On November 4, 1996, a speeding Mercedes crashed into a truck at Susurluk on the İzmir-İstanbul road. The car belonged to Sedat Bucak, a member of parliament for one of the parties in the coalition government and the leader of a Kurdish tribe that participates in the village guard corps. (These are Kurdish villagers paid and armed by the government to fight the PKK. Village guards have been found responsible for crimes ranging from theft and extortion to murder.) Sedat Bucak survived, but the three other passengers were killed. They included Hüseyin Kocadağ, director of the İstanbul Police Academy and former deputy police chief of İstanbul, and Abdullah Çatlı, alleged mafia leader and former vice president of an extreme right-wing youth organization. Çatlı was wanted for alleged participation in the massacre of seven members of the Turkish Labor Party in 1978 and was also on Interpol's wanted list for drug smuggling offenses. At the time of the accident, Abdullah Çatlı was carrying a "green passport," reserved for high-ranking civil servants, even though he was on the run after escaping from a prison in Switzerland, where he had been held on drug-smuggling charges.

   The car also contained an arsenal of weapons, including two submachine guns. High-profile figures are often heavily armed, but there could be no legitimate explanation for the silencers also found in the wreckage.

   When asked how a high-ranking police officer came to be in the company of a criminal wanted for political murder and drug smuggling, the minister of the interior (and former police chief) Mehmet Ağar's initial explanation was that Hüseyin Kocadağ had been driving Çatlı to Ankara to hand him over to the authorities. It later emerged that the four had been vacationing together at a coastal resort. Mehmet Ağar resigned as interior minister shortly afterward. Criminal proceedings against him have since been blocked, because Mehmet Ağar became a member of parliament and benefits from diplomatic immunity.

   The National Intelligence Organization (MIT) confirmed in public statements that Abdullah Çatlı had been used for "secret operations abroad." A spokesperson for MIT added, "Later we learned he was involved in drug trafficking and stopped using him. But the General Police Directorate took him on." The revelations corroborated widespread allegations that Turkish security forces were involved in blatantly criminal activities, including political killings, and that the government and administration were covering up such crimes.

16. Police intelligence unit implicated in killings and "disappearances." The government denies that JITEM exists, but it has been referred to in various official documents.

and off, whistling, blowing horns, and banging saucepan lids.[17] As soon as the public marched into the arena with drums and flutes, the army staged its February 28 coup d'état.

The problem for Islam in our country at the moment is not its leaders, such as Necmettin Erbakan, Mezarcı, and Erdoğan. The scenes people were made to watch on TV—replays of speeches given by such figures eight or ten years previously—were not the real grounds for the military intervention. The real reason was the Susurluk scandal.

The most effective way of shaking off the scandal was to divide those who were uniting against the state and the army. No fault line splits Turkish society more sharply than the secular/Islamic divide. So the military quickly grabbed their *gladio*[18] and got to work.

For Abdurrahman Dilipak's views on this subject, see Green *chapters 3 and 4.*

---

17. This countrywide campaign was known as the "one minute of darkness for enlightenment." In their book, *Turkey Unveiled* (Woodstock, NY: Overlook Press, 2000), Nichole and Hugh Pope describe the scene: "Flashing lights lit entire neighborhoods like Christmas trees. Military families in army barracks and the gleaming skyscraper towers of Sabanci Holdings headquarters joined in at times. For the first time in years, Turks felt they were no longer prisoners of fate, but could influence the course of events."

18. *Gladio*, derived from the Latin for "sword." But it is also the code name for a network of secret organizations in NATO countries—a state within the state that carried out many provocative actions. It was first uncovered in Italy toward the end of the 1980s. The network was unraveled throughout the rest of Europe shortly afterward. In Turkey, they are also known as the contraguerrillas. Turkey is the NATO country that still has not established proper control of what we call its "deep state." Well, it is up to us to get rid of them.

5. WHAT ABOUT SEPARATISTS, THEN?
WHAT ABOUT KURDISTAN?

All right, then.

Should a person be free to stand up and say, "The Kurds should separate from Turkey and form their own independent state?" Does that count as freedom of expression?

Of course it does.

The earth would not open up and swallow us if we had the freedom to say such things.

On the contrary. All our problems have arisen because we treated the Kurds' basic rights (to speak or sing in their own language, for example) as "separatism." The terrible bloodshed during the conflict in the southeast occurred because these legitimate demands were suppressed with beatings, imprisonment, and repression. Terrorism was born out of oppression, not freedom. Those who cannot abide the thought of liberty parrot the argument that "If there were unlimited freedom of expression, our nation would be divided."

Why? The bloodshed was brought on us by people who are free to say whatever they like, but who do not recognize that others have the same right.

If expression were totally free, our world would not come to an end. What would happen? Well, perhaps we, and our minorities, would have the same relationship as England and Scotland.

The United Kingdom did not repeat in Scotland the mistakes it made in Ireland. In Scotland, the Scottish Nationalist Party officially supports the separation of Scotland from the United Kingdom. Nobody closes this party or puts its leaders in jail. The party fights elections; its speakers join TV discussions and say to the English, "You are exploiting us. If we separated from you, we would be richer." And the others snort back, "That's rubbish. If we were to invest the money we are currently wasting on Scotland in our own country, England, *we* would be much better off."

So if the Scottish Nationalists do one day obtain the majority needed and separate from England, what would happen then?

That is up to them. In Czechoslovakia, the Czechs and the Slovaks separated amicably, and no blood was shed. That is what they wanted, and that is what they did. Czechoslovakia did not become a Yugoslavia. They separated. Is that better? I do not know. It is not my business.

I'll tell you a story about my personal situation. Last year, my wife, Melike Demirağ, and I separated after a marriage of eighteen years and two children. To our perverted media this was a good story, so the public learned a good deal more about this than about anything I have tried to do for human rights. Melike fell in love with another person, wanted to leave me, and so we split up.

What would you have me do? Beat her and call her "a treacherous family separatist?" Suppose I did not want us to separate. Should I have just flatly refused? Not at all. If she didn't want to live with me, I could not force her to stay. The most I could have done is perhaps to have tried to find out why she cooled toward me and tried to win her heart again. Because a shared existence is sustained by mutual consent, not force. This is as true for two communities as for two individuals. In international law, this is known as the right to self determination. (A bit further on, we'll have a look at documents from a secret parliamentary debate, and then you can see what they said about this right in those days!)

Do not forget that the government used to levy a fine per word on anyone who spoke Kurdish. Court records amply document the absurdities that passed between the police, who had to implement this law, and Kurdish villagers. And if you get bored with dry court records, try reading the books of Günay Aslan, a "thought criminal" who became acquainted with our jails at an early age.

Didn't they jail anyone who said Kurds exist? Didn't they even try Aziz Nesin for this?

Just a few days ago, the case of lawyer Eren Keskin, former president of the İstanbul branch of the Turkish Human Rights Association reached its conclusion. The court imposed a two-year prison sentence. Do you know why? Because in one of her writings she used the word *Kurdistan* to signify a geographic area! Now just look at the document below:

Turkish Grand National Assembly (TBBM) Secret Session Transcripts, Volume 3 (The original is in the parliament library.):

This is the instruction of the Parliamentary Representatives Committee to the Elcezire Front Command Headquarters concerning Kurdistan:

Increasingly, our department of the interior considers necessary the creation of regional administrations throughout the whole country in a way that will influence the popular classes. In the regions where Kurds are living, our government looks favorably on the creation of a local administration for reasons of internal and external political considerations.

It is a generally accepted principle throughout the world that nations should have the right to determine their own future. We too have accepted this principle. We estimate that the Kurds have by now completed their local administrative organization. The local chiefs and influential figures must be won over to our side. When they show their votes, they must declare they have the power to determine their own destiny and that they wish to live under the administration of the Turkish Grand National Assembly. The Elcezire front Command Headquarters is responsible for ensuring that all activities in Kurdistan will be directed toward this aim.

It has been decided that armed clashes on the Iraqi border between Kurds in Kurdistan and the French and (in the areas allotted them) the British must obstruct any possible agreement between the Kurds and the foreigners and ensure their mutual enmity. Meanwhile, we will show the need for the establishment of local administrations and in this way ensure their loyalty to us. By nominating Kurdish leaders to administrative and military positions, we will increase that loyalty.

The internal affairs of Kurdistan will brought together under the administration of the Elcezire front Command Headquarters. The front Command will communicate directly with Turkish Grand National Assembly leaders on this issue. The Elcezire front Command will regulate and coordinate the line of action to be followed by the local governors, and the chief civil servants will therefore also be under its control.

Orders concerning Kurdistan drawn up by the deputies to the Grand National Assembly are communicated as stated above to you in confidence.

We modern Turks have difficulty understanding the archaic Ottoman language, but I advise anyone interested in its meaning to do his own research because this is a document that sheds light on our heritage from the Progress and Union Party government—which took the place of the Ottoman Empire—a heritage that is still of significance today.

The point I want to emphasize is that the word *Kurdistan* appears five times in this document and that the writer would therefore be punished, if he were alive today, by a sentence five times heavier than the one imposed on the lawyer Eren Keskin, who used the word only once. So a prison sentence of ten years would await the author of this document.

Now, look and see who the unlucky writer is...none other than the founder of the Turkish Republic and its first president: President of the Grand National Assembly Mustafa Kemal.

Come on, then! Either jail Atatürk or get Eren Keskin out of jail!

Let's think for a moment. What does this document tell us? That in those days, the 1920s, the government referred to this geographic region as *Kurdistan* and to the people who lived in that area as *Kurds*. The expression *Mountain Turks* had not yet been invented.

What is the use of such prohibitions? In the late 1980s, when the Bulgarian government tried to rebrand the Bulgarian Turks as Bulgarians, we cried "tyranny" at the top of our lungs, and we cry the same thing when the Greeks try to say that the Turks of Western Thrace are "Muslim Greeks."

How would we like it if someone tried to force us to change the names of our country, our region, our city, our village, or our children? We wouldn't, yet this is precisely what our authorities did. Turkish consulates in Germany refused to register Kurdish names to Kurdish children born in Germany to Turkish citizens, and tried to force them instead to give their children Turkish names. This practice is probably still going on today.

For Abdurrahman Dilipak's views on this subject, see Green chapters 15, 16, and 28.

6. THE REAL AND THE MOST DANGEROUS SEPARATISM: CHAUVINISM

Chauvinism is the unsavory product of nationalism. Even if nationalism starts out innocently and justifiably as a people's search for identity, in the long run it always ends with "I am the greatest." It cannot resist making the laughable, ridiculous assertion that it produced the finest specimens of humanity ever. (The Turkish Republic has excelled at this stuff, but Kurdish nationalism is catching up fast.)

In recent years, the state has orchestrated the incredible growth of chauvinism and animosity toward the Kurds, with the media providing a sickening chorus. This is why the authorities turn a blind eye to the terror of "high spirits" to which our youngsters subject us and each other in the streets of our cities after soccer matches. Under normal conditions, if you made a fraction of the noise, the police would be there to stop it. Yet the car horns shriek until morning, and the fans stop passing cars and extract tribute from the drivers. Kids make the graywolf sign[19] to TV cameras and fire volleys of bullets in the air. The last Turkish soccer victory against Switzerland left six dead and God knows how many wounded.

Is this sport or the emotional discharge of a society wounded by a sense of inferiority? Perhaps we should make an effort to understand these people by considering the social factors behind their behavior, but meanwhile we should all act to prevent a form of terror the state chooses to ignore.

I want to say to those who find this behavior normal and perhaps even run into the street to seek relief in the same way: Imagine that this happened in Berlin rather than İstanbul, and it was the German team that had beaten Brazil in Rio. Who would be behaving in the same way in the streets of Berlin? What salutes would aggressive youngsters be making for the TV cameras? What slogans would they be yelling? What sort of haircuts would

---

19. The informal salute of Turkey's extreme right, particularly MHP members. It imitates a wolf's head by putting together the thumb, middle, and ring finger while raising the index and little fingers. It recalls a legendary she-wolf that led captive Central Asian Turks to freedom.

they have? If the police did not take precautions, against whom do you think their unrestrained behavior would be directed? Think about it. How many of you have relatives working in Germany?

It is not clever to get little kids to yell anti-Kurd slogans at soccer matches. It is dangerous. It is playing with fire. If the result is not that children of the Turks and the Kurds living together throughout Anatolia form gangs and cut one another's throats, and that their parents pretty soon follow suit, then Aziz Nesin was wrong. (He once claimed in an interview that 60 percent of the Turkish population was stupid; when this provoked widespread rage, he apologized and corrected the figure to 70 percent.) Well, so far, it appears that our people still possess some wit and common sense, and we should be thankful for this. But we should also call a halt to this feud between brothers and ensure that a handful of hawkish types do not drag sixty million of us any closer to disaster.

Incidentally, something has been bothering me for some time: Why do foreigners call Türkiye "Turkey"?

Türkiye means the land of the Turks, but in English, *turkey* means the Christmas meal!

When I first heard this, I was amazed. The penny dropped only years later when I heard the words of the state official, which I mentioned earlier: "In Turkey, thinking is not forbidden. Everyone is free to write and speak as they wish. But if what they write contains an offense, obviously the prosecutors and courts act swiftly and do whatever is necessary!"

We constantly complain that the world does not understand us, that we have not been able to present ourselves in the best light. Yet actually, the foreigner seems to have summed us up rather well—we who think and think but can never say what we mean. That's why they call us *Turkey*. We'd better make ourselves scarce around Christmastime!

For Abdurrahman Dilipak's views on this subject, see Green *chapters 15 and 28.*

7. I LOVE MY MIND, BUT I'M LOSING IT!

—Father, where did I come from?

—From your mother, child; she bore you from her belly.

—But how did I get there?

—A cell from my body joined a cell from your mother; then, nourished in your mother's body, this cell increased in number many times over. Nine months later, you were a little baby and when all was ready, you were born.

—But father, what is a cell, and how does it get into us?

—It is the smallest unit in the bodies of living things and is so small that it cannot be seen with the naked eye. The cells in our body make new cells from the food we eat.

—Where do the things we eat come from?

—They too come from living things. For example, bread is made from wheat. Wheat is a plant. The plants make their cells from the minerals they take from the soil with their roots.

—How did those minerals get into the soil?

—The rocks from which the world is made broke into smaller pieces under the influence of the sun, wind, and rains, and finally became soil.

—And how did those rocks form?

—It is believed that the world was a ball of fire made of molten materials and gas. When it eventually cooled, a crust formed, just like lava that pours out of a volcano and becomes rock when it cools.

—But where did the ball of fire come from?

—They say that it broke off the sun.

—And the sun, father, where did that come from?

—It is a part of a galaxy consisting of other suns like our sun, and other satellites like our earth.

—But father, where did that come from?

—Many galaxies make up the universe, which is thought to have formed as a result of a big bang. All these are different forms of existence of matter that is constantly changing and that sometimes also turns into energy.

—Well, where did matter come from?

—They say it always existed. It has no beginning and no end. Just like the dimensions in which it finds itself, space and time.

At this point, Materialist Father[20] stops talking and Idealist Uncle takes over:

—Dear boy, don't listen to your father. Can something that exists come about all by itself? If something exists, then something must have made it from nothing. A force, perhaps, or an energy. Our brains can't understand it all, but we call this force that makes things out of nothing God.

—If God created everything, who created him? Because God exists, there must be somebody else who created him. And someone else who created the creator of the creator, and so on.

—No, God always existed. He existed everywhere and eternally. He did not need to be created.

Idealist Uncle also comes to a halt. But nothing can stop the child now.

—Uncle, you said the same thing as father in the end. Father said that matter always existed and did not need to be created. You started off saying that if something exists, then there must be a creator, but then you ended up saying that God always existed and did not need to be created. If we keep coming across something that always existed, why do we need God to intervene?

At this moment, Agnostic Uncle barges in.

---

20. In everyday use, *materialist* refers to an opportunist who loves property and money and puts his own interests first. In philosophy, it has a different meaning and refers to a worldview that looks at matter as the basis of the universe and treats thought and moral values as the functions of matter. An idealist is the opposite, believing that ideas, the spirit, or God are the basis of the universe, and that these created matter. In normal usage, we think of *idealism* as a readiness to make great sacrifices for a particular thought or belief. Hallac-i Mansur (Muslim philosopher [857–922] who believed that God was present in all living and nonliving nature) was martyred for saying "*Enel Haq*" (which can be interpreted as "I am God") and Deniz Gezmiş (leader of an illegal revolutionary movement; executed in 1972) who went fearlessly to the scaffold for the sake of his beliefs were, in this sense, idealists. By contrast, it is not hard to find supporters of both philosophies who are prepared to abandon their beliefs and quickly change their tune when there's a chance of some material benefit. Agnosticism is distinct from and should not be confused with scientific doubt, to which both agnostics and dialectical materialists attribute great importance.

—You are right, my child, but both your father and your other uncle have left something out. Both base their ideas on the knowledge of their brains. Yet what we know is just a tiny fraction of all that we do not know. And what science once thought to be the truth often later turned out to be false. How can we be sure that what we know as right today will not be proved wrong in the future?

—So what's your view on these matters, Agnostic Uncle?

—I say, dear nephew, that the truth of this can never be known. We cannot know even whether matter really exists or just appears to exist.

—What do you mean, can't be known? We all eat our bread and get full. If we do not find food, we die of hunger. Irrespective of whether it can be known, we die, and therefore, bread exists!

The pious grandfather, who until now managed to keep quiet, can no longer keep his silence and enters the discussion:

—For shame! You are all straying into sinful error. How can our little brain solve such big questions? Almighty Allah, who created heaven and earth, gave us enough intellect to understand his greatness. Once you have recognized him, you can abandon this discussion about what is true and what not, and simply read the Holy Qur'an. Everything is explained there. What use is our little brain when measured against the supreme intellect of he who created heaven and earth?

For Abdurrahman Dilipak's views on this subject, see Green *chapters 5, 6, and 29.*

8. THE APOLOGY THAT CAME FOUR CENTURIES LATE

At the beginning of the sixteenth century, Galileo Galilei made an important contribution to astronomy by inventing the telescope and then proceeding publicly to confirm the theories of Copernicus: that the world is not flat but round, and that it is not the center of the universe but rather revolves around the sun together with all the other planets.

This shook medieval Europe to its foundations. Galileo's words directly contradicted what the Catholic church taught and were treated as a heresy that brought the godless rascal before the courts of the Inquisition.

The courts of the Inquisition were not like our State Security Courts. Both deal with thought crimes, but ours are satisfied with handing down prison sentences, whereas the punishments meted out by the Inquisition were worse than inhuman. Galileo was an esteemed professor with friends in high places, so the public prosecutor, Nusretio Demirali[21] (in fact, the real name of the Italian prosecutor was Nuchio Metheus Juxelli, which, as you can see, I have updated), gave him a chance to recant:

—Declare that you have abandoned this theory, or it will be the worse for you.

Galileo was a mature man. He must have thought discretion the better part of valor, because he declared that all his theories were wrong and apologized to the church. So saying, he saved his neck. But it is told that as he came out of the courthouse, he murmured to himself, "And yet it moves; the world is round and it is revolving around the sun."

Did he really say this? And if he did, who was the fellow who heard him and, instead of informing the Inquisition for a fat reward, kept his counsel and quietly passed the story down to us? Or was it that Galileo never actually said it, and we invented the story to console ourselves? I have no idea. But we know that just a couple of years ago the pope, sitting

---

21. Nusret Demiral, now retired, was a well-known State Security Court prosecutor with a reputation for harshness.

on the throne of highest authority at the Vatican, with the authority of a president, ruling his statelet from the middle of Rome, officially apologized to Galileo Galilei. An apology after four hundred years may seem ridiculous, but not as ridiculous as the situation the church put itself into before making its apology. Well, let's close this file and wait to see what they decide to do about Darwin.

What is the moral of this story? It is that the truth comes out in the end no matter what people may say. The astronomical truth was uncovered not by the scholastic[22] mentality of the Middle Ages but by the scientific method which tests its validity at every moment. Scientific thought does not look for absolute truth, which in reality can never be attained, but looks for falsifiable propositions that can be tested by repeated experiment and become part of life through their application.

"How can our tiny intellect understand these secrets? What help can I possibly expect from my inferior brain, when I can refer to the pronouncement of the intellect of the creator of heavens and earth?"

This is the kind of thinking I can never accept. Given that human progress over centuries—no, millions of years—is the work of our tiny intellect, aren't you appealing to my intellect even when making the above remarks? And is it not true that every thesis you put forward to prove God's existence begins by appealing to the *intellect*?

You have seen those touching and moving images shown on our religious TV programs. They are all taken from foreign documentaries, as far as I can tell, but they still hold our rapt attention: the endless expanses of space, protozoa whirling ceaselessly under the microscope, the beauty of a drop of dew on a blossoming flower, the picturesque grandeur of the sun setting over the ocean—you cannot take your eyes off them. What is that sublime voice saying underneath? It says, look at these beauties, look at this stunning and infinite depth, look at the laws of this universe, which do not err even by a millimeter. Consider how perfectly tuned this mechanism is, of which no part could function without all the other parts. If there were no creator, could such a perfectly organized whole have come into existence all

---

22. The scholastic tradition of the Middle Ages based its view of science on the official teachings of the church. The schools and universities taught the Bible and biblical commentaries by Christian elders. Today, Islamic thought follows the same method.

by itself? What further proof can you possibly need for the existence of God?

But note again: All these words suggest that we use our *intellect* to grasp the existence of God. The little boy's brain at the beginning of chapter 7 understood this, but didn't leave it at that. It delved deeper. Let's look at it again:

—Because God created everything, who created him? Because nothing can come into existence from nothingness, and God exists, then someone else must have created him from nothing. And someone else who created the creator....

—No, God always existed. He existed everywhere and all the time. He did not need to be created. In our sacred book, it is written so. And we cannot understand the secrets of the universe with our tiny brains. So I do not have the right to question even a single line of the sacred book while the commands of the biggest brain are there for the reading.

—Is that right, though? First, we were told to use our minds to evaluate the proofs, but then at the next step our minds were subordinated to a supermind! They ask us to stop thinking and to accept things as they are in the book. People who support this idea should make up their minds: Do we conclude that God exists by using our minds or on the basis of pure faith? If you choose the first method, then address my *mind* all the way through. If you choose the second, then *do not mention my mind.* If you try to have it both ways, then you are not being consistent.

Well, that's enough philosophy for today.[23] Actually, I do not claim to be qualified to delve into such matters. But I do think it is my responsibility to help create a context in which every person can think without fear and express what he has thought.

For Abdurrahman Dilipak's views on this subject, see Green *chapters 12 and 17.*

---

23. I advise those interested in the subject to read *Elementary Principles of Philosophy* (Paris: Editions Sociales, 1954). I should add that the writer of this book, Georges Politzer, was shot by a firing squad during the German occupation of France, while İlhan Erdost, the publisher of the book in Turkey, was beaten to death by soldiers after the September 12, 1980, military coup.

9. WHAT SHOULD I TELL MY KIDS?

I always wondered how I would respond to my children's questions about matter, the universe, existence, and God. In the end, this is the conclusion I came to: Without hesitation, I told them as clearly as I could, and tried not to influence them in any way. I told them my views in a language they could understand. That is, I told them I do not believe in God. But I also told them that others—for example, their grandmother—believe, and I advised them to hear what those people had to say on the matter. "Don't take my word for it just because I am your father. Who knows? I could be mistaken."

Of course, children tend to believe the person who is closest to them. Growing up in a house where prayers are offered five times a day, they will take that way of life to heart, and, by imitating their elders, will feel grown up and expect to be congratulated for their performance.

Patiently, I tried to explain:

"In order to make up your minds on this matter, you need a lot more information. It would not be right to decide until you have that information. Be patient. You will obtain most of the information you need at school. And you can get different views by talking with other people. Only after you have heard all these things should you make up your mind."

It was easy to discuss such things in Germany,[24] but it was a different matter when we came to Turkey. You can just imagine the problems created in our country when a child publicly and recklessly declares, "I do not believe in God." For myself, I am ready to face what comes my way, but it is impossible not be afraid of what the consequences might be for a child.

So what then? What was I supposed to do?

Should I say to the kid, "Look, sweetheart. Unfortunately, in Turkey, people are not mature enough to tolerate people who think differently. So don't say these things aloud in public"?

---

24. Şanar Yurdatapan was stripped of his citizenship by a military junta that seized power in Turkey in 1980. He lived in exile in Germany from 1980 to 1992.

I found no way out, and, to my great shame, that was what I said. I still feel ashamed, but I think we all share in this shame, and we should free ourselves from it, even if we have to pay the price. Just writing *this nation is secular* in the constitution does not make a country secular.

IS SECULARISM ATHEISM?

In 1995, Turkey is witnessing a conversation among the deaf.

There are two big communities, the Secularists and the Muslims, who see themselves as rivals. Even the distinction is laughable, as daft as saying that there are Democrats on one side and Fenerbahçe soccer club fans on the other.

Our beliefs and our philosophical ideas do not prevent us from being secularist.

Some people do not believe in the creation story or in God, and they are atheists. Some people are neither believers nor unbelievers and are left in the middle. Some people believe in God but do not like any of the available religions. They are not atheists, but they do not belong to any religious community either. And some people like one of the existing religions, monotheistic or otherwise, and order their lives accordingly.

Everyone should live as he wishes and organize his life according to his heart's desire. But here's the rub—only *his own* life. People should not try to organize other people's lives by force.

This is what secularism is all about.

Under secularism, our common lives will be ordered by contemporary laws, not by the dictates of a religion. Individuals may have their own religions and live according to the precepts of those religions, but there will be no state religion.

Let everyone dress, eat, associate, and live according to his beliefs. But as soon as one person usurps the rights of another person, the secular laws apply. For example: Muslims are free to fast during their holy month of Ramadan, but they are not free to raid schools and beat the heads of those who do not fast. Similarly, religious Germans cannot force Turks or other Germans who are not churchgoers to attend Sunday services.

Again, Muslims are free to praise their religion, but they are not free to lynch those who criticize it. And they are not free to burn down hotels, saying: "Aziz Nesin says he is an atheist, and that provokes me."[25] In a secular country, the nonbelievers have as much right to express their views as believers have to express their beliefs.

What's more, they also have the freedom not to express their views. Nobody should be forced to declare his thoughts. This can be a terrible imposition. If you want, you can declare your beliefs or thoughts. But nobody should be able to put you to the test in the middle of a coffee bar by yelling at you to list the five pillars of Islam.

Only under secularism can individuals and groups of different beliefs and ideas live side by side in peace and with mutual self-respect. *Anyone who does not nurse a primitive instinct to force others to think or act like himself is a secularist.* It does not matter whether he is Muslim, Christian, atheist, or of no organized religion.

Secularism is a prize that was achieved after hundreds of years of bloody and bitter struggle. To arrive at this point, humankind had to fight against religion because the church, which was part of the authority structure in an earlier social order, was in no hurry to give up its property or its power. In the early years of the republican revolutions, the people seized church property and distributed it to the villagers, just as they did with the property of the feudal landlords. In the Restoration, following the defeat of Napoleon, who wanted to export revolution to the world with his armies, the lands were returned to their former owners. But history continued to march forward.

In Turkey, the establishment of secularism, like the establishment of the republic itself, was a top-down process. But here, too, the accounts with religion had to be settled, because in the endless fight between the forces of the old and those of the new that has been going on since the nineteenth century, conservative economic interests used religion as their tool and weapon, refusing to recognize any other belief system as legitimate. The

---

25. On July 2, 1993, in Sıvas in central Turkey, a fanatical mob burned a hotel where Aziz Nesin was staying with a group of Alevis who had come to celebrate the unveiling of a statue of Pir Sultan Abdal, an Alevi martyr. Thirty-seven people, most of them Alevis, died in the flames.

new Turkish republic passed root-and-branch laws to establish secularism. To our modern eyes, these laws are quite undemocratic. The severity with which laws were enforced was not actually an attack against Islam but a way of defending the individual's freedom of religion against the violent fanatic forces that attempted to shape everything according to its own rules and force all to obey them. I mention these things to neither criticize nor endorse, neither damn nor defend, but as an objective observation.

I also want to make my views about Islam quite clear: I do not like this religion. I could give many reasons for this, but the most important are these:

1. Islam wants to subordinate my brain. It says, "Abandon thought, and just believe." (In fact, all religions require this, to a greater or lesser extent.)
2. It is not open to revision. It forbids interpretation of sociological phenomena that are more than thirteen hundred years old. It is "the Word of Allah," and you have to conform to it! Moreover, these are not ordinary general rules but prescriptions for the smallest details of our daily lives.
3. It defends inequality. Slavery persists in this religion, and man and woman are not equal. How can I look upon my daughter as inferior to my son?
4. It considers war as holy, and, what is more, commands it (*jihad*).
5. Again, for the sake of religion, it allows deception (*takiyye*).

So have I insulted Islam? No, I have only expressed my views. But if you call yourself a Muslim, this will be a test for you. Can you tolerate criticism of your religion? Or do you now see me as a *kafir*, a nonbeliever who, according to some verse of the Holy Qur'an, can legitimately be killed?

If a religion cannot take criticism, then it cannot claim to be the most superior and tolerant religion. Wrong or right?

But I am willing to live together with millions of adherents of a religion I do not like and to respect their right to live according to their beliefs. If you are prepared to share the world with me, recognizing the same rights for me as for all others, then please do not take offense, because, you know, *you are a secularist without knowing it.*

So!

Is the Republic of Turkey secular?

Unfortunately not!

Do not take any notice of what is written in the constitution. (As we all know, you can find a great deal written about freedom in the constitution, but when you look at our real lives, it is all just the opposite!)

In secular countries, religious affairs are administered by the respective religious communities. A secular state should not, as it does in Turkey, set up an Department of Religious Affairs and proceed to treat the majority sect as the religion of the state. The state should not open religious schools and fill civil service positions with graduates of religious schools as if they were the same as other graduates. In secular countries, we do not see graduates of religious schools settling themselves into the most elevated positions, shrieking, "We are the embodiment of Islam, as Muslim as the call to prayer!" and get votes for their party by using their position within the state. The state should not open mosque associations abroad and appoint its own officials to them and give such associations status by letting them handle state business such as passport renewals and deferment of military service for Turkish nationals living abroad.

In short, secularism should not act contrary to its basic principles on the pretext of "keeping religion under control." If there is such a contradiction, then it is up to the citizens to put it right. The thinking people of this country have a duty to protect our treasured secularism from open attack by fanatics or covert attack by politicians in their suits and ties. It is a heavy responsibility.

What would our ninth president[26] say if he were here?

"Who could have done the things you describe? Where is the culprit? When did this happen? How could such a thing have happened? If anyone has any proof, bring it forward. The state will immediately take action. Nobody should make unfounded accusations that might have grave repercussions."

Fine, Mr. President. Here is your proof:

---

26. Süleyman Demirel, who served as president from 1993 to 2000. A center-right politician who also served as prime minister six times, he was ousted by military coups in 1971 and 1980, and much criticized for having exploited religion to promote his party's electoral fortunes.

This is from a statement made by the Turkish Consulate in Münster, Germany, on October 23, 1991:

> If you are a worker or a student and you want to defer your military service, it is not necessary to come to the Consulate General. *It will be sufficient*[27] to get in touch with the religious official appointed to associations attached to the DITIB [Diyanet İşleri Türk Islam Birliği—Turkish Islamic Union of Religious Affairs] in your city or the city nearest to you and to *deliver the necessary documents to them*. A list of religious officials *who will carry out such procedures* with their names and addresses is attached. [The list gives the addresses of DITIB Mosque Associations.]

So what did we do?

A group of thinking, concerned people addressed the ambassador about this practice and about a speech attributed to the chief consul of Düsseldorf.

Ambassador Onur Öymen replied that the associations were merely giving out information. We refused to accept this response, arguing that, in the end, Turkish citizens living abroad would come to view mosque associations and imams as official branches of the consulate, contrary to the principles of the secular republic.

When the press got involved, the authorities made a statement over Köln Radio that there had been "a misunderstanding" and that in the future all such transactions would be handled by the consulate; this was reported in the news on February 22, 1992.

Nevertheless, we later heard from youngsters living in the region that the practice was continuing and that religious officials were still processing passports and delivering them to the Münster consulate.

We did all we could to respectively submit this evidence to our Atatürkist, *secular* (!?) state:

To Mr. Demirel at the Prime Minister's office.

To Mr. İnönü at the office of the Deputy Prime Minister.

---

27. Emphasis added.

To Mr. Hikmet Çetin at the Foreign Ministry.

As the Turkish proverb says, "The dog barks, but the caravan continues on its way." We barked, but it seems we couldn't stop the caravan.

The roots of this sort of practice go far deeper than Münster. Since 1985, on the basis of a Turkish Foreign Ministry directive, our embassies and consulates have organized mosque associations along the lines of the "Turk-Islam synthesis,"[28] staffing them with the Turkish ultranationalists living abroad. The idea was that mosques in Europe should not be left to the supporters of Kaplan, Hodja,[29] or Erbakan.[30] Well, who should they be left to? Surely not to the Turk-Islam synthesis of nationalists and religious orders, an arabesque mockery of the secular principles of Atatürk.

Who are the foreign representatives of the Republic of Turkey?

---

28. The yoking together of religion and Turkish nationalist identity, embodied in 1983 in the military junta's National Culture Plan.

29. Cemalettin Kaplan, who organized a network of religious-based organizations, the Islamic Society and Community Union, and later declared himself caliph of an Islamic state in exile. He died in 1995.

30. In 1972, Necmettin Erbakan headed the religious-based National Salvation Party (Milli Selamet Partisi, MSP), which participated in three coalition governments before being banned after the military coup of 1980. MSP established a pattern that was followed by two successors, under the leadership of Erbakan—the Welfare Party (Refah, 1983–1998) and the Virtue Party (Fazilet, 1997–2001)—gathering support of 24 percent or less of the electorate but holding the largest number of seats in parliament.

    The Welfare Party won the largest vote (21.3 percent) in the general election of December 1995. It formed a coalition government with Tansu Çiller's center-right True Path Party (DYP), and Necmettin Erbakan took office as prime minister in June 1996. When the prime minister signaled a change in foreign policy toward closer relations with Muslim nations, the military publicly expressed its unease. At a National Security Council meeting on February 28, 1997, the General Staff presented Necmettin Erbakan with a series of eighteen demands that, if implemented, would reverse the Welfare Party program. Those measures included abolition of religious-based middle schools and purging the civil service of members of religious brotherhoods (tarikat). Erbakan eventually acceded to the demands, but the military stepped up the pressure, and a Constitutional Court case was brought, seeking the abolition of Welfare. Deputies began to migrate from the True Path Party, and the government lost its parliamentary majority. Necmettin Erbakan resigned as prime minister in June 1997. In January 1998, the Constitutional Court closed down the Welfare Party on the grounds that it had become "a focus of activities in breach of the [constitutional] principle of secularism." Necmettin Erbakan and four other party officials were excluded from politics for five years. In June 2001, the Virtue Party was closed by the Constitutional Court for antisecular activities.

In capital cities: the ambassadors.

In big cities: chief consuls.

In small cities: religious associations and imams attached to the DITIB.

Does that look like a secular state to you?

For Abdurrahman Dilipak's views on this subject, see Green *chapters 6, 7, 25, and 30.*

10. ISN'T THE WEATHER LOVELY TODAY?

And really, it is. The full beauty of spring is in the air, in the tree branches, clean and sweet-smelling, intensely colorful. People get caught up in the spring atmosphere. Everybody is out on the streets or by the sea. I am writing these lines near a big wooded area, the sort of green space that is hard to find in İstanbul. This corner, which is free of pollution, even in the poisonous smoky nights of winter, is perfumed with fresh flowers. The park, which normally is empty, except when young lovers skip school and come wandering hand in hand in the grove, is today crowded, bursting with life. I quit writing for a while and go out, walking toward Kuzguncuk.[31] With every step, my heart fills with a little more joy of life. Now we are walking with Nazım.[32]

Today is Sunday.
Today, for the first time,
      they took me out into the sun
      and for the first time in my life
I looked at the sky
      amazed that it was so far
      and so blue
      and so wide.
I stood without moving
and then respectfully sat on the black earth,
pressed my back against the wall.
Now, not even a thought of dying,

---

31. District of İstanbul on the Asian shore, close to Yurdatapan's home.

32. Nazım Hikmet (1902–1963). Author of the twenty-thousand-line epic *Memleketimden İnsan Manzaraları* (*Human Views of My Homeland*), Nazım Hikmet is Turkey's most celebrated modern poet, widely translated. In his home country, however, he was condemned and imprisoned for twelve years for his commitment to Marxism. Following his release from prison in 1950, he fled to Russia and died in Moscow, stripped of his Turkish citizenship.

not a thought of freedom, of my wife.

The earth, the sun and me . . .

        I am happy.

Today is Sunday again, Great Nazım. Yes, almost fifty years have passed since that Sunday, but the sun that makes us happy is the same sun. What is fifty years in the lifetime of the sun? But it is the same for you too! Artists like you who leave great monuments behind can somehow never die. Every sunny spring day you look out and there are Nazım's couplets floating by, or the *saz*[33] melodies of Ruhi Su[34] in Kuzguncuk.

In Kuzguncuk this beautiful spring morning, young lovers are walking around. Some, who are enjoying every moment of the warmth of young feelings flooding through them, are afraid of being seen hand in hand, though just as afraid of letting go of the other's hand.

I whisper inside my head, "What are you afraid of, youngsters?"

They do not reply. But in my mind, I form their answer: "What if someone saw us and went to tell our father or our elder brother?"

So, what if they do? Surely their father or brother was young once.

Of course, but they are alarmed lest the neighbors talk.

And were the neighbors born already old?

"!!! For pity's sake, are you from outer space or something?" they would tell me. "Don't you know that society frowns on boys and girls wandering around together?"

So boys wandering with boys and girls wandering with girls counts as normal?

"You know very well what we are talking about. A girl can get a bad reputation."

And the boy, doesn't he get a bad reputation?

"At worst, he will be called a Casanova. Well, that much is expected from a young boy!"

---

33. A Turkish stringed instrument, similar to the buzuki.

34. Folklorist, singer, and composer, Ruhi Su (1912–1985) was frequently imprisoned for expressing his leftist views. In 1983, when he was seriously ill with cancer, Ruhi Su was offered free medical treatment in Germany. The Turkish government refused to let him leave the country.

And not from a young girl?

I think about the hell we put our kids through, and somehow I cannot understand why we behave so unlovingly toward them. In their childhood, we stretch our protective wings over them as far as we can and spoil them by doing what they ask for without hesitation. We will go without to feed and clothe them, do anything so they do not feel deprived and long for what they do not have. But when they reach puberty, the tender, compassionate mother and father disappear, to be replaced by a pair of morality police, each armed with a truncheon.

In fact, they need us more than ever in that period. Full of new passion, they are exhilarated by each other. At the same time, they are reaching out to find out who they are, while all around them the merciless pressure of life is preparing to grind them down and eventually consign their remains to the grave.

We should be very much there for our children in these adolescent days, when they need more than ever the warm understanding of their mother and father. We should not push them into the abyss of loneliness with our own hands. We should not even turn a blind eye to their snuggling up to someone of their own age because they are taking steps that could endanger the rest of their lives. Can we offer our children something more than a rat race, competing for a place at a good school, qualifications, and some petty job they must climb over each other to secure?

For Abdurrahman Dilipak's views on this subject, see Green *chapters 7 and 11.*

11. FATHER, HOW DID I COME INTO THE WORLD?

The child asks his father:

—Father, where did I come from?

The father gives the famous reply:

—The stork brought you, my child.

Then the child goes to his grandfather:

—Grandpa, where did my father come from?

Grandpa turns purple and stammers:

—Er, your father came out of an egg.

The child asks again:

—Well, where did you come from?

The grandpa's new story is that:

—They found me in front of the mosque door.

The child runs off to his friend and says:

—It's amazing! For the last three generations, there has not been a single normal birth in our family!

He is a TV child. What else can you expect? We can mumble and try to cover up all we like, but the media network reaches our children before we do. Right now, we are trying to keep my five-and-a-half-year-old, Can,[35] away from TV violence; he is a tough and quick-tempered character anyway. It is not possible or sensible to stop him from watching TV altogether. But the programs are so full of scenes of blood, death, murder, and violence that we are trying at least to make him choose the less damaging ones—cartoons, for example, which he loves. But it is an impossible task. I sit him down to watch a harmless cartoon and suddenly there is an ad trailing some horror film to be shown later that evening. Blood sprays out all over the room and dead bodies are hurled from the TV screen. Either that, or the cartoon film broadcasts terror and savagery: space monsters with molten wax faces, or giant spiders trying to conquer the world, or pop-eyed ghosts springing out of the earth.

35. Pronounced Jan.

Alongside all this junk, this colorful box also shows our children many of those life truths we are vainly trying to hide from them. Especially about sex. Let it not be misunderstood, I am not defending porno films, which simply make a profit out of our society's thirst for sex. Plainly, the premature interests or fears these films may awaken in children who are still far from the natural developing age is going to adversely affect their psychological development. (You know the story of the child who woke up in the middle of the night and witnessed a scene he was not familiar with and assumed his father was doing something evil to his mother.) This is why I find it harmful and unnecessary. But the lies we tell them about sex—simply because of our own taboos—are no less harmful and, perhaps, worse.

Yet, how can we do such a wrong to our children, whom we think we love so much? We tell them about all manner of subjects and answer their questions clearly and openly until it comes to sex, when we tell lies or change the subject, telling ourselves we are only postponing the conversation. The child grows up in a culture where "it's shameful, it's a sin, it's naughty, it's dirty," and begins to be ashamed of or repelled by a particular region of their body. Then the child grows older, nature dictates its laws, puberty arrives, and spring blooms in our children's bodies. How badly we let our children down at this special time! At this period of their life, when both body and mind are changing rapidly, we become the most distant strangers to them. These little people try to find their way in the company of others their age who are at least as ignorant as they are, leaning on each other in the dark. And these young and tender little people sometimes go through bitter experiences: miscarriages, secret abortions, even suicide triggered by shame and desperation.

I am the child of a family of readers and thinkers. I was a lucky child who could find books on every subject in the bookshelves at home and obtain serious answers to all my questions, but I also went through bad experiences and witnessed even worse. For this reason I am determined not to do harm to my children in this respect.

Now my youngest daughter is at this age. From now on, I must no longer be her father but her friend. Whatever rights I recognize for my son—or at this age for myself—I must now recognize for my daughter too. Nothing less, nothing more. I hope I can establish a real friendship with her, in spite of the generational difference between us, so that she shares her experiences and her thoughts with me, openly and without fear. She must not live in fear of my getting angry, imposing prohibitions on her life, failing to understand, despising her.

I want to be able to tell her my views and experiences, but in the end she must make her own decisions. She is living her life, not mine. I think the best fatherhood I can provide for her is not to attempt to solve all her problems, and thereby perhaps to make them even less solvable, but to support her and to encourage her to solve her own problems and stand on her own two feet in this world.

I do not know how far I will achieve my hopes, but, in general, it is clear that on this subject there is a gulf between us and our children and that we are not helpful to them. Why is this? Don't we love them? Of course we love them. They are the light of our lives. But the taboos we accept without thought or judgment, monsters of our own creation, and societal pressures have permeated us deeply. The one that strays from the flock is torn apart by the flock long before the wolf gets her!

AH, THOSE IMMORAL FLOWERS!

There is something called honor *(namus),* and in our society, once it is blotted, only blood can clean the stain. Womankind is basically the bearer of honor, but once a woman loses her honor, it is considered to have been lost by the menfolk too.

It is truly a strange item, this honor. Cats and dogs do not have any honor. When March arrives and they get fidgety, we fling them outside so they can get on with it. Of course, we can do this more comfortably if we have removed their reproductive organs with a small operation to prevent the unwanted increase of our household. When our pets return from an escapade with their male or female friends, we greet them half approvingly, saying, "You randy Casanova." I have not yet met a family that scolded a female pet as she returned from a bout outside, saying, "Dishonorable slut! We are no longer your mother and your father. We'll not have you under our roof a moment longer! Get out!"

Cats and dogs do not have honor, and neither do birds, flies, or even flowers. In flowers, the female and male organs stand side by side like fire and gunpowder. As soon as they feel the heat of the sun, they open their leaves and shamelessly show us their various parts. And then, thanks to the matchmaking of bees and insects, they do shameful deeds and then cast their young to the care of the winds, sometimes filling our hayfeverish nostrils with sneezes.

Now you are smirking. "Of course there is no honor among the animals, because they are animals. But we have honor because we are different, because we are human. And what distinguishes us from animals is the fact that we have brains and can think and understand."

Is that right? Yes, someone has called man the rational animal. Well, in that case, let's all think together and deserve our humanity. But we must live with the results of our thinking, and we must think the issue through to the end. We must not give up halfway when the going gets tough, saying, "Good heavens, our little brains can't possibly solve this big mystery." If we are going to treat our brains as pathetic and helpless, surrender to a brain of greater intellect than ours, quit thinking and make our intellect subservient to it, then the honest thing would be to do this right from the start. If you agree, then let us proceed to question ourselves.

Why is honor located in womankind? Why is it that, according to some of us, it is concentrated in the sexual parts of a woman's body, while according to others, it spreads right up to the hair on her head, which she must therefore cover? If one of our girls flirts with a boy, why does she become a slut, but if one of our boys flirts with a girl, we say, "Well, he's bound to. He is a real lad and takes after his father"?

How can we explain this sort of thing?

"Well, this is how our forefathers behaved!"

Really? It is a poor argument.

Are you ready to go on a journey into the past? If you are, then be my guest and ride the time machine. Let's go home and open our encyclopedia. What can we learn from our ancestors?

For Abdurrahman Dilipak's views on this subject, see Green *chapter 14.*

12. DID WE LEARN FROM OUR FOREFATHERS OR FROM OUR FOREMOTHERS?

Our encyclopedia says that the age of our world is something like 4,600,000,000 years old. To understand how big a number this is, try counting up from one and go on counting for five minutes: 1, 2, 3, 4, 5, 6, 7, 8, 9, 10, 11...

Your time is up. How far did you reach? I counted like a machine, but I could not reach 500. Well, 4,600,000,000 means 9,000,000 times 200,000 times 500 (9,200,000 x 500 = 4,600,000,000). Have you ever seen so many zeroes? Do you want to try to count this number? Go ahead and try. That's how long our globe has been turning in space!

It is believed that life on earth started approximately 700,000,000 years ago. These microscopic living creatures were without honor. They ate and drank their fill until they separated into two new cells, mitochrondial and amitochrondial, also referred to as mitos and amitos, which then in time split in exactly the same fashion as their parents, and in this way they multiplied. (In those days, Article 8 of the Anti-Terror Law did not apply, so everyone could be as separatist as they liked.) Then, multicellular creatures appeared, with a more complex structure, but all of these scoundrels were also quite bereft of honor—promiscuous rascals! Some were plants, some were animals, and some were something in between. Some had feet on their heads or on their bellies; some lived in water; some crept on the ground; some flew in the air—thousands of species of living things! Let us forget Darwin and his theory of evolution for a moment and focus on our ancestors, who somehow dignified this world by arriving either by constant evolution or by falling through the roof.

Before we had a chance to ask if they were monkeys or pithecanthropus, *Homo sapiens* hit the scene. (Yeah, I remember it as if it were yesterday, though it actually was *1,000,000 years ago*. Time really flies.)

Look, we are close to the year 2000 C.E. Since the invention of writing and the beginning of history, only five or six thousand years have passed. According to most calculations, everything we learned from our forefathers we learned in those years. Now let us put this story under the magnifying glass.

Please do not get stuck on Darwin and evolution. Let me call it evolution and you call it creation; it does not make any difference. Living things came to existence in the sequence specified above.

Because our topic is humanity, let us turn our attention to humans' adventure on this earth. If we treat the period from the beginning of humankind until the present day as a single year, here is what it would look like:

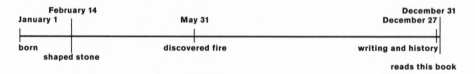

So what is the point of all this?

What we have learned from our forefathers consists, at most, of the few days from the afternoon of December 27 until New Year's Day. Yet our foremothers existed since the first day of the year. Well, we know they existed, but what did they eat and drink? How did they live?

If we look at the imaginary depictions of the Stone Age cave in the first pages of elementary schoolbooks, we see a family very much like one of today. The mother is cooking food in one corner, the child is playing near her, and the father—who, as usual, has left his wife to do all the hard work—is enjoying himself drawing bison on the cave wall. That they are all respectable, with their *namus* intact, is evident because they all wear animal skins on their backs rather than going naked. (Well, I suppose the National Education Ministry would prefer to sacrifice authenticity rather than get into trouble with parents.)

I apologize to our Ministry of Education and the reader, but I am obliged to point out that these pictures are as faithful in their representation of Stone Age caves as the Flintstones. First of all, the family of that time was nothing like our contemporary family structure, and the bloodline was not considered to pass through the man yelling "Yaba daba doooooo," but through the woman. To use the scientific term, the family structure was not patriarchal but matriarchal. The family was not like today's nuclear family, with a child and a single father and mother. Early people lived in clans, just like the natives of Africa or the Amazon basin whom we see in adventure films and whom we describe as primitive just because they continue their ancestral customs and traditions.

For these people, "production" was hunting and gathering. When we say "hunting," do not imagine hunting rabbits with a bow and arrow. Hunting larger game was a job that could not be done alone but had to be handled in groups by means of cooperation and division of labor, with the proceeds shared appropriately. One group of hunters would disturb the prey and direct it toward the trap, and others would attack it at the place of ambush. The people lived in tribal communities because they needed to hunt together and felt greater security in numbers. When the food or fresh water became scarce again, they moved on together. (Even today, we take great pride in the fact that our nomadic ancestors were born, lived, and died on horses. In some parts of Anatolia, some people still live the nomadic life. But the horses of the Turks who migrated to Germany are manufactured by Mercedes and BMW. How the world changes!)

However it may have looked inside the house, the responsibility for internal affairs was assigned to the women and the responsibility for external affairs to the men. The women handled economics, justice, education, and culture. Why was it like that? First, everybody knew that both men and women were born from the mother's womb. How they got there in the first place was still a matter of debate. It must have taken primitive man and woman quite a while to figure out the connection between sexual relations that we would consider quite without *namus* today and having a baby nine months later. Because the marital rights of women over men at that period were different from those of today, and women may have had four or more husbands, the paternity of the children was unclear while the maternity was never in doubt. This was why the bloodline passed through the mother—there was no other likely candidate.

Because the woman could bring a child out of herself, out of nowhere, she clearly possessed secret powers. Was she at that time physically weaker than the man? Who knows? Perhaps due to lack of usage over many, many years, her muscles atrophied and lost their strength. Even if that were the case, she had enough strength to clout her youngster, and as even the strongest of men grew up being disciplined by his mother since childhood, it is not difficult to understand why women were powerful in the community.

Why was the indoor world the woman's domain? She not only gave birth to the child but she also had a maternal instinct, whereas paternal feeling came later and had to be learned. Because it was the mother who took care of the child, obviously the woman had to be indoors, and internal affairs were under her jurisdiction.

In those days (I should really say in those millennia), the refrigerator had not yet been invented, so hunting and gathering vegetables and fruits were dirty, tough, and unrewarding tasks. The men had to brave difficulty and danger to hunt an animal down, perhaps lose a couple of their team as casualties, fight to stop their neighbors from snatching the meat, and in the end they had to eat the animal quickly before it putrefied and could no longer be eaten. And every day the whole business would start all over again.

Then one day, somebody smart must have thought, "Why do we kill these animals right away? While they are still alive, they do not rot and stink. So let's not hang them, but feed them!"[36] And that's what they did, and it changed everything. The livestock bred much faster than the humans, so breeding proved more productive than hunting. Pastures were periodically overgrazed, so nomadism continued, but the first major blow had been dealt to the division of labor. Why? Because outside-the-house work, previously the dirty and unrewarding responsibility of the men, had started to become profitable. Animal herds were a form of wealth. Then they discovered something else.

The seeds of these unchaste plants, which have no *namus* at all, do not lie idle in the ground but rather grow and produce another identical plant. What is more, they grow faster and in greater number than the animals. So

---

36. Ironically, this echoes the words of General Kenan Evren, leader of the 1980 military junta, in his speech of October 3, 1984: "Shall we not hang these traitors, and feed them instead?" During the following month, political prisoners Ilyas Has and Hidir Aslan were indeed hanged, but these were the last (judicial) executions in Turkey.

let us grow them, and cut and eat them when we are hungry, and save what we do not need for another day!

This discovery cost womankind dearly. The new source of wealth was *land*! And this damn thing also was outside the house in the male domain. (Your Anatolian male also discovered how to sit all day drinking tea at the village café and have the woman go off to the fields, but Stone Age man was just a primitive. He had not thought of this yet.)

To make a long story short, man, the master of all these new riches, gradually imposed his authority over women as well. Our matriarchal heritage began to disappear. Dairy farming and cultivation took the place of hunting, and nomadic life gave way to settlements. The male realized he could produce with less manpower and concentrated on cooperation with close kin rather than a broader tribe. At about this time, he also discovered how he could ensure that he was providing for his own child only.

Polygamy for men (at least in practice) became monogamy for women, and from then on, every woman had to be in full possession of her *namus*. Patriarchal morality arose only in the last week of human history, but it has really taken hold since then, pushing women around and even locking them away into Hitler's *"Kirche, Küche, Kinder"* (church, kitchen, children). Hitler limited the female zone to the three *K*s. The woman of the super-race, with German blood in her veins, entered her three-*K* cage with pride, and I am afraid that some are still imprisoned there.

PACK UP AND CLEAR OFF TO YOUR MOTHER'S!

Let us return for a moment to the matriarchal period, scientifically known as primitive communal society, and follow a prehistoric tale of love and betrayal:

Our young hero's name is Tanju, and our damsel is Serpil. Tanju falls in love with Serpil. He gathers all his belongings (his animal-skin cloak and his flints) and goes off to Serpil's clan. Serpil's clan is about fifty or sixty strong, headed by Mother Mualla. Short of two male members lost in recent hunts and fights, the whole family is pleased to welcome Tanju.

The two lovers are very happy. Canan, Elif, Nurten, and Itir, the other women of Serpil's generation, are also happy because by clan law they can claim marital rights from Tanju. The young men of the clan, Çelik, Tufan, Doğan, and Aytaç, have no complaints either. A capable new member has joined the workforce, and the new arrival can help to meet the demands for marital rights imposed by the women of their generation.

Family life goes on happily enough, and one day Serpil brings a baby into the world. We know she is the baby's mother, but nobody can be sure if Tanju is the father because Serpil can demand marital rights not just from Tanju but also from Çelik, Tufan, Doğan, and Aytaç. None of the men can bounce the baby on his knee, saying, "Jack, the lad, every inch his father's son!"

More time passes. Serpil and the other girls of her generation, Canan, Elif, Nurten, and Itır are getting old. They are beyond their middle years, and their beauty has faded. Tanju has now got his eye on young Ayla, from the next generation. Ayla clearly returns his interest. But such disgraceful behavior is against the customs of the community. Relations between people of a different generation? Shame on you! Such an act is a breach of the strongest taboo. It is not only scandalous and against the rules of the community, it may anger the God Totem and cause him to strike like thunder on the clan. (And just as an aside: Tanju will not be reunited with his Ayla for thousands of years—not until today, when he can make a fast buck and have any girl he fancies.)

No one knows who established these moral codes. Perhaps they arose because the clan wanted to avoid the problem of increasing population and having too many mouths to be feed. Anyway, this was the heritage of our foremothers. We break the head of anyone who tries to impose new customs on our old village, and we do it in the name of great God Totem.

Secretly, Tanju and Ayla go at it. They nearly get caught a couple of times, but the postman only rings twice, and the third time the game is up. Mother Mualla chairs a council of the eldest mothers of the family and they reach a decision according to Article 8 of the Totemic code. Because Ayla is a woman, after all, and she has certain flirting rights, she just gets a slap on the wrist, but Tanju is a man, so he has stained and soiled his honor. He is also from another family, so he is even more an outsider. Therefore he must go. Poor Tanju, not wanting to be left alone and at the mercy of the wolves and vultures, packs his suitcase and creeps away to his mother's house, sick with fear at how he will be viewed in his dishonored state.

So our story closes, and, because this is not a Hollywood movie, it has a sad ending.

THE MORAL LESSONS OF OUR STORY

Now, let us just review our lesson, before Father History puts us to the test.

Between December 27 and 31 on our time chart, all we learned from our forefathers was patriarchy. From January 1 until December 27, our foremothers taught us matriarchy, but we have forgotten all that.

Until December 27, families existed, though they were not like contemporary families, but the pictures in the elementary schoolbooks do not reflect this.

In the time of the foremothers, there was a clearly defined concept of honor, but the honor they devised to suit their time was quite unlike ours. According to them, we are quite disgracefully without honor.

So this thing called honor is not immutable. It is not something that does not change with the times. When the realities of life change, what is considered honor can also change—sometimes even reemerging as its diametric opposite.

So, who says that our current idea of honor will not change tomorrow?

Let us then review our values to see what is consistent with modern realities and what is in conflict with those realities.

If the values conflict with our realities, is it not time they changed?

I'd say it is! So that we propose a civilized understanding of honor befitting contemporary society:

Honor does not reside in private relations between people but in their relations with society as a whole. A man or a woman's private relations are his or her own business, and both should live their lives as they choose. Whether or not people have honor depends on the way they live, living without infringing on the rights of others or harming them, living by their own labor, contributing to the welfare of the community rather than being parasites on the back of society.

By this measure, a woman who never harms others and earns her living by working but who changes lovers frequently is respectable and honorable, but a man who swindles property by taking advantage of the political influence of his close friends or relatives and who grows rich without producing anything is disgraceful and dishonorable.

Which understanding do you think is more appropriate to today's realities?

I am not from another planet. I know that in today's world just the opposite is happening, particularly in countries whose progress has been held back, like Turkey. Scenes illustrating our current understanding of honor darken our TV screens, newspapers, and hearts every day: expensive yachts, luxurious living, violence, fights, knives, and blood. I had better not darken your hearts any further. Instead, here is a joke about honor:

Temel[37] shot his wife dead on their second night of marriage. People asked:

—Hey, Temel, why did you shoot her?

—She wasn't a virgin!

—Well, why did you kill her on the second night of your marriage rather than the first?

—She was a virgin the first night!

But this black humor freezes the smile on your lips and gives more sorrow than pleasure. Of course, because Temel is exaggeratedly stupid, the story is considered funny, and we laugh, though our laughter is hollow. If he had killed her the first night, this would not have been a joke, because in Turkey we have grown used to the many real-life cases of men shooting their wife on their first night "because she was not a virgin."

That is the blackest humor.

So, this is our world and our Turkey. On the one side, millions of poor, uneducated men are so much in the grip of ignorance that if they even see their former wife with someone else, they consider it a matter of honor to kill her. The woman goes to the grave, the man to jail! On the other hand, the very people who condemn the others to poverty and ignorance, those who have achieved super-rich status through dishonesty and immorality, are treated as highly honorable and honored.

---

37. Stories about the famously stupid fictional character Temel are a standard of Turkish humor.

So I am asking you again, even though I know the answer:

Which understanding do you think is more appropriate to today's realities?

For Abdurrahman Dilipak's views on this subject, see Green *chapter 30.*

13. WHEREVER THE HODJA STRIKES, NO, NOT ROSES, BUT EDUCATION GROWS

"Roses grow wherever the hodja (teacher) strikes."

—Turkish proverb

"No, sir, I don't get what you told us. It is not like that at all—it's like this!"

Imagine this scene at an elementary school in Germany. A tiny child does not like what the teacher said, and he puts his hand up in the middle of class and says this quite openly to the teacher's face. What happens? Here's a little test for you:

A. The teacher turns red. "What did you say, you little monkey? I'll teach you how to talk to a teacher!" (Whack, smack, and the roses begin to bloom.)

B. With great difficulty, the teacher controls himself. "Quiet now, don't show off. Just learn what I tell you!"

C. The teacher, with a mocking smile at his lips, says, "Is that right? Well, if you know better than me, come up here to the front then!" (Laughs from the class. The child sits down blushing.)

Unfortunately, you did not score any points, because none of the above choices is right. The teacher *should* take what the child says seriously and continue to defend his own views. Then the other children should join in, and the discussion should continue until the bell announces the end of the lesson. (Yes! We managed to spend the lesson chattering instead of doing our lessons!) But that is not the end of the matter. First, during the break in the schoolyard, and then on the way home after school, the children continue to discuss the issue among themselves. When they reach home, they put the same question to their mothers and the fathers, perhaps consulting books and encyclopedias as everyone seeks an answer to the question.

You may say, "How could such a thing be allowed? How can you teach anything to students in a place where classes are conducted according to the wishes of the students?" Well, we in Turkey are used to order and discipline, and while it is difficult for us to grasp this kind of "anarchy," the results are in front of us! The knowledge drilled into our heads under our educational system does not stay there. Within a couple of years it is gone, forgotten, with no visible trace, whereas the German child is not likely to forget the topic because he heard several views on it, weighed them, and came to his own conclusion. The topic and the related knowledge are his property. On top of this, he gained two other things:

1. He gained experience in expressing his thoughts without fear or hesitation.
2. Even more important, he learned to listen to opposing views and to assess them.

Are these not valuable lessons?

In Germany, whenever we watched TV, we were surprised to see how even small children could speak without shyness, not sputtering away like the television personality Mehmet Ali Birand, but naturally, fluently, and, what's more, knowledgeably. Our daughter Zeynep came to Germany when she was only one year old, and now she is sixteen (*twenty-three in 2002*), so the majority of her education took place in the German system. The foundations of her personality were laid in that environment.

In Germany, elementary education lasts four years. When the children are still only ten or eleven years old, they come to an important and difficult crossroads. At that point, what they will become in the future is about 95 percent decided. Because there are several alternative paths for higher education, they do not automatically go on to middle school and high school, as in our country; the fast track to university in Germany is via the *gymnasium*, which provides a broader education. The Germans also have other schools that are similar to our high schools but that educate students up to different levels.

I did not like this aspect of their education at all. It seemed directed toward the needs of German industry rather than towards allowing people to gather knowledge and develop themselves as better-qualified people— the German version of our "If everybody gets a university education, who will sweep our streets?" This is the mentality of people who cannot see that a society in which individuals are encouraged to realize their full potential through education could probably devise more civilized methods or machines to keep their streets clean.

Thank heavens, I am not the only one who thinks this way. Under the German Social Democratic Party (SDP) government, another kind of school was opened as an alternative to the above system. This *Gesamtschule* (comprehensive school) brings various kinds of education under one roof, so that students can easily transfer from one to the other according to their wishes and achievements. In this way, that crossroads at age ten or eleven does not determine the course of the rest of their lives. Of course, there are some problems that must be ironed out with these new schools, but they are not insurmountable. What is difficult to overcome is that the conservative parties (who have been in power for most of the time in recent years) systematically try to sabotage these schools by spoiling their reputation and generally running them down.

But for now, let's go back to the end of the four-year elementary school system. When my little Zeynep finished elementary school, the class teacher called us in, just as she does for all her students, and made her recommendations for the future of Zeynep. She said, "Zeynep is an unusual child. She has strong powers of imagination. We must not let her lose that. Without a doubt, she must go to the *gymnasium* [the fast track to university], but there she will only be looked on as a *number*, just like any other student. For this reason I am going to recommend a particular school."

When she did, we stared at her astounded . . . the school which she named was a *Catholic girls' high school.*

What? Will she really be going to a *Catholic girls' high school*? I don't believe it!

Why did our eyes open so wide with surprise when we heard the teacher recommend a Catholic girls' high school? What did we understand this to mean?

First, that boys and girls would study in separate schools, thereby sustaining the idea that the sexes should be separated. The two sexes, which tomorrow will be side by side in every walk of life, would be educated separately from each other, kept apart as firmly as the north and south poles. We saw no difference between our son and our daughter, other than what nature had given them, so we greatly resented the idea that our daughter would go to a *girls' school*.

Second, in Germany, of the two main Christian sects, the Protestants have broader views and are a community-based group whose churches are more open and active on the issues of peace and anti-racism. The Catholics, by contrast, are more conservative, more bigoted. They tend more toward ideas of separating sexes, races, nationalities, and are in general more xeno-phobic. (Most of those who applaud the neo-Nazi skinheads are not Nazis but devout Catholics.)

But the teacher insisted. "It's no longer like that," she said. She conceded that the administrators of the school were nuns with black gowns, but she said that the school also had very modern people. And the girls were often in contact with the boys from the boys' high school right next door. They could meet each other in the yard and the school corridors, and only the classrooms were separate. The main reason why she preferred this particular school, though, was that she knew the teaching staff well and she liked them.

In Germany, unlike in our country, the bond between teacher and student is not broken as soon as the child finishes elementary school. For a certain period, the teacher attends teachers' meetings at the high school where the student has enrolled and is able to pass on valuable information about the child to his new teachers. Because of this, the elementary school teachers are familiar with the upper-level schools in the region. In our case, the teacher was recommending this school as one that would protect Zeynep's powers of imagination.

To cut a long story short, we took the teacher's advice, and we went to the girls' high school. It was spotlessly clean, surrounded by a small grove of trees, a place like a little paradise. Just as we were told, the boys' high school was right next door, and the boys and the girls were together in the yard and the passages, everywhere side by side—mixed. Yes, there were nuns in their long dresses, white collars, and black and white wimples here and there, but the scene was not like one of those dark, overgrown, and terrifying medieval monasteries.

But the real surprise was waiting for us in the school corridors, where there was an exhibition of writings, enlarged photographs, and newspaper cuttings prepared by the school's final-year students. It addressed the young newcomers to the school, warning them and informing them about AIDS. From that moment on, I had no more doubts. This place was a school that aimed to bring up the girls as *equal* and *free humans*. Inside me, I felt both joy and burning sorrow. Joy, because this school promised me hope and peace of mind about the future of my daughter, and sorrow, because I could not help thinking of the millions of children in my own country who are deprived of all this. It was the feeling you might get as you swallow a mouthful knowing that someone nearby is hungry.

Then, for a moment, a fictional scene materialized in front of me. Suddenly this was not a Catholic girls' school but its rough, European equivalent: an *imam hatip* school. Instead of nuns in long black dresses, there would be lady directors wearing the *turban* (the headscarf), and on the walls the same exhibition warning of the dangers of AIDS! (It is indeed our imagination that sustains us and keeps us going in this world.)

(Years later, when I went to offer my support to the year 2001 Marmara University Faculty of Religion girls who were barred from their classes because they were wearing the *turban*, I remembered that beautiful school and the principal in her jet-black clothes. That I will tell you about a bit later.)

As we went through those corridors that gave us so much joy and peace as well as sorrow and sadness, we reached the office of the principal. She was a Catholic sister who was waiting for us in her spotlessly clean office—like all other offices in Germany—furnished with classic furniture. She had long white hair that stretched down behind her black and white wimple, deep blue eyes that smiled warmly from behind her narrow-rimmed glasses, and she spoke perfect English. She told us that it was not problem for them to accept a Muslim (!?) girl into their school. There was only one difficulty, and she hoped we would be understanding on the subject.

We should have no doubt that she herself and the school itself assuredly respected freedom of belief. They would never, ever exert pressure on any student to educate them against their beliefs. But there was a concrete, practical problem, and they did not want to relive the stresses and strains they had experienced with the child of a Moroccan family.

There were religion classes at the school. The school was attached to the Catholic church, but Protestant children were registered there as well.

When the time came for classes in religion, the class would divide into two, and the children would receive religious education from their respective teachers, Catholics in one classroom and Protestants in another. But the Moroccan girl who came last year had confronted them with difficulties. The parents did not want their daughter exposed to Christian religious propaganda, and they had made their wishes known to the school administration. The administration found this request reasonable and considered it normal that the girl might not want to take religious education classes with either group. So what happened then? During the religious education lessons, the Moroccan girl was all by herself in the empty corridors, but because the administration was responsible for each student as long as they were at school, they were worried about an increase in the number of unattended students.

We told her to feel comfortable about this. Because our daughter was living in this country, she should get to know the culture of the people here. These religious education classes, which were not included in the curriculum of the public schools in secular Germany, were part of the reality of contemporary German society, inculcated into every German child as a part of their culture. So let them explain their views to Zeynep, and we would explain ours. When the day came, she would be able to choose her own views for herself.

TWO TURKISH GIRLS SAYING "NO TO WAR"! ONE IN GERMANY AND ONE IN TURKEY

Years have passed since that day. With time, we realized that Zeynep's elementary school teacher had sent us to the right place. Something we experienced during the Gulf War strengthened this conviction. At that time, the whole of Germany was in a fever. There were protests against the war and against Germany's joining the war. Every thinking person, and everyone on the side of peace, was on the streets.

Major Helmut, a neighbor who lived opposite us, came over to our house with a bundle of papers. He was conducting a signature campaign. He wanted us to sign the petition and to help collect more signatures from our circle of acquaintances and friends. Of course, we accepted and took the forms. Zeynep also asked for some forms. She wanted to collect signatures at her school! Helmut did not want to discourage the child, so he gave her a couple of forms. After two days, the results were fantastic. Our little one, with over eighty signatures, had collected more names than anyone else in our area.

"How did you do it?" we asked. She had first gone directly to the principal and asked for permission. The woman liked this very much and in addition to giving permission, she gave the first signature herself. Of course, once the principal had signed, the teachers, the students, and even parents visiting the school signed Zeynep's forms. After that, they hit a snag. One or two conservative parents created a fuss, saying, "It is wrong for such a thing to be going on in this school." But our Catholic sister made no concession. "Our duty is to raise our children in such a way that they are not afraid to think freely and express their opinions!"

At about the same time, an exactly opposite event was happening in Turkey. A fifteen-year-old student named N. A. was arrested by the police and roughed up in the police station because she had written "No to war" on the wall of her school. When we returned to Turkey, we wanted to meet N. A. My brave reporter friend Mustafa Ekmekçi, who had stood up for her in his writings, gave me her phone number, and I called her. Unfortunately, her family had been badly scared. They asked us to leave their daughter in peace. That is what I did, but is she in peace? I am not sure.

In 1992, we moved from Germany to İstanbul, and little Zeynep started the 1992–1993 school year in İstanbul. From the first day, she was in conflict with the Turkish education system. One of the lessons on the very first day at school was Citizenship Studies. In my day, it was called Homeland Studies, and we covered such topics as court verdicts, how court decisions are executed, and what the responsibilities of the accounting office are. But Zeynep's teacher started out with a nationalist tone. He went on and on, explaining what a great a privilege it is to be a Turk and how they should all be proud of it. While he was talking, Zeynep's hand was in the air. "Yes, but whatever society a person is brought up in, they feel a part of that society. Most of us in this class grew up in Germany, should we now feel sorry for that?"

The answer of the teacher was heartbreaking.

"Whoever feels they belong over there, they should go and live there!"

In other words, "Like it or leave it."

Zeynep sat down, her face burning. I expect the teacher puffed up, pretty proud of his reply. But if he had accepted that his students might have their own opinions and if he had asked for them, he might have gotten some disturbing answers, such as, "What are you talking about? It is clear that you have never been out of this country, because if you had, you would understand what it means to be a Turk from the moment you crossed the frontier. Especially in Germany. Being a Turk is not a reason for being proud there. Quite the opposite: In many places we are looked down on and pushed around. Our worth is counted by the value of the money in our pocket. What is there in this to make us feel proud?"

Forget empty talk about being proud, whatever benefit that is supposed to bring. Let us think seriously about just how independent a nation can be when daily transactions are conducted in foreign currency. Members of parliament who give lengthy speeches describing Turkey as the "independent Turkish state" must be aware, at least at some level, that just down the road in the shop windows on Necatibey Avenue, the price tags are marked in U.S. dollars.

But we should get back to our topic. The Turkish system of education, under which all our members of parliament were educated, is based on rote-learning and unquestioning obedience. I am not talking about schools only. This system of education, which fears thought, which represses thought, and which permits only the parroting of official truths, starts at home. The child fears the mother or the father, or both of them. This situation at home foreshadows the fear-based discipline outside, for at school, the same pattern continues. This time it is fear of the teacher. Once out in the world, fear of the boss, the director, or the principal takes over. Everywhere and all of the time, fear of the police, the state—and as if that were not enough, we are introduced to fears about the afterlife and Allah, and so our fears soar even beyond the physical limits of the world.

And we Turks wonder why we produce so few scientists, writers, artists....Science, art, and literature all require free and creative brains. When we do manage to produce independent thinkers, we drag them into court and let them rot in prison. Everything is in place to turn the next generation into unthinking imbeciles. We tell our children, "Study your lessons well so that you can give the right (?!) answers to the questions in the examination and pass." Did the child do research in order to learn his lesson?

Did he discuss the topic with others? That is not important for us. And if the student happens to question some issues—and especially if he is not on the teacher's good side—we have ready words of advice: "It doesn't matter who's right and who's wrong. Just write what is in the book and get good marks. You have to toe the line, my child, until you have crossed this bridge!"

But by the time our children have crossed all their bridges, they have become as conformist as everyone else.

For Abdurrahman Dilipak's views on this subject, see Green *chapters 20 and 21.*

14. THIS IS THE ONLY WORLD THERE IS, BUT THIS ONE IS ENOUGH FOR US ALL!

Today is May 19, 1995. I am on a train in Germany. I am sitting in an ultra-modern railcar watching the green fields, the trees, the superbly clean and organized roads, and the pretty houses in well-kept gardens as they flow past on either side. But I have mixed feelings. Despite living so many years in this country, I just have not got used to it. As I look at this spotlessly clean and painstakingly well-organized landscape, with its lines as straight as if they had been drawn with a ruler, I feel endless admiration but also extreme sadness.

I feel admiration for the achievement of humankind in its one million years of struggle with nature. How can we not admire such a victory of intellect, science, and technology?

At the same time, I am raging inside because just a very small part of the world is rich, clean, organized, and well-kept in this way. The rest of the planet is living under the tyranny of hunger, disease, poverty, and ignorance—and the fire, death, resentment, and hatred engendered by endless, ceaseless wars.

Today, nearly six billion of us live on this blue sphere. Look how we are *not* sharing this beautiful world, with its abundant blessings and favors, which are more than enough for all of us:

The wealthiest 20 percent of the earth's population has laid its hands on 79 percent of the world's income. The remaining 80 percent of the population is sharing the remaining 21 percent.

To put it more bluntly, while one person in five is eating four loaves of bread, four other people are fighting over the last single loaf.

How does the proverb go? If one eats and the other looks on. . .[38]

Do not believe the superficial excuses they give for wars. The Arabs and the Jews, the Turks and the Kurds, the Catholics and the Protestants, the Sunni and the Alevi, the Hutu and the Tutsi—there are plenty of exam-

---

38. The Turkish proverb, which continues, "trouble before long," suggests that if there is no social justice, then social disharmony will soon follow.

ples, but if you look beneath the apparent reasons for these conflicts, at the bottom of them all lie this same merciless exploitation and the same greedy interests.

Poverty, instead of decreasing as technology advances, is actually increasing. In the 1970s, the number of the people living below the poverty line (earning less than $1 per day) was approximately 200 million—but in the 1990s, it reached two billion—that is, poverty increased exactly tenfold. But the population of the earth did not increase tenfold in those twenty years.

The main sources of raw materials—oil and minerals—are under the control of the wealthy North. And nowadays, more of these resources that could feed hungry mouths are being spent on arms. The countries that are being kept underdeveloped are all arming themselves to the teeth. Each country is either at its neighbor's throat or internally at odds. Especially after the collapse of the Soviet Union and the socialist bloc, devils broke loose from their bonds and stalked abroad in the world as if the lid had been lifted from Pandora's box.

But those who hold power like to create a bogeyman and blame all their troubles on him. It always pays to keep fear of an external enemy alive.

And in the end, the poor nations of the world do not eat or drink but instead ceaselessly labor, greasing the wheels of the rich countries that manufacture arms. Because the poor nations waste their time and limited resources fighting wars instead of working and producing, they become consumers for the Northern industries.

Yes, this is the kind of world we are living in.

WHAT DO THE NUMBERS SAY?
Numbers, the swaddling clothes of babies
numbers, the coffins of cities
those killed
those about to be killed
numbers are seeds in the palm of our hopes
numbers tell us something is approaching
numbers tell us something is drifting away
what is approaching us

what is drifting away from us
world war: I
world war: II
from '14 to '18, from '39 to '45, 10 years, 54 million dead
49 million crippled
the country of the dead and the crippled
is a country with a population of 103 million
and along with its oxen its madmen its scorched stones
and one of the departed was from our house
he went and never came back
I can't remember whether he was 19 or 40
came back with two blind eyes
I can't remember whether he was blue-eyed or black
He came back with his leg cut at the knee
he returned but could not find the door of his house
from '14 to '18, from '39 to '45, 10 years, 54 million dead
49 million crippled

—Nazım Hikmet

Yet the scientists say that if the resources of the world were used pro-
ductively, they could feed twice the present population. The problem is in
the system. The world economic order is now the *shah*, the king, the dictator, the supreme ruler, and the shape of the new world order is particularly
aggressive and domineering. Yet the institutions of this same order (the
World Bank, the International Monetary Fund) were giving warning sig-
nals just before the collapse of the socialist bloc. They were saying:

"What we are doing is very dangerous. We bury the Third World up to
their throats in debt and impose such difficult conditions on them in
exchange for a helping hand that there is no way they are ever going to
stand on their feet. Let's stop giving them a dollar and asking five in return.
Let's ease up on them a bit, or else the whole system may collapse and we
will all pay for it."

But the system did not collapse. On the contrary, the opposing system
collapsed. And once again we, the have-nots of the world, lost out. When
the master of the new world order, the United States, let everyone see on
TV that it was not willing to leave the Middle East oil reserves to anyone

else and bravely stood up for the independence of the Kuwait sheikhdom, a leftover from medieval times, we all understood that if we defy the boss, we will end up like Iraq. Here and elsewhere in the world, people sitting comfortably in front of their TVs would watch the Cruise fireworks exploding in the skies over İstanbul. Between mouthfuls of Coca-Cola and popcorn, they would see our buildings pulverized—but not the people dying under the ruins, because CNN does not show those scenes.

Yes, that is the new world order for you. It is tragic that the people crushed by the pressure of this economic order are going for each other's throats. The situation today reminds me of a story I heard from Aziz Nesin:

When the stray dogs of İstanbul became too numerous, the municipality used to collect them, pack them into sacks, and throw them into the Sea of Marmara.[39] It was observed that before they were thrown into the sea, the dogs in the sacks attacked each other. "The poor creatures did not understand the calamity that was befalling them and blamed their fellows in the sack," said Aziz Nesin.

It is an awful but graphic picture of our situation. Here and elsewhere, people pinched in the vice of the world order start attacking others in exactly the same position because they do not know the reason for their catastrophe. Meanwhile, the facts of the situation are continually obscured to ensure that nobody ever realizes what is happening. If someone comes along who does understand, the public prosecutors and courts move into action to prevent him from explaining it to others. For those who are alert to what is happening, the prison gates yawn, leaving the rest of us to doze in quiescence, lulled by the colorful dreams piped down to us by our satellite dishes.

"We are the greatest. Nobody's greater than us!"
"Dance, baby, dance."
"Win the goose, win the goose."
"We are giving away two hundred brand-new cars."
My people, O my poor people,

---

39. A ship traveling from the Aegean Sea into the Black Sea would first pass through the Dardanelle Straits, then through the small Sea of Marmara, then through the Bosphorus Straits and into the Black Sea. İstanbul is situated where the Bosphorus meets the Sea of Marmara.

if the mothers are telling lies,
if the aerials are telling lies,
if the books are telling lies,
if the poster on the wall and the notice on the lamppost are telling lies,
if the naked thighs of the girls on the white screen are telling lies,
if prayers are telling lies,
if your mother's lullaby is telling lies,
if the dream is telling lies,
if the violinist in the bar is telling lies,
if the moonlight in the night of hopeless day is telling lies.
if the voice is telling lies,
if the word is telling lies,
if everything and everyone is telling lies
apart from your hands
your hands, obedient as the potter's clay,
your hands, blind as darkness,
your hands, stupid as sheepdogs,
so that your hands may never rebel,
and so that, of course, in this world of life and death,
where we are such brief visitors
this sultanate of greed merchants, this tyranny, should never end.
—Nazim Hikmet, 1949

Is it really that difficult to live in peace, side by side, in this world? As I watch from the window of the train and see all this beautiful countryside, the deep blue sky, and the sun (which does not show his face so often in Germany), all these thoughts pass through my mind. It hurts to think and understand, but when I ask myself if I would rather not think and understand, my heart answers *no* every time. It is easy to be born human, but to deserve being called human is not so easy. If we want to wear the honor of being human, we must pay the price, even if it costs us dearly.

For Abdurrahman Dilipak's views on this subject, see Green *chapters 26 and 27.*

15. DOES XENOPHOBIA EXIST ONLY IN GERMANY?

Here's Germany for you, a great country, with its smart and highly polished exterior! And underneath the polish? How many of the people living in these spotlessly clean houses with their well-kept gardens are willing to pay the price for being genuinely and fully human? This society paid a heavy price for following the Nazis like tame sheep to great disaster seventy years ago. It sacrificed millions of its children in a crazy war. The country was burned and devastated. So where have these blue-eyed youths come from, with their shaved heads and leather jackets, their arms tattooed with swastikas? We could say they are just a handful of misfits, but if that is the case, why are the ordinary Germans in the street so bereft of humanity as to give their silent approval and even occasional support by applauding them? In truth, the isolation and pain suffered by thinking people in Germany is probably greater than ours.

Xenophobia, or to put it more precisely, intolerance of those who are different, is not found only in Germany. You can find few societies anywhere in the world that tolerate people who are different from the majority and recognize their right to live among them. In most societies, the rule is simple: "Join the herd or clear off!"

But really, the differences in any society, different traditions and customs, different behavior, sounds, and colors, constitute the cultural wealth of that society. We in Turkey are heirs to a broad cultural mosaic. People ignorant of this heritage may look askance and grumble, "Mosaic? What mosaic?" but it is nevertheless true that we are living on a piece of land that has hosted a great many civilizations in the course of history. It is also, sadly, true that we have already squandered much of our great human inheritance. After each conflict, we have driven away part of our population, and apparently consider it some kind of achievement to have done so.

Have you ever been to the Kuzguncuk district of İstanbul? If you have not, make a point of passing that way to see the mosque and the church standing together on the main street like next-door neighbors. They are like monuments to past respect and tolerance between two cultures. I say "past" because unfortunately, peaceful co-existence is now just a beautiful memory. The Armenian church in Kuzguncuk no longer has a congregation, and its doors are locked. The same goes for the beautiful Greek church in the marketplace too, with its white bell tower. The people who have lived in this neighborhood for centuries are now burying their last children in the soil on which their ancestors once lived, leaving İstanbul a little lonelier.

We drove them away with our slogan "Turkey belongs to the Turks" and with campaigns including the notorious "Citizen of Turkey: Speak Turkish" and rampages such as the attacks of September 6 and 7, 1955.[40] We used those Greeks living in Turkey, who did not want to desert the land of their birth, as chips at the bargaining table over Cyprus. Baselessly accusing them of "sending money to EOKA terrorists"[41] or of being spies, we deported them with a single suitcase and $100 in their hands. Friends who happen to pass through Athens witness the nostalgia felt by our former fellow citizens, who when they hear there are visitors from İstanbul at once gather around them and with tears in their eyes ask for news, saying, "Tell us about İstanbul! I spent my youth in Kurtulus. I have never got used to living here in Athens. How is it there in İstanbul nowadays?" In İstanbul they were looked down on as "the filthy Greek militia," but after they were sent off to Greece, they were also despised there as "İstanbullers." Just like our second-generation immigrant children who are pushed out and called "dirty Turks" in Germany and "Germanists" in Turkey. Is it only xenophobia? Once you have discrimination of any kind, in the end it will return like a boomerang to strike the discriminator.

For Abdurrahman Dilipak's views on this subject, see Green *chapters 16 and 28.*

---

40. Following a bomb attack on the house in which Atatürk was born in Thessalonika, now part of Greece, there were widespread attacks on the substantial Greek minority in İstanbul. Mobs burned thousands of Greek homes and looted Greek churches and shops. Sixteen Greeks were killed in the violence.

41. EOKA (*Ethniki Organosis Kyprion Agoniston*, National Organization of Freedom Fighters), an armed organization founded in 1954 by George Grivas, a Cyprus-born officer in the Greek army. Its aim was to achieve Cyprus' union with Greece, an aim opposed by the island's Turkish minority.

16. KNOWING HOW TO LOOK AT HISTORY

Two days ago was May 29, and we celebrated the Ottoman Turkish conquest of İstanbul 542 years ago. While certain newspapers and TV channels treated the anniversary as a sign of how far we have come, others with a different ideological bent said it was a reminder of how far we have fallen from our historic ideals. Readers on both sides of the argument had their prejudices confirmed. They all huddled closer to their own clan, uneasy at witnessing the aggressive arguments of the other side, their sense of security further eroded. Who gains from this sort of polarization?

What I am about to say will annoy both sides. But, unfortunately, our perception of history from both sides is skewed. As individuals and as a society, it is our right and duty to know our own past, to put it in the album kept by our family or our society, with all its faults as well as its merits. We gain nothing of value by denying the parts of our history we do not like or by exaggerating the parts we do like, just to make us feel proud and superior to others. On the contrary, denial makes us all losers.

Think about how we as individuals behave in such matters. Photographs of our parents and grandparents decorate our family albums and the walls of our living rooms. In the faces of these people, most of them now dead and gone, we see our own roots. We show them to our friends, saying, "Halide Hanım was an angel, God rest her soul. They say my great grandfather Ali Riza Paşa here was a ruthless character. He was known as Ali Riza Paşa the Cruel and earned the curses of many people of his generation. And this is my youngest uncle, a completely worthless character. A swindler and a crook, he was no good to himself or anyone else."

It is like this when we are chatting among ourselves or talking to close relatives, but if someone from outside our circle were to intrude and say, "His great grandfather Ali Riza Paşa the Cruel was a murderer, and his uncle was a worthless swindler and a crook," we would be deeply affronted and try to punch the person in the nose, saying, "Scoundrel! How dare you insult my ancestors?" An insult directed against a family member is a personal insult, so we go on the offensive. Why do we behave like that?

Is this some kind of defense mechanism, or what? Yet, if the statement were not about our relatives and us, we would think it ridiculous to assert that someone should take the blame for the shortcomings of a relative. We would say, "Well, the father may be a scoundrel, but we can hardly blame his poor children for it."

As a society, our relationship with our past is much the same. Once we start to comment on something in the past that has a bearing on our current affairs, we are incorrigible. For example, we were always told that the Ottoman (or *Osmanlı*) Turks treated their subject populations well, respecting their rights and beliefs. This is written in all our schoolbooks. But if one day your travels take you to Greece, Bulgaria, Hungary, or Austria, you will see a museum with an exhibition showing Ottoman oppression. Or perhaps you read a novel describing a similar history of oppression. You feel angry and say, "This is a conspiracy to slander the Turks and the Muslims!" And you are not completely wrong. Today, even in countries considered among the most civilized in Europe, the average person has all sorts of prejudices, and some of these prejudices are officially encouraged, or at least winked at.

But whether we like it or not, certain facts are out there. Should we not investigate these facts and accept our ancestors whether or not they turn out to be guilty? Yes, they were our ancestors, and, if they were good, they were good, and, if they were bad, they were bad. Remember also that the concepts of good and bad have not stood still over history. What was once very bad has now become a virtue and vice versa. When we look at history in this way we will see incidents that by today's standards look very bad indeed. Our ancestors hanged people and cut other people's throats, but were they the only people who did such things? No. Some things that are considered shameful today were understood as the right of anyone who had established power by force of arms. Investigating matters impartially and accepting history "as is" does not belittle any society. Quite the opposite.

Was it an "Armenian massacre" or a "massacre of Turks by Armenian guerillas"? To deny that Armenians were massacred would make us look absurd. I myself heard old men, forty or fifty years after the event, telling me their memories, telling how they "murdered the Armenians in this valley," or when they "took the Greeks away, a good number of them remained in this forest."

To claim that the Ottomans did not hang and murder people in the lands they occupied would amount to disrespecting the facts as well as ourselves. They made positive contributions to those countries and left behind stories of oppression. And was the other side any better? The Romanians exploit Voyvoda Vlad, Count Dracula, as a tourist attraction. He was known in his day as Vlad the Impaler because any Ottoman he took prisoner in the war he would impale, alive, on a stake. So should we Turks and Romanians go after each other now just because our ancestors did? No. The Vladimir of today is not responsible for the atrocities of Vlad the Impaler, and young Osman, the apprentice mechanic, is not responsible for the barbaric actions of some Ottoman general. We, contemporary Turks and Romanians, are responsible for our friendship and our peaceful coexistence today and tomorrow.

To accept the negative side of our history as well as the positive is a necessary condition for sharing this world with others and living side by side in peace. If we can put ourselves in the place of the people opposite us, and if we can look at events through their eyes, then we have taken the first step. Come on, let us go back to our elementary schoolbooks and remember how the Janissary corps, the nucleus of the Ottoman army, was recruited.

The healthiest children in captured territories were selected. These children were abducted and given to Muslim families to be brought up, and then they received their army training. Janissaries lived permanently in army barracks. They never married, never had families or children, and lived all their lives as soldiers.

Now read the paragraph above once again, substituting the term *New Soldier* for *Janissary* and *Christian* for *Muslim* and see how it sounds to you.

I will paint the picture for you.

American troops enter a defenseless Iraqi village with the most modern fighting equipment. Acting on General Norman Schwarzkopf's orders, they take away nine or ten of the healthiest boys from the bosoms of their families, to the accompaniment of their mothers' tears. These boys are sent to trustworthy Christian homes in Kansas, Nevada, and Ohio. As they grow up, they forget their true identity and become good U.S. citizens. The day comes, and they graduate from the West Point Military Academy as crack American troops. They then make raids all over the world to protect U.S. oil interests.

As fate would have it, one of these boy soldiers one day comes to the same Iraqi village whence he was taken to collect more New Soldier candidates! While he is forcibly tearing an old woman's grandchild from her arms, perhaps his helmet falls to the ground and she recognizes the birthmark on his forehead and cries, "You—you are my Mustafa!" Of course, the New Soldier is not able to make any sense of this. Perhaps he hits the old woman with the butt of his gun, shouting, "God damn you, crazy hag." He removes the child by force and puts him in the army vehicle. Then, with the satisfaction of a soldier who has completed his mission, he returns to his barracks.

Now, how does history look to you? If you want to bring it even closer to home, substitute Turkey for Iraq. If soldiers were to come to your house and take your child away, what would you say or do?

Should we feel ashamed of this and go around with our heads bent? No. It is history. It is in the past. Even if those who did it were our grandfathers, *we are not them.* Those who captured Africans and took them to America as slaves were James's ancestors, *not James.*

James and I are responsible for the world of today. James is responsible for what the United States is doing today, and we are responsible for what Turkey is doing today. If we give our support to inhuman actions, or if we say, "I don't like what they are doing, but if I oppose them, I might be declared a traitor, so I had better keep quiet," then we bear responsibility for those things.

But there is another side to this. If we treat the evil actions of our ancestors as virtues to be proud of, then it is as if we are saying, "We should do the same things today," and in that case, others would be right to stigmatize us.

Now we are ready to look at the conquest of İstanbul:

Five hundred forty-two years ago, one state swallowed the lands of another and captured its capital city. If Byzantium had had the strength, it would certainly have conquered the Ottoman cities of Bursa and Edirne. This was the name of the game in those days: Might was right!

But that does not mean that we should make this historic incident a cause for pride today. Would we feel comfortable if Greece proudly celebrated its capture of Edirne in 1913 or Bursa in 1921? What if Germany celebrated the capture of France in 1940 or Russia the capture of Berlin in 1945? The end of World War II is remembered not as the day a particular city was conquered but as the liberation of humankind from the curse of war. War is remembered as a lesson and a warning, not as a clever thing to be proud of.

Now the Muslims have something special to say on the matter. "Yes but, there is a *hadith*[42] that the Prophet urged the capture of this city." I cannot comment about that. I said right at the start that I can only appeal to your intellect, and you must do the same when you address me. If I am at fault, that is the only way I can correct my error. But if you tell me, "This is the command of my religion. I cannot even think of questioning any recommendation made by my prophet. My intellect is limited, but the supreme intellect is always right," then all I can say is, "If Christianity, Judaism, Buddha, and Confucius had commanded the capture of İstanbul, what would humankind have done—destroyed itself fighting over our beautiful city?" But this, too, is a thought addressed to humankind's intellect. So again I repeat, "Our intellect is our most precious treasure." We should not subordinate it to anything or anyone.

What we have done with Ayasofya also strikes me as seriously contradictory.[43] We are always saying the Ottoman Turks were respectful toward the religions and customs of others and emphasize that this is how they behaved toward the Christians of the city after the conquest of İstanbul. (Actually, the Byzantine historian Dukas tells a different story, but Dukas's writings also have to be treated with caution because he was a fanatic Protestant who claimed that what had befallen the city was God's punishment for its citizens having strayed from their religion.)

We should not readily give credence to assertions that are manifestly debatable. In the case of Ayasofya, it is a clear fact that the Church of Hagia Sophia was converted to a mosque, as you can see from its appearance today!

---

42. A saying attributed to the prophet.

43. Church of Hagia Sophia (constructed 532 C.E.), the largest church in Constantinople at the time of the conquest by Mehmet the Conqueror in 1453 and converted by him into a mosque.

The Ottoman sultan turned this church, the foremost place of worship of the Orthodox world, into a mosque, probably in order to demonstrate his own political power to the world. For him, this gesture of power was more important than showing respect to other beliefs. Would it have been so difficult to build a new mosque? Obviously not, because the İstanbul skyline is replete with mosques, each as elegant as the next one. Was there no other way of saying "I'm in charge here now"? Was it not enough to take down the flag of the Byzantine Empire and raise the Ottoman flag in its place?

Well, never mind; he did what he did! And with a generous gesture, the secular republic converted Ayasofya into a museum, and it now lives as a historic monument visited by thousands of people of all beliefs and religions from all corners of the world. If, as some are urging today, we were to turn it back into a mosque, we would be inviting the condemnation of the world. It would be difficult for us then to maintain our claim that "The West is prejudiced against Islam."

Does it really make sense to complain about the intolerance toward different beliefs, modes of thinking, and ways of life that we see in Germany and then behave exactly the same way to others in our own country? How intolerantly we behave sometimes, not only to people of different faiths or ethnicity but even to our own children.

Some years ago, the older generations used to give young men who grew their hair long and wore earrings a really hard time: "What is this long hair and this earring? Are you a woman, or a heathen, or what? Shame on you. Did our forefathers behave in such a way?"

And, of course, when we look in school textbooks, we see that Sultan Süleyman the Magnificent actually did wear earrings! History does not tell us if our Central Asian grandfathers wore their hair shorter than our Central Asian grandmothers, but we still watch TV and admire the luxurious mane of the actor playing the great Turkish hero Tarkan.[44] Even if it were not our traditional custom, what business is it of ours how long a person wears his hair or whether he puts rings in his ears? They are *his* hair, *his* ears, *his* own private life, and it is *his* right to do what he wants with them!

---

44. Comic strip adventure hero embodying the archetypical virtues of the Turkic warrior, created by Sezgin Burak (1935–1978).

Let us allow him to wear what he wants and to live as he wants. Do we like it when Germans try to interfere with our way of life in Germany?

There are many nations on the face of the earth, and in each nation are millions of people. Let us allow each freely to develop his own identity and his own individuality. Our world is like a many-cultured, colorful flower garden. Let us help it grow that way so we too can live in this garden the way we want and the way we believe.

For Abdurrahman Dilipak's views on this subject, see Green *chapters 9, 10, and 28.*

17. ADDITION: FREEDOM OF THOUGHT: THE SHORT STORY OF A CIVIL DISOBEDIENCE ACTION

In 1995, Yaşar Kemal[45] wrote an article[46] for the German magazine *Der Spiegel* in which he strongly criticized the government's handling of the conflict in southeastern Turkey. He was duly indicted for separatism by the İstanbul State Security Court. Our signature campaign started as a reaction to this court action and turned into a civil disobedience movement. One thousand eighty intellectuals republished Yaşar Kemal's article and nine other articles whose authors had been dragged into courts or sentenced to prison. Under Article 162 of the Turkish criminal code, to republish an offensive article is to commit a further offense, carrying the same sentence as that imposed on the original author.[47]

The publishers declared their own guilt by informing the prosecutor. But the prosecutor was reluctant to bring legal action against them because this would spotlight the absurdity of the law, so he prolonged the process to such an extent that after two and a half years he had not even finished taking the preliminary statements. In the end, Mesut Yılmaz's government rid itself of this embarrassing case, as well as the Işık Yurtçu[48] case, with a conditional amnesty for publishers—a cosmetic measure that froze cases and released some prisoners without actually changing the law under which they had been tried and imprisoned.

---

45. Yaşar Kemal (1923–) is Turkey's most renowned and celebrated contemporary novelist. His first novel, *İnce Memed* (*Memed, My Hawk*), like many of his other novels, was a powerful critique of injustice and inequality in a rural setting. Kemal was imprisoned several times for his left-wing opinions.

46. "Campaign of Lies," *Der Spiegel* (January 10, 1995). Also published as an op-ed piece, titled "Turkey's War of Words," in *The New York Times* (May 6, 1995).

47. Turkish Criminal Code, Article 162: Publishing a publication that is considered criminal under law constitutes an offense in its own right, and the perpetrator shall be subject to the same punishment. The publisher of such a publication shall not be exempt from responsibility by claiming that he did not approve of the contents of the publication or that he published it together with a warning, or that another person took responsibility for the publication.

48. Editor of the Kurdish daily newspaper *Özgür Gündem*. He was arrested in December 1994 and released after a conditional amnesty in 1997.

In response, we changed the tactics of our resistance. Instead of a single sensational case with many accused, we started to open many cases with small groups of one to five defendants. Our aim was to flood the system with as many cases as possible and to bring them to a conclusion as fast as possible.

We published a new booklet, first every week and then once a month; the backlog of legal follow-up increased, and in each case the publishers participated in the offense of the latest "thought criminals." We have been able to provide a "publisher" to offer this support for every case of thought crime since 1995.

Among the 1,278 persons who participated in these actions and acted as publishers of the forty-three offensive booklets were people of widely differing views and identity who appeared side by side in print and then in court. There were people being tried because of their views about the Kurds, and there were Atatürkists, who certainly did not share their views. There were devoutly religious people and atheists. There were songwriters and caricaturists. What held this odd assortment together?

The answer to this question lies in the text we have printed above the signatures since the first signature campaign was started. It paraphrases the words of Voltaire, one of the vanguard of the French Revolution:

"I do not share any of your views. But I shall defend to the last your freedom to express them."

WHAT HAPPENED THEN?

A total of 1,278 individuals became publishers and denounced themselves to the courts for the publication of forty-three booklets. (*Freedom of Thought No. 32* had mass participation, and 1,117 teachers participated in the "crime" of the teacher İlknur Birol.)

The public prosecutor decided not to prosecute in nine of the forty-three booklets. Prosecutions were opened against six of them. Two of these cases ended with prison terms. And one of these sentences was upheld by the Supreme Court.

While investigations were continuing into the other booklets, all the sentences and the cases and the investigations were suspended under Law 4454 of September 28, 1999. That put us right back where we started!

But the case in *Freedom of Thought No. 38* (the republication of the statement by conscientious objector Osman Murat Ülke, which we always refer to as the soup of the soup of the rabbit, after Hodja Nasreddin's story)[49] was not covered by the suspension law because it was published after the cutoff date of April 23, 1999, laid down in that law. My reporter friend Nevzat Onaran and I were sentenced to two months' imprisonment each for republishing the statement which "undermined the institution of military service." The verdict was upheld by the military Supreme Court and at the end of the year 2000, we both spent time in prison.

Because we had exhausted judicial remedies in Turkey, we had a right to open a case at the European Court of Human Rights (ECHR), and this is what we did. We have not the slightest doubt that we will win this case, which is still continuing. You may remember that in one of its decisions, the

---

49. NASREDDIN HODJA AND THE RABBIT GANG:
AN OLD TURKISH FABLE
(Nasreddin Hodja is a well-known Turkish wit and scholar, and tales about him are told not only in Turkey but also in Egypt, Syria, Pakistan, and even in Europe.)
One day, the Hodja had an unexpected visitor. He and the visitor were not personally acquainted, but the visitor had apparently heard of the Hodja's fame and had come to visit him. Well, Turkish hospitality meant inviting the visitor in and offering him at least a glass of tea. This visitor had brought a present with him—a skinny rabbit. Now the Hodja had to do more than just offer a glass of tea to such a generous guest. But the Hodja was a poor man, and he did not have much in the cupboard. So he skinned the rabbit, cooked it, and made a tolerable dish, which he offered to his guest, who downed it with relish.

They chatted until the visitor took his leave. Aleykum Selam.

Not long after, another visitor arrived and presented himself as a friend of the man who had brought the gift of a rabbit. Hodja felt bound to please him too and managed to treat him to a bowl of soup as well.

Then another visitor came who said that he was a friend of the friend of the man who had brought the rabbit. A few days later, a friend of that friend came by for his bowl of soup. But the Hodja had had enough of the rabbit gang and decided to teach them a lesson.

He welcomed this latest guest in and sat him down, talking to him in a polite and friendly manner. He asked the visitor to wait while he went into the back kitchen to prepare something. After a long time and much clattering of saucepans, the soup arrived on a tray brought by the smiling Hodja.

The visitor could not make out what the soup was made of—it looked suspiciously like a bowl of warm water—so he politely asked the Hodja, "What kind of soup is this, Hodja?" And this was the question the Hodja had been waiting for.

"This is the soup of the soup of the soup of the rabbit that the friend of the friend of your friend brought me."

And, of course, that was the last visit from the rabbit gang!

ECHR ruled that a defendant's right to a fair trial had been infringed because one of the three judges at the State Security Court was a soldier. When Abdullah Öcalan was put on trial in 1999, they hastily changed the composition of the State Security Court bench, even though this move required an amendment to the constitution. But in our trial, *all* the judges were soldiers; in fact, one of the judges was not even a lawyer but an ordinary noncommissioned officer!

We hope this spells the beginning of the end for the double standard in the justice system we have had in Turkey for so long.

BUT THAT IS NOT THE END OF THE STORY

Under the suspension law, our trials and sentences were suspended on condition that we did not commit the same offense in the subsequent three years. Our activists saw this as simply sweeping the problem under the carpet, a way of avoiding making the necessary legal reforms, and before seven months had passed, they republished all the same articles once again in a book called *Freedom of Thought 2000.* At a press conference, the author and actor Yılmaz Erdoğan introduced this book, which also told the story of the campaign. After the meeting, all the publishers went together to the State Security Court and denounced themselves to the public prosecutor.

The book was banned, but the State Security Court issued an acquittal in the case against fifteen of the accused (Cengiz Bektaş, Yılmaz Ensaroğlu, Siyami Erdem, Vahdettin Karabay, Ömer Madra, Etyen Mahcupyan, Lale Mansur, Atilla Maraş, Professor Ali Nesin, Zuhal Olcay, Hüsnü Öndul, Yavuz Önen, Erdal Öz, Salim Uslu, and Şanar Yurdatapan). We, and also the public prosecutor, appealed the decision. The decision was overturned by the Supreme Court and the case is still being heard today. But cases relating to this book that were heard in three other courts (Üsküdar Primary Court, Üsküdar Criminal Court, and Ankara General Staff Military Court) also ended with acquittals. Needless to say, we appealed them too.

The most laughable of these was the acquittal issued by the Military Court, because this very court had twice before found me guilty for the same two texts (as author of the booklets *Freedom of Thought Nos. 16* and *38*). The first of these convictions had been suspended under the suspension law, while the other was upheld by the Supreme Court. But now we were republishing the same text together with fourteen well-known people. According to the letter of the law, the government had no choice but to give each of them two months' imprisonment, and four months' imprisonment to me. Throughout the proceedings, all the accused refused to defend themselves because they were civilians being tried by soldiers. They merely repeated that their right to a fair trial was being infringed in that court.

The Ankara court decided we would be acquitted whether we liked it or not. But we are going to take this acquittal to the ECHR; it will be interesting to see whether they take the same view.

FREEDOM OF THOUGHT: FOR EVERYONE

Once the wheels of the law have started turning, nothing can stop them from grinding both the thought and the thinker. It is like the story of the Sorcerer's Apprentice, who is told to wash the floor while the master is out but learns the magic words that can make the buckets and mops wash the sorcerer's castle by themselves. He says the words and the buckets and mops start bringing water in, but the poor apprentice does not know the words to stop them, so the buckets just keep on bringing in water until the castle is flooded. These courts (the State Security Courts) are just the same. Once someone has set the system in motion, they do not seem to know the magic words they need to stop it again: "I do not share any of your views. But I shall defend to the last your freedom to express them."

The banned leader of the religious Refah (Welfare) Party, Professor Necmettin Erbakan, was also bitten by the snake he neglected to get rid of while he was in power. He was prosecuted under Article 312 of the Turkish criminal code. And the most ridiculous aspect of this was that he was not prosecuted for Islamic fundamentalism but for "Kurdism."

Our civil disobedience movement has been spreading to wider circles. Two other party leaders were under the same threat as Erbakan. After a two-month signature campaign, 77,663 people jointly published a book, titled *Freedom of Thought: For Everyone*, which included the words responsible for the sentencing of the three party leaders (Professor Erbakan of the Welfare Party, Hasan Celal Güzel of the center-right Rebirth Party, and Murat Bozlak of the People's Democracy Party, which has a largely Kurdish membership), as well as two other famous thought criminals

(Akın Birdal, former president of the Turkish Human Rights Association, and Eşber Yağmurdereli, a lawyer who was one of Turkey's longest-serving political prisoners). A committee of prominent individuals submitted 550 copies of the book to the Turkish Parliament (which has 550 members). The tens of thousands of publishers went in groups to the State Security Court prosecutor's offices to make their statements. The court proceedings started in October 2001 and are continuing.

For Abdurrahman Dilipak's views on this subject, see Green *chapter 5.*

18. ISN'T IT FINISHED YET?

An Update, August 2002

No, it is not finished yet!

In spite of the fact that 2001 brought us newspaper headlines saying "Thought Is Finally Free," State Security Courts and other courts are once again doling out sentences for people who express thoughts the state does not like to hear. People from all walks of life have been put behind bars. You have the owner of the *Yeni Asya* (*New Asia*) newspaper Mehmet Kutlular, who said, "The earthquake of August 17 [1999] is not a natural event but a punishment from Allah," and you also have Dr. Fikret Başkaya, well known for his leftist views, and Ahmet Turan Demir, vice president of the mainly Kurdish HADEP party. All three spent time behind bars in 2001. Emine Şenlikoğlu, Neşe Düzel, Ahmet Altan, Ali Bayramoğlu, Gülay Göktürk, Fehmi Koru, Yılmaz Çamlıbel, Can Dündar, Eren Keskin, İlyas Salman, Sabiha Ünlü, and many more were tried for expressing their opinions. Some were sentenced, others had their trials suspended, and some were acquitted. But the law was tarnished with each such prosecution.

And the minister of justice, Hikmet Sami Türk, with his peculiar views, is one of our great statesmen and has excelled in bringing the law into disrepute. According to him, the courts should prosecute anyone who criticizes the new F-type isolation prisons[50] or petitions for Kurdish to be

---

50. The Justice Ministry had long planned to move prisoners held for State Security Court offenses from their traditional large wards holding forty or more prisoners into small group isolation in newly constructed, cell-based, F-type prisons. In December 2000, twenty-eight prisoners and two guards died during Operation Return to Life, when ten thousand police officers carried out the violent transfers. Some prisoners burned themselves in protest, but others were deliberately killed. Police officers beat and tortured prisoners during the transfer and on arrival at the F-type prisons. Eight male prisoners formally complained that policemen anally raped them with truncheons on arrival at Kandira F-type Prison. F-type prisons have produced many allegations of ill treatment, and despite some concessions made by the Justice Ministry, most prisoners are still living in conditions of isolation. Since December 2000, more than seventy prisoners and their relatives have died in hunger strikes. The most recent was Özlem Türk, who died on January 11, 2003.

accepted as an optional course in universities. But he says they should be tried not under Article 8 of the Anti-Terror Law[51] nor Article 312 of the Turkish criminal code[52] but rather under Article 169 of the Turkish criminal code[53]—offering shelter and assistance to terrorists. The logic is surreal: "Who opposes the F-type prisons? Terrorist organizations. So terrorist organizations benefit if anyone opposes F-type prisons, and the defendant has therefore *assisted* terrorist organizations." Similarly, because some congress of the PKK declared that it wanted to run a campaign of civil disobedience, anybody who uses techniques of civil disobedience is purported to be assisting the PKK.

Please do not laugh. Students and parents who exercised their constitutional right to submit petitions to state functionaries are everywhere being tried for doing just that. And many of them are in prison while their trials proceed.[54] Members of the teachers' trade union Eğitim-Sen are on trial because they said that education in their mother tongue is a right. Officials of the Turkish Human Rights Foundation and the Medical Association are being tried because they gave medical assistance to hunger strikers. The Human Rights Association and Mazlum-Der (The Association for Solidarity with Oppressed People) are being tried. The writer of the book titled *Cell* has been tried and convicted. Its author, Nevin Berktaş, is already in prison serving a thirteen-year sentence for another offense.

Still, things are not so bad. What if the PKK had held a meeting and passed this resolution: "The Turkish parliament should have an extraordinary meeting and pass laws needed to conform to the European Union, and we must have early elections right away?" Then what would the Justice Minister, the Honorable Hikmet Sami Turk, have done? (In fact, that almost happened, because the Parliament lifted the ban on education in Kurdish.

---

51. Maximum sentence: three years.

52. Maximum sentence: three years.

53. Maximum sentence: seven and a half years.

54. From January to August 2002, police detained 3,621 students or their parents for giving petitions asking for Kurdish to be taught as an optional subject in universities. Of these, 536 were formally arrested and committed to prison; 446 were charged with assisting an armed illegal organization.

Perhaps PKK supporters have become the majority in the Parliament without us noticing).[55]

In 2001, the İstanbul State Security Court collared the celebrated professor of linguistics and merciless opponent of U.S. foreign policy Noam Chomsky (or perhaps the opposite more accurately reflects what happened). A prosecution was opened against the book *American Interventionism*, which the ARAM publishing house translated into Turkish and published. I do not know whether the prosecutor had ever heard of Chomsky, but believing he would not be able to haul a foreign unbeliever into court in Turkey, he opened his prosecution only against the publisher, Fatih Taş (in spite of the fact that under Article 16 of the Press Law, both author and publisher share primary responsibility for an "offense"). When Chomsky learned about this and about our seven-year civil disobedience story, he agreed to come to Turkey. Moreover, on the day he arrived he presented a request to the State Security Court explaining that he accepted responsibility for his book and wanted to be tried. The next day we witnessed the fastest legal proceedings in Turkish history. The court avoided putting Chomsky in the witness box and, at the prosecutor's own request, acquitted Fatih Taş.[56] Next door, mind you, Neşe Düzel was being tried for writing a newspaper article, and there was no acquittal for her.

Chomsky was not satisfied with this victory, though. Because he had come all this way to the State Security Court, he made himself a publisher of *Freedom of Thought 2001* and presented himself (together with Professor Mehmet Bekaroğlu, writer Abdurrahman Dilipak, and the president of the İstanbul branch of the Human Rights Association, lawyer Eren Keskin) to the public prosecutor, denouncing himself and requesting that a court case be opened against him in accordance with Article 162 of the Turkish criminal code. He also wanted to give a statement, but the prosecutor did not

---

55. In August 2002, the Parliament passed a law removing constitutional obstacles to Kurdish being taught. However, there are still legal obstacles to it being taught in universities. For the moment, there is permission for private schools only to teach Kurdish, and only to children of school age.

56. The previous record holder for speedy acquittal was Kurdish writer Mehmet Uzun, who lived in Sweden. When he was indicted, observers poured in from Sweden to watch the case tried at İstanbul State Security Court. He was acquitted of all charges in a single hearing.

deem it necessary (because he could easily reach Chomsky any time he liked, so why bother himself now?). In fact, he did not want to accept the declaration of guilt, but when everyone, including Chomsky, insisted this was his legal duty, the prosecutor was left with no alternative but to accept it.

In *Freedom of Thought 2001* you can find the "guilty writings" of the following:

Celal Başlangıç, Professor Noam Chomsky, Abdurrahman Dilipak, Emine Şenlikoğlu, Eren Keskin, Fehmi Koru, Dr. Fikret Başkaya, Mehmet Kutlular, Yılmaz Çamlıbel, Nevin Berktaş, and the youngsters who submitted petitions asking for lessons in Kurdish.

The peculiarity of this book is that the writers and the publishers are the same (except for Professor Mehmet Bekaroğlu and Şanar Yurdatapan, who joined to give a helping hand). We wanted to send two messages. The first is that the individuals, by repeating their crime, are saying to the state, "We do not accept that this is a crime. Here we are doing it again. You can do whatever you want." At the same time, they come from such widely differing political, cultural, and religious viewpoints that all are publishing at least one or two views they definitely reject. So even though it is 250 years since Voltaire, it is a good feeling to erase the blemish on our society's forehead by standing shoulder to shoulder with our opponents.

We will repeat this every year. *Freedom of Thought 2002* will be published on January 23, 2003, which is the anniversary of the birth of our movement. On that day, the writers of the "guilty writings" and supporters will cut a birthday cake in the courtyard of the State Security Court and take the book to the public prosecutor and denounce themselves. We will publish *Freedom of Thought 2003, Freedom of Thought 2004*. . . . How much longer will it have to go on?

We finally got a prosecution opened against *Freedom of Thought 2001*.

And this started some fun. Chomsky was one of the publishers. The prosecutor wanted to save himself and the state the embarrassment of prosecuting Chomsky. After procrastinating for a couple of months, he did the worst thing he could have done: He opened cases against just two of the publishers (Yılmaz Çamlıbel and me). As for the others, he decided not to prosecute on the grounds that they had not participated in preparing the booklet. There is nothing in the law specifying that only somebody who physically prepares a book should be prosecuted. What it does say is that the writer and the publisher are equally responsible. Professor Mehmet Bekaroğlu, Abdurrahman Dilipak, Eren Keskin, and Noam Chomsky all went to the prosecutor and said, "We are publishers, too; open a case against us as well." These requests are sitting in the case file, document numbers 30–33. But our prosecutor tried to keep them out of the case on the grounds of irrelevance. Sadly, we had to submit a complaint against him to the High Council of Judges and Prosecutors, the committee that looks after the personnel matters of judges and prosecutors, including promotions and appointments. The president of this council is the minister of justice, and its secretariat is at the Ministry of Justice. Our supposedly independent judiciary is supervised by the executive. And the decisions of this committee—just like those of the High Military Council—are not subject to judicial review. There is no way to object to its decisions, and no appeal against them—except at the European Court of Human Rights in Strasbourg.

They say that "All roads lead to Rome," but these days, in our justice system, all roads seem to lead to Strasbourg!

AUGUST 2002

The second half of 2002 brought surprises. The demands that the European Union imposed on new members, the Copenhagen Criteria,[57] were incompatible with the recommendations of the military members of the National Security Council, and this incompatibility was compounded by the multiple obstructions of the MHP (the right-wing National Action Party), which was unwilling to accept these conditions. Suddenly, the country was gripped with panic. "Oh no! We are going to miss the European train!" Big capital, in particular, had come to believe that if we stayed outside Europe, all its wealth would soon slip through its fingers, so it moved into action with all its institutions, with research reports by foundations, and pages and pages of newspaper advertisements, and this finally got the results they wanted.

---

57. The Copenhagen Criteria are the political criteria all European Union applicant countries must meet before they can begin negotiations for membership. They include the requirement to show "stability of institutions guaranteeing democracy, the rule of law, human rights, and respect for and protection of minorities."

First of all, some changes were made to the constitution, but this was not enough, and they had to find a way to pass some new "harmonization laws," that is, to revise the old laws in order to conform with the revisions in the constitution. Also, something had to be done about the government, which was being obstructionist. The two problems were solved at once. While Prime Minister Ecevit's Democratic Left Party was noisily crumbling to pieces and the Özkan, Cem, and Derviş trio[58] blossomed as the new darlings of the media, the TBMM quickly held an extraordinary session. And while the MHP tried to curry public favor by opposing abolition of the death penalty, saying, "What, shall we not hang Apo[59] but feed him?" the "harmonization laws" were quickly passed by the Parliament.

Yes, the death penalty was abolished.[60] It was replaced by a longer life sentence. Yes, the prohibition against education in Kurdish was abandoned. There were to be no elective Kurdish courses in the universities; however, it would be possible to start private courses.

Yes, Kurdish radio and TV broadcasting were allowed—under the control of the RTUK,[61] by the government, for a few minutes a day.

Yes, an addition was made to Article 159 (insulting state institutions) to the effect that statements "would not be considered an offense, if there was no intention of insult."

Yes.

---

58. Hüsamettin Özkan, former deputy leader of the Democratic Left Party; İsmail Cem, former foreign minister of the Democratic Left Party; and Kemal Derviş, former deputy president of the World Bank and former economy minister under Ecevit. They looked in mid-2002 as if they would form a party that would capitalize on İsmail Cem and Kemal Derviş's popularity. Instead, İsmail Cem and Husamettin Özkan formed the New Turkey Party, but Kemal Derviş joined the Republican People's Party (originally founded by Atatürk). The New Turkey Party failed to win any seats at the November 2002 election. The Republican People's Party is currently in opposition.

59. Abdullah Öcalan, leader of the PKK, who was under sentence of death. There had been no judicial executions in Turkey since 1984, so the debate surrounding abolition in August 2002 focused almost exclusively on Öcalan, whom the MHP said they wanted to see hanged.

60. Except in times of war, or near war. By abolishing the death penalty in peacetime, Turkey met the standard required by the European Union on this issue.

61. High Council for Radio and Television Broadcasting. A representative of the military sits on the council.

Yes, BUT—there was a pile of *buts*.

Our lawmakers exercised their usual skill to make it look *as if* something were changing while ensuring that business would continue as usual. The question is: How will the lower courts and the Supreme Court interpret these new laws? We will have to wait and see.

Unfortunately, our justice system does not have a good record on such matters and does not promise a particularly bright future. But I hope I am wrong.

So now let us look at how the situation stands, practically, in August 2002:

The Kurds: Every party they open gets closed down. A case for the closure of HADEP is currently under consideration by the Supreme Court. And one of the problems for Prime Minister Ecevit is this: "If HADEP gets enough votes to get into the Parliament at the next election,[62] what will happen to us?" Kurdish cultural associations are constantly raided and their members arrested on empty pretexts. People are arrested at wedding parties for singing in Kurdish and "patted affectionately" by the police. Students and parents who submitted petitions are still spending their days in court. Hikmet Sami, the minister of justice, told us on television on the very day that the "harmonization package" went into effect that it would not cover them and that "there would be no change in their condition" because they were being tried under Article 169. Business as usual.

The Sunnis: Since February 28, 1997, they have seen the real face of the regime. Their parties are constantly under threat of abolition. The struggle over the headscarf continues. Women students' rights of equality under the law, freedom of conscience, and the right to education are being openly flouted.

The Alevis: The Union of Alevi Bektashi Institutions has been shut down, and the case against them is currently pending before the Supreme Court. Using the word *Alevi* is regarded as a form of separatism. The Office

---

62. Elections were held on November 3, 2002. The news was not good for Ecevit's DSP, which was completely wiped out of Parliament. The new government was formed by the center-right Justice and Development Party, which describes itself as "not Islamist but Muslim Democrat, the equivalent of Europe's Christian Democrats."

of Religious Affairs, which claims to be secular, recognizes no Muslim religious identity other than the Hanefi school of the Sunni sect. So, they ask, what do you need a Cem Evi[63] for? It is unnecessary. If you want to worship, come along to the mosque. Think of the equivalent for Sunnis in Germany. The German state bans mosques and tells Muslims, "Those who want to worship are welcome to come to church!"

The Minorities: Ethnic and religious minorities are supposed to be under the protection of a number of international treaties, including, in particular, the Treaty of Lausanne.[64] In reality, they face various pressures, but, as minorities, they find it difficult to raise their voice. (They remember the riots of September 6–7, 1955.) They are probably thankful that their situation is no worse in a country where the MHP, a strongly nationalist party, was recently the biggest party and a member of the coalition government.

Selma Koçiva, author of a book that mentions the Laz culture and identity,[65] and her publisher have been brought before the State Security Court. This is also true for Omer Şükrü Asan, author of *The Pontus Culture*,[66] and its publisher, our very dear Ayşenur Zarakolu. (We lost her recently, and I wonder if the State Security Court, where she was a regular customer, has branches in the other world too. I should ask Dilipak; he may have connections over there!)

Over the years, ways have been found to seize property belonging to Armenian charitable foundations in İstanbul. It is true that the right to such properties was restored to them in the last "harmonization law," but with a little deception: This only applies to property they will acquire in the

---

63. Cem Evi (Gathering House) is the traditional meeting place for Turkey's Alevis.

64. The Treaty of Lausanne (1923) concluded the war with Greece and superseded the Treaty of Sèvres (1919), which had more or less destroyed Turkey, reducing it to a rump state in central Asia Minor. Lausanne established Turkey's borders close to those of the present day, and also included protections for Christian and Jewish minorities in Turkey and the Turkish minority in Greece.

65. The Laz people of the Black Sea coast speak a language related to Georgian.

66. Pontus is the former Greek kingdom of the Black Sea region around Trabzon (Trebizond) that fell in 1461. The Black Sea coast had a substantial Greek population until the exchange of populations with Greece in the 1920s following the Treaty of Lausanne.

future. So those who usurped the Armenians' property will continue to sit on it.[67]

Women: While the principle of joint ownership of property was finally recognized in the amendments to the Civil Code, our fine male members of Parliament again did their male duty by making the rule valid only from then onward. So if a woman married her husband forty years ago and is unable within a year to convince him to reregister their possessions in their joint name with a notarized document, then she will get nothing if they ever separate or divorce. So look out, all you ladies whose husbands have been treating you unusually nicely lately! Don't say I did not warn you.

And of all the women who have been sexually assaulted by the security forces in police stations, in prisons, or out in the villages, how many have dared to come out and talk about the calamity that befell them? Of those who did speak out, how many were able to have their molesters prosecuted? In how many of those cases, opened after extreme difficulties, did the law manage to get the accused policemen to turn up in court? Asiye Güzel Zeybek,[68] whose complaint brought no results, could explain what happened to her only when she was brought to court for her own trial. And

---

67. In fact, in a further "harmonization law" in early 2003, the law with regard to non-Muslim foundations was changed to offer full protection for the charities. It is worth noting that Mazlum-Der, a human rights organization mentioned earlier in this chapter, which has a devout Muslim membership, championed reform of the law for non-Muslim foundations—a graphic example of opposites side by side.

68. Asiye Güzel Zeybek was editor-in-chief of the radical leftist magazine *Atılım (Surge)* and worked on a related publication, *İşçinin Yolu (Worker's Path)*. In February 1997, police detained her for participating in a demonstration protesting alleged links between the Turkish mafia and the government. She was imprisoned and charged under Article 168 of the Turkish criminal code for membership in an illegal armed organization, the Marxist-Leninist Communist Party (MLKP). During a hearing in October 1997, Zeybek reported that she had been raped during interrogation. Her complaint against eight policemen was accepted after a medical report confirmed that she showed signs of psychological trauma. In October 1999, the prosecutor decided not to prosecute. In October 1999, she published *İşkencede Bir Tecavüz Öyküsü (A Story of Rape Under Torture)*, (İstanbul: Ceylan Publishers). Zeybek was injured during the violent transfers into F-type prisons in December 2000. On June 5, 2002, after spending five years and four months in prison, Zeybek's trial continued. In October 2002, İstanbul State Security Court sentenced her in absentia to twelve and a half years in prison. At the time the sentence was announced, Asiye Güzel Zeybek was in Sweden to receive the PEN Tucholsky Award, granted annually to writers who have been persecuted, threatened, or in exile. She remains in exile in Sweden.

you all know what happened to Sema Pişkinsüt,[69] president of the Human Rights Commission of the Turkish Parliament, who was working to combat such abuses.

Workers, civil servants, trade unionists: Most employers want European standards for their own gains and interests, but when it is their employees' turn, they find the European standards far too generous. They thought the Employment Security Law gave too much away, and we should be thankful it became law at all. But when workers try to demonstrate or strike or press for their rights in other ways, it is not only Allah that knows what they will be faced with. We know too. We have watched it on TV thousands of times.

Journalists, writers, publishers: I do not think I need to add anything further.

Now we will test what mathematical knowledge we have left from our school days and try to balance the equation.

Well, 90 percent of the population is Muslim, either Sunni or Alevi.

Kurdish citizens of the Turkish Republic number twelve to fifteen million. There are also Greeks, Armenians, Jews, Syrians, Assyrians, the Laz— a lot of people who would like to express their ethnic identity but dare not.

---

69. A member of parliament from the DSP, Dr. Sema Pişkinsüt was president of the Human Rights Commission of the Turkish parliament from December 1997 until November 2000. She took an uncompromising stand against torture and carried out unannounced visits to police stations. In May 2000, the commission released a series of reports on its visits to places of detention in various provinces of Turkey. The reports document the torture of women, children, and people accused of common criminal offenses, as well as people detained under the Anti-Terror Law. The commission collected various instruments apparently used in torture. The commission also reported the adulteration of custody records, an abuse that not only destroys evidence that might be used in subsequent prosecutions but also was a contributory factor in the wave of "disappearances" that swept Turkey in the mid-1990s. Responsibility was placed squarely at the top of the chain of command: "As for those who are in reality responsible for such abuses, it is not, as people believe, the police station commanders and executive officers and other lower- and middle-level positions. Rather, it is the governors and chief public prosecutors who are to blame. This is because both these positions have the authority and duty to supervise and inspect the entire system. The fact that they do not carry out their duties and avail themselves of their authority should never be excused and should be investigated as extreme neglect of duty. We should have the political determination to resolve this issue without further hesitation or deviation." (Commission quoted in *Turkish Daily News*, May 27, 2000). Dr. Pişkinsüt subsequently expressed regret that she was removed from the presidency before being able to complete her project to stop torture in Turkey.

Actually, it is difficult to put these numbers on either side of any equation because some of the Kurds are Sunni and some Alevi, even Christian. But no matter from what angle we look or how we add or subtract, just about every sector of society in Turkey is under pressure, each in its own way.

In Turkey, the state is at loggerheads with all parts of society.

But how can this be? It contradicts the first rule of military strategy.

My father, Lieutenant General Daniyal Yurdatapan, was a soldier, with quite a few medals on his shoulder. Of course, when he was giving us kids advice, he used examples from his own professional experience: "Listen, son, if you can avoid fighting, do so. But if you find yourself forced to fight, then make sure you fight only on one front at a time. Keep your back against the wall, because nobody can fight on all fronts at once. First go and cut some deals with those who are not your main enemy. Make sure they are neutral, and then fight your fight on a single front."

But what we see today in Turkey contradicts this simple military logic.

So how come the fight still continues? The answer is not complicated. Because we are all fighting just for our own individual rights and keeping quiet when others' rights are trampled underfoot. Sometimes we are even pleased to see others come in for their share of trouble.

The Alevis watch the headscarf struggle from a distance. They think to themselves, "You burned our coreligionists in Sivas, so now you have some idea how it feels." (As if those who committed the Sivas murders had not come to Sivas from outside. As if they were not the same evil force that carried out the murders at Başbağlar.[70])

The Sunnis keep quiet when Alevi organizations are forced to disband, thinking to themselves, "Well, these are just *kızılbaş* [redheads] anyway."[71]

---

70. On July 5, 1993, three days after the massacre of Alevis at Sivas, thirty-three Sunni Muslims were massacred at Başbağlar, near Kemaliye in Erzincan province. Responsibility for this massacre has never been satisfactorily established. Some claim the PKK committed the killings; others that it was an Alevi revenge action; still others suggest that it was an action carried out by the state within the state to promote conflict between Alevis and Sunnis.

71. The followers of the Sheikh Junayd (d. 1460) wore red turbans and thus earned their name. Junayd was from a branch of the Shiite Safavid ruling family in Iran that influenced the growth of ideas among the Turks of Azerbaijan and Anatolia, which eventually grew into the Turkish brand of Alevism. The term *kızılbaş* is a pejorative term for Alevis (some regard Alevism, with its special regard for the caliph Ali, as a form of Shiism).

The secularists, and especially the Kemalists, look on impassively as police forcibly remove the headscarves of female students at the universities. Afraid that Turkey will be turned into a theocracy like Iran or Afghanistan, they say, "If those Islamists come to power, they will forcibly cover our heads. So I do not care what you do to them." In fact, in adopting this position, the secularists are accepting that the state has the right to cover or uncover people's heads by force. That is actually pressing a saw into the hands of the state so it can cut the branch that this species of secularist sits on. I am particularly shocked that some leftists should think this way. How quickly they have forgotten how this argument was used to suppress their freedom of expression by means of Articles 141 and 142 of the Turkish criminal code,[72] and how quickly they took up positions on the opposite side of the argument. For years the state said, "Communism will not recognize rights for anybody else, so why should we recognize the rights of anyone with leftist views?" And consequently, some of the most promising young people this country produced wasted their youth in prison in the 1980s.

The Kurds are watching what is happening to the Sunnis and the Alevis, thinking, "When our parties were closed down, when our members of parliament were being violently carried off, when we were being lynched by people making the graywolf sign, you watched without mercy or pity for us. Your parties even worked deliberately against us. You deserve now whatever is happening to you."

When the Christian minorities are under pressure, the Muslims make not the slightest protest, voicing instead the traditional anti-Christian comments—"We don't want them selling snails in the Muslim quarter."[73] And there are also headlines in the press, saying, "Missionaries are spreading Christian propaganda, trying to convert our children. It is a scandal." And this prompts the TV stations to hold studio discussions where a lot of

---

72. Articles 141 and 142 of the Turkish criminal code outlawed any expression of communist or separatist ideas. They were abolished in 1991, but a new provision was passed simultaneously under Article 8 of the Anti-Terror Law so even nonviolent advocacy of separatism remains punishable by up to three years' imprisonment; this is still the case today.

73. Snails are among the foodstuffs, including pork, that are forbidden to Muslims.

nonsense is exchanged, and then the prosecutors swing into action with court cases.[74]

And weren't we supposed to be defending *everybody's* right to freedom of thought, expression, and conscience? If a Christian thinks his religion is the best, of course he may want to pass this belief on to others. When our compatriots in Germany manage to persuade their neighbors to accept Islam, we broadcast it in the newspaper headlines, but the Catholic and Protestant churches in Germany do not get on the TV and protest, "These Turks are turning our children into Muslims. Get the prosecutors to teach them a lesson."

True or not? Do you need more examples?

So this is how millions of people are being divided and ruled. This is the real separatism.

It is clear what we have to do. Wherever our society has been cut and separated, that is where we should begin to glue our community back together again.

For Abdurrahman Dilipak's views on this subject, see Green *chapters 4, 16, and 19.*

---

74. "There is no law that explicitly prohibits proselytizing or religious conversions; however, religious groups that proselytize occasionally are subject to government restrictions or harassment. Many prosecutors regard proselytizing and religious activism on the part of evangelical Christians, and particularly Islamists, with suspicion, particularly when such activities are deemed to have political overtones. Police sometimes arrest proselytizers for disturbing the peace, 'insulting Islam,' conducting unauthorized educational courses, or distributing literature that has criminal or separatist elements; courts usually dismiss such charges. If the proselytizers are foreigners, they may be deported, but they usually are able to reenter the country." U.S. Department of State, *Country Reports on Human Rights Practices*: Turkey, March 4, 2002.

19. OPPOSITES SIDE BY SIDE

Is that an easy thing to do? Of course not.

Our social differences were stoked up to white heat for so many years and transformed into an enmity amounting more or less to a blood feud, with bloodshed on Bloody Sunday,[75] in Kahramanmaraş,[76] Çorum,[77] Sivas, Başbağlar, Lice,[78] Şırnak,[79] and Hakkari[80]—it is clear that we are not likely to overcome these obstacles in a moment.

Yes, it will take time to move beyond so much fear and distrust. But if we assume that it will take ten years, then we should start today, so that we will reach our goal ten years from today. If we start tomorrow, it will be ten years from tomorrow. We must get started immediately.

Our proposal is as simple as this: *opposites side by side.*

This is a hard thing to do, but at the same time, we have it in our tradition.

Our festivals are traditional occasions for making peace among those who are angry with one another, the joining of hands by those who have

---

75. Murder of two leftists and the injury of hundreds more by police and right wingers who attacked a demonstration in the Taksim district of İstanbul protesting the presence of the U.S. Sixth Fleet in the Bosphorus.

76. Massacre of Alevis in Kahramanmaraş (Maraş) by right-wing mobs on December 24, 1978. One hundred eleven people were killed.

77. Massacre of forty-eight leftists and Alevis by right-wing mobs at Çorum between May 27 and July 4, 1980.

78. Lice is a small town in Diyarbakır province that was the scene of several attacks by security forces on civilians during the 1990s. The PKK was founded in 1978 in a village near Lice.

79. In March 1992, troops fired on thousands of townsfolk who had gathered to celebrate the Kurdish new year (*newroz*). Thirty-eight people were killed, including one police officer. In August 1992, most of the population of Şırnak fled when security forces went on a rampage in the town, shooting up buildings with small arms and tank fire. Twenty-six were killed, including one police officer and three enlisted men.

80. The farthest southeastern province, home of the Yeşilyurt gang, which allegedly comprises police officers, village guards, and former PKK militants who turned state's evidence; responsible for hostage taking, drug smuggling, and at least one killing.

hurt one other. Even the most hard-bitten character cannot push away the outstretched hand of a former friend on a festival day. Even if he really wants to reject it, he cannot do so while he is in that setting because he knows that such hardheartedness would be poorly received by onlookers all around. Once the *selam* (peace greeting) has been spoken, it cannot be left in the air; it must be returned with another *selam* in response. And there is another proverb to set beside this ancient tradition of peacemaking: "For a fool, every day is festival day." Well, let them call us fools, and every day will be our festival of fools, as we all stretch out our hand of friendship to our *social opposite*.

I am not saying you should in any way stop being yourself. Just stop trying to make your opposite just like you. You continue to be yourself and live as you choose, and your opposite continues to be himself and live as he chooses.

Of course, whether we like it or not, we all have to breathe the same air, walk on the same earth, and drink the same water. When the developers succeed in their aim of selling off the forests around İstanbul, and the forests that hold the water for the city are destroyed, then all of us will be left with the water shortage. Disasters like that do not distinguish between right and left, Muslim or secularist. Yes, environmental disaster is already on its way, disturbing the equilibrium of the atmosphere, bringing rising seas, changing climate, drought to Africa, floods to Europe. It does not matter whether you are a Muslim or a Christian; death does not discriminate!

So Dilipak and I together decided that this year our most important effort will be in this direction: *opposites side by side*.

So come on, wherever you are, at home, in your home district, your town, your province: Do not wait for leadership or a signal. Make your own decision, if you agree with our idea. Go and find the person who does *not* agree with you or share your ideas. Go find your opposite, stretch your hand out to him, and say, "Greetings, Opposite, how are you? How is your health? What are you eating and drinking? Take care of yourself, because what would I do without you?"

They say, "There is only one İstanbul." We can expand that a bit if we want:

"There is only one homeland. There is only one planet Earth."

We must love it and take care of it. As the Native American saying goes, "We did not inherit the world from our ancestors; we borrowed it from our children."

Şanar Yurdatapan
August 2002

THE GREEN

BY ABDURRAHMAN DİLİPAK

CONTENTS

1. INTRODUCTION

"I think, therefore I am."

I must render my existence meaningful.

Therefore I must think.

I know I can be wrong, but still I must think.

Because I can learn whether I am wrong or not by thinking.

If I am, my existence has a reason. Every being has a past history, and every action must have an agent. If you continue to think, you will reach the first cause that will force the limits of your intelligence. That first cause is the creative force. The mind cannot grasp that force. In fact, if we could understand it, it would not be God.

I exist as much as my intellect. I am a human being insofar as I have intellect. I shall believe as much as my intellect, and I shall be myself as much as my intellect.

He who has no intellect has no religion—nor opinions nor ideology.

Every category or classification that the intellect can think of is an obstacle in front of humankind in our struggle to be human.

Man is man, together with all his sins and all his good deeds.

This is a reality from the moment we are born.

We are sharing this world together.

We do not choose the parents or the soil of our birth, or the time of our birth either. So we did not choose this world or this country! And this is not a matter of regret for us. Yurdatapan (patriot)—an interesting surname, is it not, given by his father, and, the way I see it, one of life's pleasant ironies. I, Muslim Dilipak, I chose this religion. Islam is a sacred preference for me, and He who created me knows me better than I know myself. This is a reason for me to be grateful, and to praise my Creator.

When Yurdatapan and I found each other, we noticed that we were living in this world together.

We were different! Our religions, our languages, our cultural backgrounds, our ethnic origins and personalities, our fears and our hopes—everything about us was different.

But we knew this much: that if we tried to understand each other, instead of validating ourselves by tring to invalidate the other, we could establish a more humane order between us.

And we could do this only by speaking and writing to each other.

Instead of seeking happiness in the other's sorrow, or triumphing in the other's defeat, we noticed that sorrows decrease as they are shared. And happiness increases.

We could live together, humanely, in peace and freedom!

Perhaps we would not share each other's beliefs and ideas, or perhaps we could. We could still be productive together, and we could share what we produced.

We had to start by getting to know each other.

Instead of devising a definition of the other and forcing him into it like a straitjacket, could I not set aside my value judgments, and allow him to bring his own definition of himself?

Let everyone's religion, beliefs, and ideas be his own.

If problems arise from our co-existence, we can solve them fairly with a peaceful approach.

We want a better world and we believe there is much we can do to that end.

Perhaps we are singing the same songs, but in different languages. Perhaps we are searching for the same thing.

We come from the same roots. In this world, we shall return to the same soil.

This work is a product of shared concerns and efforts.

Our beliefs are different, our ways of seeing things in this world, our hopes, and our fears are all different.

But today we live here and together.

Instead of making this reality into a nightmare or this world a hell for each other, we think that together we can work to shape a happier future.

At least, we can find common words between us.

At least, we can agree on certain virtues.

Surely we must have things in common; we must find them and bring them to the fore.

Instead of cursing the darkness, we must light candles.

Darkness is just the absence of light.

Everything is in our minds and hearts.

We share a common hope that if we can learn to share what is in our minds and hearts, many problems may solve themselves.

The land is our mother.

We want flowers of freedom to blossom in this land; this will be our mother's smile to us.

This is the debt of the child to its mother.

We are either brothers in faith or fellows in flesh.

We are human beings.

2. CONCERNING FREEDOM OF BELIEF AND THOUGHT

Freedom of belief, thought, conscience, expression, organization, and the right to education. These come at the head of fundamental rights and freedoms.

The freedom of belief and thought are fundamental freedoms that even take precedence over the right to life.

This may seem ridiculous, but it is my opinion that the right of belief and thought do precede the right to life. At first glance this may not appear to make sense, but it must be stated straight away that when you have abolished the freedom of belief and thought, life no longer has meaning.

What makes our life meaningful and sacred is our belief and thought. If you strip us of our belief and thought, what is left behind is nothing but a biological event. The fundamental difference that makes us human, what sets us apart, is our belief and our thought. If you exclude this, what you have left is just a living creature no different from any other. It is for this reason that the ancients described the human being as "the reasoning creature."

You manage animals according to the degree of their harm or benefit to you, and in doing so take away from them their right of existence. When you do away with a human being's freedom of belief and thought, then what remains is just another living creature: You have done away with the fundamental elements that make that person's life sacred.

For this reason, the freedom of belief and thought comes before the freedom of existence or life.

For this reason also, belief and thought on their own do not constitute an offense.

In this sense, the idea of "ideological offense" is not a correct or healthy way of thinking.

Those who consider belief and ideology "offenses" are enemies of humanity, enemies of the values that make a human being out of a person. This is an offense against the sacredness of the human being.

One cannot here consider cursing and insult as products of belief and thought.

Belief is the knowledge of reality; it is the fundamental knowledge concerning the way we perceive and comprehend the world, ourselves, the past, and the future; it is the fundamental tool for the judgment of values. And thought expresses the response of a particular individual's mind to reality as experienced at a certain time, in a particular place and around a specific event.

Hindering this response in any way amounts to hindering the evolution of humankind, and it is this hinderance, rather than belief or thought, that should be considered an offense against humanity.

There is always a benefit in remembering this: My distance from you is equal to your distance from me. Your ideas will be as strange to me as mine are to you.

Here, one side attempting to silence or overpower the opposition or to limit or punish belief and thought is no different from one claiming lordship or divinity over the other.

Without a doubt, imposing beliefs and thoughts is just as serious an offense against humanity as limiting them.

Belief and thought are not offenses; they cannot be and must not be.

Allow people to live as they believe and to freely express their thoughts.

If what they say is true and beautiful, let us share it with them; if what they say is wrong, let us be able to correct them, so wrong ideas do not grow and spread among them.

Let them express their thoughts, let them live their beliefs, so we can see what kind of people they are—their identities, their personalities, and their values.

Pressures on belief and thought undermine people's character, make them hypocrites, practicing double standards.

People without character are the worst possible disaster for society, for everybody.

Belief and thought are unconditionally free. That is how it must be.

Do not forget that whatever you want for yourself, you are obliged to promise to others, and whatever you promise, you earn the right to ask for. Respect is mutual. Justice requires this.

Putting limits on the liberties of others means others putting limits on your brothers.

Every arrow you shoot in this tent of a world will come back and find you.

Once I was afraid too. How terrible it is to fear whoever is not like you. This makes man aggressive. You place yourself at the center of life, and you want everybody to be like you.

In fact, only in an environment where others exist do I have the possibility to determine my difference, my personality, and my individuality.

We need our opposites to express ourselves and to display our trademarks, our distinguishing characteristics.

When we eliminate our opposites, in a certain sense we eliminate ourselves as well.

Even in order to fight with our opposites, they must first exist. That is why the devil is an indestructible opponent. Light is the absence of darkness. Well, how can you even negate this absence in the name of negating darkness? Isn't turning absence into presence tantamount to self-abnegation? If you trust yourself, why would you be afraid of your opposites? In reality, you excel by defeating your opponents. By overcoming difficulties and by climbing peaks, you can develop yourself.

Everyone will be himself, herself.

Moreover, how could we destroy such differences? Our differences are what establish our individuality as separate persons. In time, differences may turn into opposition. As morality takes shape, you can begin to define immorality. And by defining immorality, you are simultaneously defining morality.

Bitter and sweet, good and bad, hot and cold are all opposites. And yet life, color, light, *everything* finds its own expression in this interplay. Our intellect, our impressions, our opinions and values, the land we were born in, our religion, our ideology, our genetic differences, our sex, our social standing all make us different.

A monotone world in which opposites did not exist would hardly be meaningful at all.

Therefore, let us appreciate the value of our differences. Let us accept this worldly life, opposites and all, and realize that we should not oppose the nature of life itself.

For surely a day will come when we will have to account for all we did in this world—a day when we shall see the reality of things we argued about while in this world.

For the views of Şanar Yurdatapan on these subjects, see The Red *chapter 3.*

3. THINK, BUT KEEP QUIET—DON'T LET ANYONE HEAR YOU

We have to produce ideas in order to define ourselves, to understand others, and to communicate with others. You have to think, define what you are thinking about, ask questions, give answers, exchange knowledge, test knowledge, and in doing so, evolve.

We are thinking, living beings; putting limits on our freedom of thought is equivalent to putting limits on our being human.

Hush, don't speak!

Among the family, in society, almost everywhere, it is considered wrong to speak near your elders, wrong to contradict your father and wrong to stand up to your bosses. You must listen and obey.

But isn't this just blind obedience?

Well, we are going to question and criticize, and by putting forward our opinions, we shall establish an identity for ourselves.

Freedom of thought is certainly *not* the right to have dreams that must not be shared. Imagination is the mother of reality, and dreams are the external expressions of our subconscious and of our feelings, so of course we will share them with each other. If we think of something and believe it, we are going to express that too. How can we test it if we do not express it? Obviously, we are going to tell others our ideas and even try to convince them of the merit of those ideas. This is a contest, a means to become strong and happy. We must be able to form organizations with other people who believe and think as we do. That is to say, people who are like us not only in thinking, but also in expression and organization: All these are parts of a whole process.

What is important is to be able to live together in peace in spite of our differences, to be able to act together on subjects about which we agree without violating each other's basic rights. And then to be able to excuse each other on subjects about which we disagree.

Do not forget that in the end, in the other world, Allah will show us the truth about all the things we have kept discussing in this world?

Let the people speak so we can learn who they are. If what they say is correct, we can benefit from their words, if what they say is not right, we can try to correct them.

Besides, aren't others as distant from us as we are from them? Our ideas are just as strange to them as their ideas are to us.

Some people are morally weak; they have the spirit of a dictator because they are interested in safeguarding their material advantages.

This is why countries like ours are riddled with prohibitions. For example, some are trying to take away in thirteen lines the rights given to us in the constitution in only three lines![81] Constitutions and laws aim not at restraining the members of the ruling class who possess wealth, guns, and power, but at keeping our society under oppression.

That is why they deem books, thinkers, and ideas criminal. Associations, foundations, and unions are all regarded as potential nests of criminality.

Thoughts are born in the mind and rule over the mind and heart. Any current of thought that could give rise to action against the establishment is viewed by some as dangerous and threatening.

Once, in every public square there was a made-up quotation,[82] attributed to Mustafa Kemal, which read, "Communism is the greatest enemy of the Turkish world; it must be crushed wherever it is seen." Those slogans have now disappeared, and been replaced by new ones describing the threat of *irtica*.[83] Certain individuals perceive society's various religious, ideological, political, and ethnic preferences as a source of conflict from which they profit, garnering authority and riches for themselves on the blood, tears, and stolen labor and sweat of the children of the same country.

---

81. The 1982 constitution imposed by the military junta, currently still in force, though somewhat modified since that date, appeared to grant broad rights but then scaled them back with extensive undemocratic reservations.

82. There is some doubt as to the authenticity of some of the statements attributed to Atatürk after his death. When the far-left Turkish Labor Party was founded in the early 1960s, the writer and journalist Çetin Altan sent a copy of the manuscript in which this text appeared to the Swedish Criminal Institute, for comparison with the manuscript of Atatürk's Oration (*Nutuk*) 1927, and the report indicated that the two texts were by a different hand.

83. Literally "reactionism." Used, particularly by the military, as a label for Islamic fundamentalism.

First destroy our identity, reduce us to ignorance, keep us in poverty, remove our sense of responsibility, and then incite us to take up arms against each other...

As a result, neither is the rightist a true rightist nor is the leftist a true leftist, neither is the Alevi a true Alevi nor is the Sunni a true Sunni...

If people are enemies of thought, it is because they are ignorant and incapable of love, and they want to see the entire population transformed into systematically retarded bionic robots.

For the views of Şanar Yurdatapan on this subject, see The Red *chapter 4.*

4. WHAT? WILL IT BE ACCEPTABLE TO WORSHIP SATAN TOO?

For 1,500 years a minority group, the Yezidi sect, has been living in Turkey. They attribute a different meaning to Satan, and respect him as "the Peacock Angel." For 1,500 years, the Muslims have been going to Mecca to stone Satan.[84]

For 1,500 years there has been no known war with the Yezidis. For 1,500 years, they have not been subjected to genocide. And they still continue their existence in the very midst of a people who shower curses on the founder of the religion, Yezid, long since dead.

Wasn't Satan granted a fixed term, to do his worst until the Day of Judgment?

Satan exists, and he will continue to exist.

Satan's existence is not the reason why we sin.

Those who worship Satan also will continue to exist.

At least we know who they are and what they believe. But what about those who worship the established regime? And those who worship political leaders? Let's leave even them to worship as they please. I have my path and they have theirs.

I will not worship what they worship, and they will not worship what I worship. Let them worship a cow if they like, or Buddha, or their political leader. It makes no difference to me. Let them make a religion out of their ideology if they want...as long as they do not try to impose it on others.

Let them be believers or unbelievers...communists or liberals.

The day will come when we shall be shown the reality of those things that we keep arguing about in this world. We shall be made to account for all we did or did not do, all we said or did not say.

That day will surely come!

Let them be believers or unbelievers

To believe or not to believe is something the individual must decide.

---

84. The Stoning of Satan (throwing seven pebbles at pillars representing Satan) at Mina, near Mecca, is a ritual that forms part of the Muslim's *Hajj*, or pilgrimage.

You can perceive life as either two-dimensional or one. If you evaluate matter and meaning at the same time, if you see spirit and body as two realities of life, if you accept that your reality is limited by your intellect and senses and that there is a reality outside them, then you are a spiritualist.

Intellect on its own may not always be able to comprehend reality. Man's instincts are just as important as his intellect in finding the truth. Obviously, you can believe to the extent that your intellect allows, and those lacking in intellect are exempt from the responsibilities of belief. They live in darkness regarding the revelations associated with Allah's rites of creation, which are also called the laws of nature. But intellect alone cannot be the source and the measure of reality. Is that not evident from the conflicts witnessed in the past thousands of years of humanity? Even today, some very intelligent people are quite unable to come to terms with each other.

Why is it difficult for humankind to believe in the reality of a creator? If nothing was created from nothing, what came first? Those who say "matter" are in error. Matter is a concentrated form of energy. In that case, there was in the beginning a field of energy. But when we talk about such a field, where in time and space was it? Doesn't the idea of something existing independent of time and space clash with the scientific mind?

You must, therefore, be talking about an energy beyond time and space. It follows, then, that this energy must be a primary treasure existing everywhere and at all times, a source of nature, able to transform itself into anything—a force that gave rise to everything around us. It cannot be more logical to believe in an entity devoid of intellect, knowledge, form, time, and space than to believe in Allah the Creator.

This is only an example of the internal contradictions and inconsistencies regarding atheism.

To some it may initially seem meaningless to believe in a God, Allah, who is a creator, possessing will and desire, never begotten or born, who had no beginning and has no end, and is the source of absolute power. In fact, if he were not of such a nature, it would not be necessary for us to worship him. We know of his nature from his own description of himself (in the Holy Qur'an). If it were possible to understand him merely with our intellect, we could divide him, break him into pieces, add, subtract, criticize, and give him new forms. But he is a treasure beyond the understanding of the human intellect, one that we can only feel in ourselves, in our soul and

spirit, in our own substance and reality. If he were to be understood, measurable, weighable, describable, then he would not be Allah. Therefore, we
worship something beyond the grasp of our intellect. Yes, that is why we
bow down before Allah.

Intellect understands things by proportion, comparison, measure...
but Allah is *Sübhan*, the Most Holy, unlike anything he has created. Because
he is supreme and superior to everything, he has no equivalent in the for-
mat and vocabulary of the intellect. It would be like asking a computer to
perform a function it was not programmed for.

In the other world, Allah will show us the reality of all the things we
keep arguing about in this world.

To deny is to reject something whose existence is known. It is just not
logically possible to say, "There is no Allah" since it concerns the denial of
an actuality and because both the denier and his mind are proofs of the
existence of Allah. Without Allah, he is alone with his desires, fancies, and
whims, trying to live in the universe created by Allah without paying his
dues, within the sphere of his command, but without his approval.

Belief is a matter of acceptance. But for believers, it is not enough just
to believe; Allah wants them to live according to the rules he has conveyed
to mankind through his prophet and in his book. As a recompense for this,
he will reward us with paradise, and in the life to come he will reveal some
of the secrets about himself at a different level of perception and understanding.

When a person accepts the existence of Allah, he confronts a crowded
world that includes such things as angels, jinns, Satan, prophet, and the
Book. That person's perception of the world changes. The reasons for his or
her own creation and the differences in the commentaries about religions
begin to interest the believer.

The mentality that sees man as a product of nature, a purposeless biological event, inevitably sees man as an evolved animal. Man's world of
spirituality and intellect, his understanding, feelings, and compulsions, are
all brought down to the level of biochemical reactions. Humankind is
reduced to a bionic robot. According to this mentality, there is no Allah,
and you are free to do as you like. But is that so? Or is it just that those who
do not serve Allah become the slaves of Satan? Satan, who has set up his
throne in their corporeality. If you believe in an Allah who is one and only

and is the master of the Day of Judgment, then it means you also believe that on that day you will have to account for all the things you did and those you did not do, the words you uttered and those you did not. Allah knows what passes in your heart. He sees, hears, and knows you. And one day you will be asked to account for all you have done.

For a Muslim, humankind is Allah's seeing eye, hearing ear, outstretched hand, and crying voice on earth. For this reason, a Muslim begins whatever he does by saying *Bismillah* ("in the name of Allah"). That means that anything he touches in the name of Allah is sacred, and therefore he treats it with respect. The Muslim knows that Allah wants to punish the oppressor and to help the oppressed through him. Allah wants to make him his inheritor on earth and to reward him.

What Allah wants is for people to live according to the purpose of his creation. And for this, he will reward them.

He is the creator of fate, destiny, sustenance, and death. He possesses real authority and judgment. He has left humankind free on earth within the domain of certain rules. He has shown us what is right. He has cautioned us. He has set up marker stones that alert the intellect to the true reality of the natural world. He has sent a book that is a guide for those who have understanding.

For the views of Şanar Yurdatapan on this subject, see The Red *chapters 4 and 9.*

5. THE QUESTION

Who are we? Where have we come from, and where are we going?

What does it mean to be a servant of Allah?

We did not choose our mother and father, nor the time or the place of our birth. Yet this is the environment into which we were born and our lives are limited by the opportunities offered by this environment.

Our parents determine our genetic/racial identity. The place where we were born decides our national identity. And the period in which we were born determines our opportunities.

All of this is according to the will of Allah.

In the genetic sense, we belong to a homeland. Our second homeland is the political state in which we live, and our third homeland is the cosmos, which shapes the time we perceive.

In the profoundest sense, we do not know exactly where or when we are living. So we define for ourselves a zone of responsibility of relative time and place that is within our understanding. We do not fully understand even the world in which we live, for our level of perception is limited by our senses.

The world as defined by materialists is meaningless. According to the evolutionists, the initial Big Bang was followed by the evolution of matter.

But according to Islamic belief, the creation was Allah's work. The philosophy of Descartes starts by saying, "I think, therefore I am." Because I exist, I owe my existence to a cause. And whether this first cause happened by itself or whether it was the work of a superior will is the subject of a fundamental conflict between the materialists and the spiritualists.

If there is no God, then there is no such thing as creation. Neither can you then talk about an aim associated with the creation nor about a way of life ordered by the Creator.

Let us quickly point out that throughout the history of humankind, no current of ideas has been as strong as religion, and no development has ever been able to render religion meaningless or useless.

Religion, the absolute need to believe, is the way of living that the Creator reveals to the created. Accordingly, in its essence, religion cannot contradict nature or the scientific truths hidden in nature, and Allah cannot engender fundamental antagonism among the elements of his creation, because this would be contrary to the divine law, or *shariah*—the declared will of God—on which religion is based. Perfection cannot be composed of absurdity or deficiency, and therefore it is impossible to speak of haphazardness in the divine system. Allah cannot be ignorant of any part of his own creation.

It must not be forgotten that the world in which we live is very limited and cannot reflect the whole of reality. On Judgment Day, Allah will explain to us the truth about the contentious issues of this world. If we were able to understand Allah in his entirety, we would be in a position superior to him. It is not logical for something temporary and limited to understand the absolute and infinite. But Allah gave us sensory organs, intelligence, and feelings and we therefore have the ability and the responsibility to understand the existence of Allah and practice the way of life he has revealed to us.

In this sense, intellect is not the source of truth but the center wherein we understand truth and apply it. Just as those who lack intellect do not need religion, people can believe and do works according to the limits of their intelligence. To one who has no intellect, belief is not an obligation.

Science is composed of the rules that the Creator has hidden in the substance of his creation, rules that man grasps, and accordingly controls nature. A material object is a revelation emerging from Allah's creative nature, and to decipher knowledge hidden within material objects is to interpret that revelation.

Just as Muslims do not possess the right to not see, hear, or know what is happening around them in the world, they will be made to account for all they have done or not done, uttered or not uttered in this world. All of them will be rewarded or punished for their good and bad deeds, no matter how small.

Perhaps *cennet* (paradise) will offer back to us the happiness that issued from our deeds in this world, but multiplied manyfold (ten times, one hundred times, or even seven hundred times over) and *cehennem* (hell) will make us taste, many times over, the sufferings we caused on earth.

This world is not made up merely of what we perceive.

In reality, there is no color, no light, no heat, no sound, and no taste. We also do not know where in the universe and in what time period we are located. It is all a question of frequencies. We possess a system that transmits or receives these frequencies. Color, sound, light, taste—everything takes shape in our minds. The sky is not blue, and fire is not hot to the touch. Those created in the form of humankind perceive things this way. Other living creatures do not experience the same taste as we do, they do not see things in the same light, they do not hear the same way. Perhaps what seems so long to us—this worldly life—is only a momentary, dreamlike realm. We have little knowledge beyond that granted to us. We do not have reliable knowledge about the science of existence and the existence of objects. We know very little. The discovery of DNA and the advent of the computer do not mean that we now know everything. Relatively speaking, we are actually growing more ignorant. The more knowledge we acquire, the more we realize how much we do not know. In the same way, if we give a child a spoonful of food to make him grow, we also make his appetite grow.

As we climb high hills, we come across higher ones.

In fact, there is no such thing as matter. Everything can be reduced to the size of an atom. Atomic density yields the characteristics of matter. The atom's nucleus is made up of the neutron and the proton. That is to say, there is no evolution in the essence of matter, for matter retains the same essence that it had at the point of original creation.

Soul and cognition are something altogether different. There is no credible explanation for the formation and the evolution of the soul and the intellect. The materialists abandon this problem when their mind cannot provide a satisfactory answer. They regard it as unknowable.

Religion, however, possesses many explanations for these matters. Angels, jinns, Satan—in reality, we are living on earth with other living creatures that have different abilities of understanding and come from other dimensions.

We have certain faculties called the soul, the intellect, and the anima.

The materialists try to understand man by reducing him to an animal. As they distance themselves from belief in Allah and the world beyond by denying the existence of the angels, and as they reject the idea of being a servant of Allah by submitting to the servitude of the devil, whom they also deny, they are transforming the world into hell while searching on earth for heaven and an eternal life.

We are like a country with angels, jinns, and devils wandering through every vein, brimming cell by cell with living creatures, each one embodying revelation. Man is the most perfect of those created, the most honored of all created, the thinking, living creature that is the summary of all creation. Mankind is therefore the regent of Allah on earth. He moves and acts with Allah's permission and in his name. In this light, the Holy Qur'an is a regent's agreement with Allah. Allah is he who reigns over fate, destiny, providence, and death, he who has absolute authority, he who is one and unique, single, without partner, he who did not beget and who was not begotten, and there is nothing before or after him.

He tests us, at times increasing and at times decreasing our property, our lives, and our loved ones. Those who believe in him and those who deny him will one day be brought before his throne to account for every moment of their lives. This universe is his property. Everything done without his consent will be punished, and every work done with his consent will be rewarded many times over.

Allah wanted to make men inherit the earth. He wanted to make them excellent and to reward them. Therefore, he arranged this world as a place of testing and trial.

There is only one religion, and it has been the same since the first human. As for the differences among religions, we devised them according to our own preferences, so any problems that have arisen as a result of these differences can be blamed on our ignorance and our worldly desires and not on religion itself.

For the views of Şanar Yurdatapan on this subject, see The Red *chapter 7.*

6. THOUGHTS ABOUT GOD, CREATION, AND EVOLUTION

Religion (*Din*) is the way of living revealed by the Creator to the created through his prophet. The true religion is Islam (surrender to the will of Allah). Islam is the common name of all the divine religions from the time of Adam, the first man, until today. *Shariah* defines the commands and the prohibitions of this religion—that is to say, its legal code.

As for *religio*, it defines the discipline of life that man has formulated for himself in line with his thinking about God and the Last Day.

Today Christianity, to a great extent, consists of *religio*. It is a project designed by the religious leaders regarding their idea of God, and basically possesses human and humanlike characteristics.

The intellect is the mark of being created human and of the faculty designated to receive the revelations. The intellect is what qualifies man's power of disposition over other living creatures and things. Science, on the other hand, is the act of uncovering the laws hidden within the essence of matter by means of the intellect, investigation, and experimentation. Religion does not conflict with this pursuit of science. If there appears to be a conflict, then the scientific finding or the religious explanation is deficient. If the scientific result is conclusive, then the religious interpretation must be changed. Conflict between religion and science is quite impossible.

Just as Allah cannot be in error about what he has created, there is nothing he does not know about his creation. The Creator does not incorporate contradictory elements into the constitution of his creation. Contradictions that may develop between religion and the intellect or science and the intellect should be resolved in favor of science.

The intellect manifests itself as a response in the mind of an individual to a particular event at a particular time in a particular place. The intellect may occasionally deviate from the limits of reality due to deficiencies or errors in the given data. The intellect is important, but it is not absolute. Neither religion nor science would be possible without the intellect. Otherwise, so many intelligent people would not be able to agree on fundamental issues.

Here we can speak, in the spiritual sense, of an endless process of perfection. It is not credible to argue against an evolutionary process concerning the human intellect, its ability to grasp truth and to examine extremely complex phenomena, themselves governed by evolutionary principles. Evolution and development within a species is possible, but the idea of one species developing into another is not very convincing.

The Holy Qur'an informs us of men who were transformed into monkeys as a punishment, but not of monkeys that were transformed into men. Even if some interspecies forms were to be found, they would be special cases born out of a punishment.

Today the efforts by scientists to produce inter-species clones or creatures cannot be conceived as examples of the normal process of evolution, but as human interference with nature's balances. It is not possible to describe the similar characteristics among various species as a product of natural evolution within a single species.

Finally, there remains the reality of creation: Everyone is free to believe or to reject what they wish, but on the Day of Judgment, everyone will get what he deserves. Those who believe are not losing anything by living in accordance with their belief. The laws of religion are also considered right and good by those who have intellect, and in paradise we shall have our reward. As for those who deny the truth and the reality of Allah, just as they are making an error in this world, they will be at a loss in the life to come because they will have made no preparation for it.

For the views of Ṣanar Yurdatapan on these subjects, see The Red *chapters 7, 9, and 12.*

7. WOMAN AND MAN

Woman and man.

We share a common ground: We are both human.

We clothed our souls with a body when we came into this world. Our soul has no gender. We are wearing the costumes necessary to meet the trials of this life.

Only true faith and piety bestow superiority.

Neither man nor woman is necessarily right or superior. Whoever is genuinely right is right irrespective of gender, and if the woman is right, then all men should defend that woman, and if the man is right, then all women should defend him.

The question here is: What is right and what is the source of that rightness? In my mind, the essential thing is the contract. Religion is a contract between Allah and humankind on the question of our regency. Believers must abide by the terms of that contract. If there is no such contract, then common rights upon which they agree must form the basis of the relationship. In the area of freedoms, first the side that has been wronged must be specified, and then a solution must be found on the basis of the rights and freedoms of the wronged party.

In the eyes of Allah and of justice, man and woman are equal.

Of course, there are areas wherein one is superior to the other. There may be various reasons for this. For example, man has more muscle power. Woman has more developed senses. In such areas, certain men and women are superior to certain other men and women.

It must not be forgotten that every man and woman is the work of another woman. Women do not only give birth to children, they give birth to society.

It is important to resist patriarchal or feminist approaches. Perhaps every human being is deficient and finds his or her true character and purpose within the family.

According to İbrahim Hakkı of Erzurum,[85] woman is superior to man in forty points, and man is superior to woman in forty points. Just as a man may be superior to forty women, a woman may be more clever, more industrious, and more honest than forty men. But beyond this, we are as equal as the teeth of a comb. But because different people merit different things, equality of treatment could be a form of oppression. Are those who merit particular things and those who do not equal? Would it be equal and just to load the same weight on the backs of a child and a thirty-year-old to give them both the same fee and the same amount of food? What sort of justice would that be?

In this sense, justice comes before equality.

Our rule must be as follows: We shall take the side of the oppressed against the oppressor no matter where the injustice originates and no matter who is wronged.

Is it true, as they claim, that in Muslim societies women have no right of inheritance and that a man can divorce his wife simply by saying, "I divorce you."

Uğur Mumcu[86] was right when he said that, unfortunately, most people have opinions before they have knowledge. Few people take the trouble to inform themselves about Islamic law concerning slavery and women servants before airing their opinions on the subject. They know nothing about women's rights to money and property, as defined by marriage laws. They know nothing about women's rights regarding inheritance. For example, even if it seems at first glance that a Muslim woman is given less than her brother at the first division of property, this woman has the right to ask for the difference and perhaps more as dowry from the man she marries. Meanwhile, the brother will end up giving the surplus money he received to the girl he marries.

According to this understanding, money and land won't be split into many ineffective pieces, change hands, and be taken out of circulation alto-

---

85. Also known as İsmail Hakki Erzurumi (1703–1780), writer, poet and thinker, author of the *Marifetname* (*Account of the Sciences*), an encyclopedic survey of astronomy, mathematics, anatomy, psychology, philosophy, and Islamic mysticism.

86. Prominent journalist and columnist, much respected for his integrity, who probed abuses by state agents as well as by the PKK and violent Islamist groups. His murder by a car-bomb in 1993 provoked nationwide grieving and protests.

gether. The quantitative growth of the money is also prevented, so the woman will be desired for her own character, not for her wealth.

In addition, the woman has a second dowry right: If for any reason she becomes destitute, she will be taken care of, and this acts as insurance for her. The woman may even be given more than the man at the first division. The situation here involves more advantages with less risk, and in this way the woman does not become someone desired only for her money or for her income. This is important, for she has an especially honorable position because of her role as a companion and a mother, charged with the noble task of bringing up a decent family. Minimizing risk and stress is an important means of happiness and comfort for the couples.

For the views of Şanar Yurdatapan on this subject, see The Red *chapter 10.*

8. OFFICIAL IDEOLOGY, OFFICIAL HISTORY, AND CIVILIAN SOCIETY

Any official ideology imposed upon society is a religion invented by the sacred state. In countries in which this happens, society is enslaved to those in power, and those in power are treated as if they possessed the spiritual character of saints, and the leaders as if they were demigods.

In such countries, there is an official history in which everyone is either a hero or a traitor, a book of damnations and praises. Such countries afford no space for civil society or civil awareness. Everyone is imprisoned by the official ideology of a single party state, though in some cases it may *appear* to be a multiparty system.

Draft laws are sent as a matter of formality to parliament, where they are accepted unanimously and without discussion. The votes in parliament are conducted by open ballot with secret counting. Laws intended to silence the opposition are passed secretly. Courts are established whose decisions cannot be challenged. First they hang, then they judge. The regime passes laws to which changes may not even be proposed, for it is illegal to do so. Yes, they pass laws but they themselves do not abide by those laws. In such countries, privileged individuals, ideas, and institutions are protected by laws. The political parties are like family businesses and their leaders like demigods. The party chief is also the ideological leader, and it is as if the leaders appoint the members of parliament. Behind the mask of democracy hides the oligarchical dictatorship of the leaders, who are, in turn, controlled with carrot and stick by deep forces within the state.

Ceaselessly, these leaders pump hope and promise salvation. But in truth, not even prophets have the power to offer salvation; they can only *speak* to show the path that leads to salvation. But the leaders promise that if you give them your votes, they will be able to act like gods and change your destiny and give you your daily bread. You are heroes, they say, and all you have to do is give them your vote. If it were in their power, they would make everybody into party members. They try to turn all civil social organizations into agents of political society. This is a treacherous betrayal of civil society, for *civilian* serves as an alternative not only to *soldier*; but also to *political* and *official*.

Everybody must think about the meaning of being a member of civil society, a party member, and a militant. There have always been people who pretend to be civilians, but intend to manipulate the civilian opposition in order to take over authority. In a country that does not motivate itself to build, but contents itself with criticizing what others have built, and that also runs away from paying the price and taking responsibility, civilian society cannot be realized. No matter which party wins, in the end the winning party forms not only the government of those who gave it votes, but also the government of the whole nation. For this reason, the party should listen to and serve the entire nation. For this reason it is important to make appointments on the basis of merit.

So whoever forms the government, that government should not be so big as to be beyond control or supervision. The best government is one that governs with the fewest laws and whose existence is the least felt. The more rules there are in a country, the more freedoms are restricted, and the more taxes there are, the more incompetent government officials are, and the more poverty there is likely to be. In addition, the more area covered by the informal economy and informal political rule, the less justice there will be in that country.

In my opinion, even if from time to time people with above-average intelligence are needed in the fields of politics and bureaucracy, generally speaking these are the province of people of average intelligence. As a rule, politicians and bureaucrats should be knowledgeable, honest, and courageous, and they should be the sort of people who bring fame and respect to their position rather than demanding the dignity of their position. Unfortunately, such people are rarer than is generally believed.

For the views of Şanar Yurdatapan on these subjects, see The Red *chapter 6.*

9. HISTORY

History should not be a book of praises and curses.

History is there to teach a lesson from past events.

Just as countries and nations each have a history, humankind also has a history.

History is the common memory and cumulative experience of a society.

We must know the fate of the peoples who came before us so we do not make the same mistakes as they did and so we can improve on whatever they did that was worthy.

There should be no such thing as official history.

Instead of starting new fights based on events whose participants are long gone, we should be deriving lasting lessons from history.

Historians should seek truth, rather than covering up the past errors of their nation and inventing heroes and villains. We should own up to the history that is our common heritage, protect historical documents, and submit them to the historians so everyone can benefit from them.

Obviously, we should evaluate historical events on the basis of the values of the age in which they occurred. We must read history not to invent heroes and traitors, but to understand the past as well as to learn lessons for today and the future.

We fulfill our responsibilities to history and society by acknowledging the accumulated knowledge of the past, the hopes of tomorrow, and the responsibilities of today. So those who content themselves merely with pride in their past are a lost generation.

What is more important than what our ancestors did is the lessons that we take from them and, in the end, what we do based on those lessons. It should not be forgotten that for Allah, all times and places are equal. We shall be brought to account based not on what our ancestors did but on what we ourselves do. If we are evildoers, it is no benefit to us even if our fathers were prophets. And if we follow the path of goodness, it is irrelevant that our fathers may have committed treachery.

Societies that do not know their past cannot have a bright future.

Besides the knowledge of reality, Allah gave humanity the knowledge of truth. He taught us the names of things. He gave us the knowledge of the past and of the future. He gave us wisdom. Knowledge is not only the product of our own experiences. If you were to take away religion from the life of humankind, today would not be as it is. The essential value that makes a human being out of a person is religion. All errors and sufferings are the results of life lived outside religion. History speaks of religious wars, the Crusades, and crimes committed in the name of religion . . . but all of this is not the result of religion, but of deviations from it.

History is not only made up of what was done by the main actors of past events; it also comprises the contributions of the historians who interpret, understand, and evaluate history.

For the views of Şanar Yurdatapan on this subject, see The Red *chapter 16.*

10. BEING ANATOLIAN

Anatolia is the country of the prophets Adam, Noah, and Abraham. With its climatic range from –40°C to +40°C, its summits and valleys, it is a place where almost every kind of vegetation and animal life can exist. It is probably the only place on earth where all four seasons can be thoroughly enjoyed. It is the only country where three continents meet, that is surrounded by three seas, and blessed with so many flowing rivers, springs of fresh water, lakes, underground sources, and sweet waters.

This place is the common homeland of humankind. It is the source of many peoples and nations.

This place is Media, the country of the Median peoples. It is the place from which Mesopotamian peoples migrated and, in the neighborhood of the Caspian Sea, met the peoples coming from Indo-Europe. It is the intercontinental passageway by which Alexander the Great made his Macedonian-to-Mongolia expedition. This place is the Silk Road. This is why, from ancient times, people called this place *Media*, the central region—because any knowledge that falls into the soil of this geographical region will reach all the world.

Anatolia is Media.

It is the cradle of the most ancient civilizations of humankind. No other country on earth is rich with so many mineral treasures.

Well, then, why are we so poor as a nation? Only three hundred years ago, were we not the richest country in the world? Our collapse has taken longer than the development of the West's modern civilization! By comparison, both the French Revolution and the American Revolution happened just a few days ago! While our country was collapsing, the West managed to squeeze into these three hundred years modern colonialism, two world wars, many coups, and two atomic bombs.

We have little money, but we are richer by far in our pockets than in our faith, and we are richer in faith than in intellect. We believe what is handed down to us without thinking.

This is the land of the prophets Adam, Noah, and Abraham!

This is the common home of all humankind, its motherland.

This country is the cradle of civilizations and humanity. Let everybody in Adam's land worship according to his own religion, speak his own language, and think his own thoughts—as long as he does no harm to others. Let's find a way to live together in peace and harmony in spite of our differences.

Chauvinism is death for peoples living in this land.

Looking for authority, wealth, and happiness at the price of each other's blood and tears means working for free as a voluntary laborer for hell.

Let this land, the source of many peoples, be a blend of religions, races, and ideologies. Let our life be as brightly colored as the fields painted with wildflowers.

Let a new order be established with many religions, many voices, and many cultures.

Let people worship Allah or Satan, as they wish.

Let everybody's religion be his own. Let people believe or deny as they choose.

Don't doubt—one day all of us will be shown the result of our work.

We shall be asked to account for everything that we have done or have not done (but should have) and for everything that we have said or not said (but should have).

Show a little patience!

Every soul will surely taste death, the only path of return is unto him.

Unfortunately, most of the unbelievers who are deprived of the truth of the revelations are subjected to anger and reproach by ill-informed and prejudiced people who are swayed by the ignorant claims and false practices circulated as true religion.

In the ambience of freedom and peace, we all will choose to do what we like, and we will reap the harvest of our choice.

To each his own religion and to each his own language. . . .

This country is the land of the prophet Adam, of the prophets Abraham, Noah, Daniel, Joshua, Hızır[87] and Elijah.

---

87. A saintly figure in Islam, much revered in Anatolia (though he is not mentioned explicitly in the Qur'an) as a helper in time of need. The spring festival Hıdrellez is celebrated in his honor on May 6.

The cradle of the oldest civilizations of history.

Poets ask, "Is paradise underneath or above this land?"

Our country is like a ship floating on top of an ocean of oil. Over centuries, hundreds of peoples, religions, and cultures intermingled on this soil. There is no country in the world with more potential for wealth. Together with South Africa, it is the country with the richest gold reserves.

But so many Anatolian religions, tongues, races, cultures, and civilizations have lost their luster—we allowed all of them to fade. Now the Arabs are no longer Arab, the Kurds Kurd, nor the Assyrians Assyrian. Our Albanians cannot speak Albanian, our Chechens do not know Chechnyan. We have become a people without a tongue and without culture. The Aramaeans, Chaldeans, and Assyrians are emigrating now. Yet, these lands are Media, the common homeland of humanity.

Every human being is in some small way Anatolian.

This place is the birthplace and wellspring of many peoples.

We must have freedom. Nothing else will do.

Perhaps the need for freedom is a more fundamental need for us that the need for water and bread. Freedom!

For the views of Şanar Yurdatapan on this subject, see The Red *chapters 6 and 16.*

11. LANGUAGE

What is the meaning of the existence of an object?

How do we understand it?

Or, how do we attribute meaning to that thing?

Tongue—is it the piece of flesh in our mouths, or does it signify a language, or, as in the old adage, does it have something to do with our heart?

Have you ever thought about how many words you know? How many of those words are nouns and adjectives, how many of them are terms, and how many concepts?

What fraction of them did we produce?

Can you imagine a civilization without language?

I don't know whether you know this, but it is said that in Turkey, our women speak with only three hundred words, our men with five hundred. But, with less than two thousand words, it is not possible to understand our religion, this world, our rights, and our responsibilities. It is said that in the Kangal District of the province of Sivas, on the shores of the Black Sea in northeastern Turkey, they have taught dogs to respond to three hundred separate words of command. A parrot has reportedly been trained to say one hundred and fifty words in three languages.

Of the words, terms, and concepts that we know, I wonder how many we use correctly.

Can you express your thoughts clearly? Do you understand correctly what you hear?

I hope the fact that civil peace has not been achieved is not due to a bad communication problem! Do you think those who show their respect and friendship know what they are saying?

If you cannot express your thoughts, or you cannot understand the complaint of the person in front of you, what is going to become of us? When we cannot find a solution to our problems with intelligence and words, what else can we do but solve them with brute force? And that is what we seem to be doing.

Think. What does this mean? What does it mean in a land when *thought* is an offense, when your words and writings can put you on the witness stand as a defendant, when books are criminalized, when the intelligentsia are all viewed as potential criminals, and when fewer than seven million out of our population of seventy million people read newspapers?

According to research, the number of words used by elementary school students are: Germany—79,000; United States—71,681; Saudi Arabia—57,000; Turkey—only 4,994.

Need I say more?

For the views of Şanar Yurdatapan on this subject, see The Red *chapter 4.*

12. UNDERSTANDING AND INTERPRETING RELIGION WRONGLY, OR, MYTH AND THE REALITY ABOUT RELIGION

Any precious thing can be misused—religion included. The Holy Qur'an, which was a source of justice in the hands of the caliph Ömer,[88] was turned into a means of threat in the hands of Yazid I.[89]

In Islam, the elements regarding the necessity of faith and those elements governing proper deeds and worship are separate. Deeds and worship may be classified as *helal* (permitted), *haram* (forbidden), *sunnet* (the way of the prophet), and *mekruh* (abominable and therefore forbidden), there are also the categories of *vacip* (recommended) and *mustehap* (good, laudable). The unchanging and the absolute truths are those founded on the revelations. Religious commentary, on the other hand, being related to time and place, is limited by the knowledge and life experiences of the commentator.

Oftentimes, the ignorant bundle up their fears and raw imagination with fairy stories, and then cloak them with religion. Much that really has nothing to do with religion has become part of accepted religion over time.

There is only one true religion in the world, and that is Islam. The other religions are described as *religio*, signifying a means whereby people show their thanks to God. Real religion is directly connected to Allah's revelations. *Religio*, however, is an attempt by local people to describe God and faith according to their own limited perception.

To put it more correctly, all the monotheistic religions, from the first man, the prophet Adam, until the last prophet, Muhammed, have only one name, and that is Islam. The other religions were reinterpreted locally and became mere *religio*.

---

88. The second caliph (successor or deputy, leader of the Muslim community) following the death of the prophet. He captured Jerusalem, and is traditionally celebrated for his justice and humility.

89. Yazid I (680–683), the son of Mu'awiya and was the second caliph of the Ummayyad dynasty. Yazid's reputation was permanently stained because he was held responsible for the death of the prophet's descendant Hussain and his family at Karbala, causing a permanent split between the Sunni and Shia sects of Islam.

Religions have only one purpose, and that is to summon all human-kind to behave in accordance with the purpose of their own creation. And the path to achieving this is to reconcile our intellect with our conscience, by following ways approved by the Creator for the created in line with the revelations sent to the prophets and exemplified by the prophets.

That is why another name of Allah is *Selam*, which means "peace." The word *Islam* is from the same root as *Selam* and has the same meaning, "peace."

Note that there can be no *içtihat* (scholarly commentary) on that which is revealed as fixed and certain, because *içtihat* does not deal with the fundamental realities of religion but with its interpretation.

It is good to remember that in Islam, a moment's deep insight is worth more than a year's nonobligatory prayers. We can only believe to the extent that our intellect or understanding permits, and we can only do good works to the extent that our intellect permits. Religion and knowledge are never in conflict because Allah cannot be in error or deficient in knowledge about what he created. If we worship him, this is not something he feels a need for. Our prayers, our fasting, our sacrifices, and our pilgrimages are not for his benefit. These are things that benefit us; they symbolize the disciplines associated with our obedience. Our going to his presence and praying five times a day, expressing our thanks to him, our glorifying him, our asking forgiveness for the wrongs we do, and our promising to walk on the straight path only show that we recognize his absolutely superior power.

Only Allah can tell the devout from the hypocrite. Many people fool themselves and others by saying, "We believe." Some of them (the hypocrites), when they gather together with others like them, mock the genuinely devout. When they are told to believe like those who are truly devout, they say, "Do you expect us to behave like those backward fools?" In reality, although they do not realize it, they themselves are the backward fools. When they are told, "Don't cause trouble in this world," they say, "Oh, we are only peacemakers." In fact, they *are* the troublemakers, and they do not know it.

For the views of Şanar Yurdatapan on this subject, see The Red *chapter 8.*

13. OH, THE WEST, THE WEST, AND AGAIN THE WEST!

Do you know who first discovered America? I suspect you do not!

The first travelers to America were the Berbers of North Africa. The arrival of the Brazil tribe from Mauretania and the Berber Banu Huveyre tribe in America and the civilization they established there influenced the West via the Islamic society of Andalusia[90] and was the source of inspiration for the European pioneers.

Did you know that when Christopher Columbus prepared to sail to America in 1492, there was already a Native American bride in İstanbul?

And that Christopher Columbus came to İstanbul to hire sea captains as guides?

And that he completed his voyage of discovery with the assistance of these guides?

The generally accepted information about going around the Cape of Good Hope (the southern tip of Africa) is also wrong!

Why do they show America to the west of Europe? You can take it and put it near Japan and observe the virtual continuity of land toward the east to America. Or you can even challenge your perceptions by turning the map in your home upside down and seeing how the world looks from that perspective.

What does *Middle East* mean? According to whom is it the Middle East? That is what it looks like if you regard the world from England's perspective.

If you listen, you will find that our own people frequently curse the Middle Ages. When "medieval thoughts" start to be discussed, there is no holding back the rage. Turks think of themselves as being locked away in the darkness of the European Middle Ages. They think of the Inquisition. They are not aware that the Middle Ages of their own history was a brilliant age. They know nothing about the magnificent, impressive achieve-

---

90. Al-Andalus was the territory ruled by Islamic dynasties on the Iberian peninsula 711–1492. At the height of its power, Al-Andalus encompassed most of what is now Spain and Portugal.

ments of the Chinese, Indian, and Islamic civilizations in science, freedom, and arts from that period.

And the West! It is considered the most splendid civilization in history!

But what has this two-hundred-year-old civilization cost the world in real terms? The French Revolution occurred only just over two hundred years ago in 1789; that is as little as three times the lifespan of a person!

In this short period, the West gave us two world wars as a present. Everyone knows what the West did in Hiroshima and Nagasaki. The West has also consumed two-thirds of the world's known strategic raw materials. They have polluted the land, the air, and the waters. They established a horrifying colonialist order all over the world. Marxism and fascism are both children of the West.

We have to remember the holocaust suffered by the Native Americans who are now under protective care like a threatened species, the enslavement of the African-Americans, the Asians whose sweat was stolen as cheap labor....

So the West is a civilization that has risen from the blood of the Native Americans, the tears of the black-skinned, and the stolen sweat of the yellow race ... The flipside of all this wealth is colonialism and exploitation.

If you don't believe me, then read Montaigne's lament for the sacking of the New World in the sixteenth century: "So many goodly cities ransacked and razed, so many nations destroyed and made desolate, millions of innocent people of all sexes, stages and ages, massacred, ravaged and put to the sword, and the richest, the fairest and the best part of the world topsy-turvied, ruined and defaced for the traffic in pearls and pepper. Mechanical victories."[91]

Likewise, Chief Seattle said, "[The white man] steals the land from his own children...His appetite will devour the earth and leave behind only a desert...The Whites, too, shall pass; perhaps sooner than other tribes. Contaminate your bed, and you will one night suffocate in your own waste."[92] And Albert Sarraut[93] said much the same: "Why do we need to

---

91. Michel Montaigne, *Denemelar* (*Essays*), translated by S. Eyüboğlu (İstanbul: Cem Publications, 1989), "On Coaches."

92. Chief Seattle's 1854 letter to U.S. president Franklin Pierce.

93. French colonial minister (1872–1962).

keep secret the future? Colonialism was not the first civilized movement. It was a movement of force and compulsion driven by interests."

Do you want to hear Jean-Paul Sartre's testimony too? It is tragic. In order to criticize the West, we need the testimony of Westerners. Otherwise, how could we dare to criticize the West? The West is sacred and untouchable. It is the source and center of truth. Everything will be done for the West, according to their orders, and by the West. Because the West is the culmination of history: "You know well enough that we are exploiters. You know too that we have laid hands on first the gold and metals, then the petroleum of the (new continents), and that we have brought them back to the old countries. This was not without excellent results, as witness our palaces, our cathedrals and our great industrial cities."[94] And do we know anything about the civilization of Isfahan, in Iran? How much do we know about its architecture, art, technology, and science?

We know nothing, and what is worse, we do not know that we do not know. Because we are supremely ignorant about our own beliefs, history, and culture. Even Westerners know more about it than we do.

Do we have any knowledge of the historical documents about the science, art, and politics of our own civilization? Many of us know about the Magna Carta, but what about the letter of the caliph Ali to Malik al-Ashtar?[95] Or the writings of Sultan Mehmet, conqueror of İstanbul and Sultan Süleyman the Magnificent concerning human rights? How many of us know the important documents, and declarations of our own history? In this regard, it is useful to look at Ismail Cem's history of how Turkey became a Third World country,[96] especially with respect to Ottoman documents on human rights.

One last witness: Louis Masignon. "We destroyed all they had. Their religion has been destroyed. They no longer believe in anything. They fell into a deep abyss. They became just right for anarchy and suicide."

Well, that's the modern West for you!

---

94. Jean-Paul Sartre's introduction to Frantz Fanon's *The Wretched of the Earth* (1961).

95. Letter from the fourth caliph Ali to the newly appointed governor of Egypt, which outlines the principles of justice and good governance.

96. *Turkiye'nin Geri Kalmisligin Tarihi* (*The History of Turkey's Underdevelopment*), by Ismail Cem (İstanbul: Cem Publications, 1978). Ismail Cem served as the Turkish foreign minister to the Ecevit government, resigning in 2002.

Western countries have no principles, only *interests*. Neither the Organization for Security and Cooperation in Europe (OSCE), nor the Paris Charter,[97] nor the Helsinki Final Act[98] have any importance or value if they do not accord with Western interests. We have seen in Bosnia, Karabağ,[99] Chechnya, and Palestine that these documents don't have any value—not even as much value as rolls of toilet paper! Democracy and human rights are valid only to the extent that they serve the interests of those who advocate them. Who supports the Saudi government, helping kings and princes maintain themselves in power over and against the population? And in Algeria, who is keeping the junta, the military regime, in power against the masses?

Democracy and speeches touting human rights are doing a good cosmetic job in hiding the ugliness of the political face of the West.

The insistence on Westernism is a fascist attitude.

Every civilization is a product of its own social truths, history, belief, and culture.

Of course, people are entitled to choose and adopt beautiful things, because wisdom is humankind's common work. To locate virtue exclusively in the West by attempting to obtain the same results as the West through copying its history, culture, and beliefs is an injustice to the character of humankind, and to the past history, beliefs, and cultures of peoples.

I talked of the poor of the East stoking the welfare of the West; the West is a civilization of exploitation. I am convinced that the West, squeezed into a space little longer than one man's life, a very brief period in relation to the full history of mankind, has come to the end of the road. And that relatively short span may have been the bloodiest and costliest in the history of civilization. This is a civilization that, in the name of the welfare and happiness of only a

---

97. Charter of Paris for a New Europe 1990. A declaration of some of the principles concerning human rights and democracy that it was hoped would shape post–Cold War politics in Europe and the world.

98. The Helsinki Final Act of 1975 was an agreement between members of the Organization for Security and Cooperation in Europe (known at that time as the Conference for Security and Cooperation in Europe), which laid down specific principles for the conduct of relations between states, including among others, respect for sovereignty, renunciation of the use of force for settling disputes, peaceful settlements of disputes, respect for human rights, and the inviolability of frontiers.

99. The territory disputed between Azerbaijan and Armenia.

few million people of the West, has been raised on the blood, tears, and stolen sweat of the billions who make up the rest of the family of humankind.

For every person in the West who has benefited from the freedom and welfare of Western civilization, in the rest of the world at least one person has lost his or her life, and ten more have served as slaves of this civilization.

Today the West is still benefiting from the unearned income of modern colonialism.

That is today's reality as far as I see it!

For the views of Şanar Yurdatapan on this subject, see The Red *chapter 14.*

14. THE QUESTION OF NAMUS (HONOR)

Guarding one's honor is one of the five fundamental necessities of religion.[100] This can also be defined as the safeguarding of a person's chastity, which is related to the innocence with which one comes into this world.

In Islam, as in the Jewish Torah and the Christian Bible, adultery and fornication, and all behavior leading toward them, are forbidden. The abuse of sexuality is unlawful in the religious sense. In its most general usage in Islamic terminology, *namus* expresses everything that is considered sacred. For example, the common Turkish expression, "The flag is our *namus*," can mean both that we value the flag and that it carries a symbolic meaning.

In the most common usage in the Muslim world, *namus* expresses the sexual innocence or virginity of a man or woman. Contrary to general public opinion, there is no distinction between the chastity of men and of women. An illicit relationship pulls apart families and negatively shapes the life and character of the next generation.

Today in the West, the family is sustaining serious wounds in the name of sexual freedom, and, as a consequence of incestuous relations, psychological and genetic problems are on the increase. For this reason, Islam forbids any and every form of illicit sexuality.

Namus encompasses sexual purity, morality, and discipline. It can also refer to people's physical and spiritual innocence. Because of the potentially disruptive effects of sex and its influence on moral development, *namus* is placed among the five attributes that must be safeguarded, according to Islam.

No doubt, economic factors also contribute to the decay of moral values. But the fundamental cause is moral poverty. It is a weakness in the sense of chastity or *namus*. When there is no purity, when *namus* is removed from both the economy and politics, we are left with the unpleasant realities of today.

---

100. *Shariah* traditionally defines the five necessities as belief and thought, life, family life, honor, and property.

Yes, animals have no sense of chastity. Or self-respect or dignity either. They say that a female spider eats its male partner after they mate. They also say that a cat eats its baby if it is very hungry. Animals do not have either flags or family feelings...so perhaps *namus* is one of the characteristics that distinguishes humans from the animals.

For the views of Şanar Yurdatapan on this subject, see The Red *chapters 10 and 11.*

15. THE SIX ARROWS,[101] AND BEING A NATIONALIST!

What is left of the Six Arrows?

What were those six arrows? Republicanism, secularism, populism, nationalism, statism, and reformism.

The world is changing fast.

Yesterday, labor was the most important; today, it is money.

Yesterday, independence was cardinal; today, it is mutual dependence.

Yesterday, republicanism was all the rage; today, democracy.

Yesterday, state and society were valued; today, it is the individual.

Yesterday, the nation mattered; today, it is the people.

Yesterday, the majority was important; today, the trend is pluralism.

Today in Germany and France, being a republican is synonymous with being a neo-Nazi or a fascist.

Democracy was not one of the Six Arrows. Republicanism is not one of the conditions for democracy—in England, for example, there is neither secularism nor republic.

Even in the European Union (EU), France is the only country that has secularism written into its constitution. In the rest of the EU nations' constitutions or legal texts, it is not religion that is written, it is a particular religious sect! In England, the monarch can only be a Protestant!

Holland, Belgium, Sweden, and many other European countries have neither secularism nor a republic. But there is democracy in all those countries, and what is more, these countries are considered the cradles of democracy.

According to the original Kemalists, "Democracy would bring back Babıali,[102] and liberalism would take us back to Galata and the Capitula-

---

101. Atatürk enumerated his principles for the development of the new Turkish republic in the form of six "arrows." They are used in the emblem of the Republican People's Party, founded by Atatürk.

102. The Sublime Porte, seat of government of the Ottoman Empire.

tions.[103] Democracy is a hell of anarchy. As for the Italy of Mussolini, it was corrective dictatorship that liberated the Italian people from the Latin backwardness."

Today I doubt whether the average Turkish intellectual or politician could clearly distinguish the difference between the republican system and democracy!

To talk all day about democracy or to regularly celebrate the Turkish Republic Day[104] is not sufficient to learn the meaning of such ideas. Many believe that republicanism is populism or rule by the people, but you could hardly claim that every republican system of government had a democratic structure. Today nobody talks about republicanism; everybody talks about democracy. They talk about a Second Republic. They talk about the restructuring of the state. All the concepts and the institutions upon which the state is based are open to discussion: the constitution, the office of the president, the parliament, the government, the laws, the political parties, justice, the army, the treasury, the economy—everything but everything is being discussed!

On the walls it is still written that a republic is a virtuous system, but the people cannot see in their daily lives what kind of virtues it imparts to their daily lives.

What they see is violence, blood, and poverty. What they see is bribery and corruption. What they see is incompetence and defeat.

The people want to make peace with their own history, beliefs, cultures, and identities; they are not getting anywhere by being alienated from themselves.

Unfortunately, however, those who control the state will not permit this.

This cannot be called a republican system; this is an oligarchy.

From a monarchy we passed into an oligarchy in the guise of a republic.

And in the name of secularism, we are facing religious intolerance.

---

103. Galata is the district on the European shore of İstanbul that was virtually colonized by European commercial interests that exploited the Ottoman Empire through a system of trading privileges known as the Capitulations.

104. October 29.

It was the authorities that laid the groundwork for the Friday Crises.[105] The state has established control over religion. Now it is impossible to talk about secularism in Turkey.

Perhaps you can talk about a Kemalist theocracy. Or if you disagree with that, then you can say that we have a Byzantine structure. And if you insist that it should be called secularism, then what we have is a Soviet-style Jivkovist Bulgarian type of secularism.[106]

To call it populism is not convincing either, because the present ideology is antipeople, looks down upon the people, rejects the people's identity, and suppresses their culture.

An old Kemalist notes that Kemal Atatürk believed only in reforms. He believed that life was a dynamic flow. Of the Six Arrows, only reformism genuinely reflects Atatürk. The first intellectuals of the new Turkish Republic went to Europe and Asia in search of an official ideology for the new Turkish state and submitted a report to İsmet İnönü.[107] From these, a composite of sorts was created. The principles of state and populism were taken from Russia, nationalism from Italy, secularism from France. *Republic* was included in the name of Atatürk's political party, and Reformism was provided by Atatürk.

Who is statist today? The mixed economy has replaced the original state of the early days. Those who pledge oaths of allegiance to the spiritual heritage of Atatürk and his Six Arrows are actually betraying the principle of statism when they espouse today's free market ideas. Is it not strange that those people, whose own pledges to statism are completely empty, feel no guilt or discomfort in denouncing certain members of parliament as traitors for refusing to pledge allegiance to the Constitution?

---

105. Periodically in recent years, police have been stationed outside key mosques throughout Turkey at times of tension in order to prevent worshippers from holding demonstrations after Friday prayers. The very presence of the police provoked the regular disturbances, according to some observers.

106. In the 1980s in communist Bulgaria, the state under President Todor Jivkov attempted to forcibly assimilate the Muslim Turkish minority and limit its freedom of worship.

107. İsmet İnönü, a general who was Atatürk's right-hand man during the War of Independence, he became president of Turkey after Atatürk's death.

Nobody is statist. Those who are quite ready to condemn statism as a backward and anachronistic ideology still continue to take oaths of allegiance to this principle and condemn those who refuse to do so!

The same people often describe nationalism as an empty, old-fashioned concept. Who can claim that they remain loyal to nationalism while they are at the same time seeking a future in the EU?

It appears that the Six Arrows have now completely lost their relevance and yet we cannot remove them from the constitution—in fact, it would be illegal to propose such a move. This is just because the Six Arrows are among the unchangeable principles of the constitution.

The same is true for the laws concerning the long-since-closed *tekkes* (dervish lodges), *zaviyes* (the Islamic cells or convents), and the wearing of the hat. Exactly like the laws that prohibit the use of the pre-Republic, old Ottoman titles such as *bey* (Mr.), *efendi* (sir), *hacı* (pilgrim), *hodja* (teacher), and *paşa* (general).

Yes, it is true: In this country it is illegal and forbidden to use the titles *bey, efendi, hacı, hodja, paşa*!

And yet the secular state passes laws to assist people with their pilgrimage to Mecca.

According to some people, by doing this, the government is making concessions to the *shariah*, and according to others, the government is preventing the profits of this business from going into the pockets of those who support a return to the *shariah*.

The Six Arrows persist in the constitution and party emblems as though they were a lucky charm to ward off the evil eye.

It is true that there is a law against proposing changes to these principles, but the statute protecting this particular law is itself unprotected and open to revision.

In other words, you can change the statutes upon which the law is based and then proceed to change the principles. Well, they do say all things are possible under democracy.

Lastly, Derviş[108] came from the World Bank to save the sinking Turkish economy and put a fine gloss on all this maneuvering. The resulting Repub-

---

108. Kemal Derviş, former deputy president of the World Bank, who was lionized when he returned to Turkey as a government minister, and later entered party politics as a member of the Republican People's Party, elected to the opposition party in 2002.

lican People's Party is a Turkish-style, capitalist party of the left that enjoys the support of the United States, the International Monetary Fund, the World Bank, and MUSIAD.[109]

How happy is he who calls himself a leftist![110]

For the views of Şanar Yurdatapan on this subject, see The Red *chapters 5 and 6.*

---

109. The Association of Muslim Employers and Industrialists.

110. This echoes the slogan "How happy he is who calls himself a Turk" that is frequently displayed in public buildings and public spaces—particularly in the mainly Kurdish Southeast.

16. THE PROBLEM OF THE OTHER: ENMITY TOWARD FOREIGNERS AND KURDS

As I remarked before, we should stand with the oppressed against the oppressor no matter where injustice originates, and no matter toward whom it is directed. The religion, the race, or the gender of the oppressed should have no bearing in this.

My distance from someone is equal to that person's distance from me.

My ideas are as strange to him as his ideas are to me. And for that person, I am "the other." We must walk in the other person's shoes. If we want to consider ourselves moral individuals, then we should seek for others whatever we seek for ourselves.

Remember that respect is mutual; we should not throw stones at someone else's idol, lest they should curse our lord.

If this were not the case, how could the Süriyanis, the Armenians, and the Yezidis have lived peacefully in these lands for the last fifteen hundred years? Today, unfortunately, the same understanding does not seem to hold sway. Somebody once asked my opinion on these issues and my reply was: "Promise to the Arabs in Turkey whatever it is that you want the Turks in Kerkuk to have. Let's give the Greeks in Turkey the same thing we want for the Turks in Greece, on the basis of equal justice."

I do not think that there is a Kurdish problem in this country. But there is a problem that people are not able to live as they would like or express what they think freely.

Everyone should be able to learn, speak, and teach their mother tongue. People should also be able to learn the languages and local dialects necessary for communicating with the people of their area and establishing their rights and responsibilities. People should also be able to protect and develop their native culture and identity.

This land is the source of many nations. It is the land of the prophets Adam, Noah, and Abraham. We are living on soil that was left to us as a legacy by an empire of many different peoples.

I say this not just because the Kurds are currently struggling for their identity; *all people* in all parts of the world should be able to speak their own chosen language without having to pay a price for it. Let's not look at it as the Kurdish Rights, Gypsy Rights, Women's Rights, or Workers' Rights; instead, let us regard this as a question of Human Rights. All should benefit from fundamental rights and freedoms, regardless of whether they are Kurd, Turk, Arab, Albanian, Circassian, Georgian, Armenian, Greek, Christian, or Muslim.

Let's defend one another's rights. If all of us try to take away the rights of others by claiming our own rights, by attempting to get rich from the poverty of others, and by delighting in the sorrow of others, we will quickly find ourselves at a dead end.

Happiness increases as it is shared, and sorrow decreases as it is shared. Happiness must be our common goal and our common ground—a place that we shall conquer not in spite of each other, but together.

For the views of Şanar Yurdatapan on this subject, see The Red *chapters 5 and 15.*

17. CONCERNING SECULARISM, THEOCRACY, BYZANTINISM, TRUCE, CONTRACTS, AND SHARING

When someone in our country is described as *secular*, we understand him to be a person who does not have much to do with religion. Or we understand him to desire the separation of the state from the mosque. But secularism is not external to religion, and it certainly does not mean separation of state and religion.

In the West, the word *secular* describes someone who does not belong to the clergy. A very religious and devout person, even a regular church-goer who pays church dues, can honestly describe himself as secular. What is more, in the mind of a secular or Western person, secularism in no way implies separation of church and state, and especially not antagonism between church and state.

In religions with a clergy class, secularism regulates the relationship between the government and the council of clergy. Thus, it is wrong to think about this only in terms of *church-state relations*. Religion existed before the state, and people set up governments to protect and develop their fundamental rights and freedoms. Religion was one of those rights and freedoms. For this reason, the approaches that separate religion from the state either sanctify the state and place it above the church or else render the state irreligious.

According to some, only the state, and not the individual, can be secular; according to others, only the individual can. According to still others, neither the state nor the individual can be secular, while according to others, both of them can.

These discussions are like a fight between two blind men.

The assertion that there is a relation between religion and the state is questionable. When discussing the religion-state connection, we must carefully examine how a particular religious institution is defined. Is religion just a sacred book or is it instead Allah himself? With this in mind, we should not talk about a connection between religion and the state, but rather about the state's view of religion, or the character and duties of the state required by religious principles. When devout people have citizenship rights, they will make demands of the state to bring about and maintain a social structure that does not conflict with their religious needs, and they will quite naturally do all they can to protect and promote the religious values that render their lives meaningful, and for whose sake they would even be prepared to sacrifice their lives.

The politicization of such issues is a proper development. Politics is a tool for solving problems. If you push a problem outside politics, you effectively open a door to illegality. Religious, philosophical, ideological, cultural problems, and those of conscience create demands for social rights, and politics is the art of reaching compromise on the basis of law.

For religion, the world is a place of testing and practice for life after death. Any attempt to divorce religion entirely from societal life is a covert effort to do away with religion, for both religion and politics intersect in the lives of individuals. According to Islamic belief, all people will be brought to account for everything they have or have not done and said in this world.

If we go back to the heart of the church, that is to say, to the council of clergy, then certainly we will be speaking about a relationship between the temporal ruler and the earthly representative of God. Secularism encompasses three possible definitions for this relationship. The first of these is theocracy, the second Byzantinism, and the third secularism.

Theocracy is the structure whereby the clergy dominates the state, as in the presecular period. For example, during the presecular period, in addition to maintaining its spiritual role, the Catholic church possessed wealth, arms, armies, and authority. During the French Revolution, the people in revolt wanted to lay their hands on wealth, arms, and power. The people were not unreligious or enemies of religion or the church. They wanted to give the rights of God to God, and the rights of the king to the king. This was the dilemma for the Christian world. The church was to look after the human soul, and the monarch was to deal with worldly issues. God and Jesus were to be accessed through the holy spirit. The pope was the shadow of God on earth, and Jesus represented the reality of God on earth. In order to be deemed sacred, the monarch had to be sanctified by the pope, and the monarch had to protect the pope. If the two joined forces in this way, the holy spirit would protect them.

Initially, the church held power in the name of God, and this was called theocracy. That is to say, the government of God was government in the name of God. Secularism was a reaction to this theocratic rule, following a clash between the church and the people, when an authority outside the church finally took shape based on a truce between church and state. The people who revolted against the church wanted the church to relinquish its governmental role to the new state that they had established. This was achieved by force. Blood was shed and, with the intercession of secularism, state and church laid down their arms.

In France, therefore, secularism represents a truce. In countries like Germany, by contrast, the state and the church determined their areas of responsibility with a contract, without resorting to arms. As a result, these countries are called *contract countries*, and the relationship of the two sides is bound in a contract which both sides had to honor.

Another solution, as seen in Italy, is the sharing of sovereignty—that is to say, the church and the state share sovereignty equally, with each side determining its own sphere and with both sides accepting the arrangement. The emergence of the Vatican, in fact, was based on such an understanding.

The Vatican is the proprietor of all the lands owned by the Catholic church throughout the world. There are two equal and sovereign parties coexisting within a single system, with political and diplomatic rights, forming a universal organization providing economic, social, cultural and religious services. The chaplains in the armies of the West are just as responsible to their own church councils as they are to their commanders, and the military authorities may not impose demands on them concerning the activities they perform and the demands they respond to in their spiritual capacity.

Secularism in Turkey is quite different. In Turkey, the Religious Affairs Department is attached to the government. Religious trusts are directed by people appointed by the government. The mosques are under the authority of the government and receive a great deal of money from the national budget. Religious education as well as Qur'anic schools are also under government control.

Secularism, of course, was quite unnecessarily put on the agenda of the National Assembly during the one-party period of the 1920s, during a period of emergency, and accepted without discussion, after it was accepted by Atatürk's party's congress. At a time when nobody had the faintest idea what secularism was.

From the point of view of religions with a clergy class, secularism is an indispensable institution, but in Islam, which does not have a clergy class, there is no place for secularism. In Islam, the political or religious leaders, called caliph and Şeyhülislam, are not the representatives of either the religion or of Allah; they are regarded only as great Islamic scholars and as representatives of the Muslims. Allah's representative on earth is man himself. Humankind is what is sacred.

When we talk about fundamental rights and freedoms, we are actually talking about two different things.

The laws focus on freedom of belief, thought, and conscience.

Belief is the inborn knowledge of truth.

Thought is the knowledge of reality. Ideas are produced or chosen. Conscience governs feelings, including our tendencies and preferences in life.

The Arabic word *Haq* (referring, in Turkish, to rights and justice) is a description of Allah. *Haq* is the totality of the privileges Allah bestowed upon man when he sent him to earth. It expresses the multiplicity of rights that Allah, the Creator, gave man, his creation.

In Islamic thought, these rights are listed under five main headings: belief and thought; the right to life and freedom from torture; the right to family life; the safeguarding of the sacred, including *namus* and everything related to it; and the protection of property justly earned by the sweat of one's brow.

There is a difference between a right and a freedom, since we cannot talk about a person's right to drink alcohol, only the freedom to do so.

If I try to prevent a priest from eating bread dipped in wine during a church sermon, or if I attempt to prevent a Christian from drinking alcohol or wine in line with his religious teachings, then I violate his freedom. Freedom is a right, because Allah left us free to choose and gave us the right of freedom. But Allah did not give us the right to drink alcohol. The man who drinks alcohol does so by using his freedom, not his right.

Judgment belongs to Allah, and in the universe there is nothing beyond or outside his will. Muslims believe in the singularity and absolute power of Allah. Good, evil and Satan are all under the command of Allah. Everyone and everything in America, Russia, Israel, or Turkey are within his control. Good and evil are all products of his creativity. Man is called into God's approval as a test, and in order to be rewarded on his path of limitless perfection.

Drinking alcohol is not a preference that Allah chooses for us. This is not behavior that Allah is summoning us to. This is a road we choose without Allah's approval, but even when doing so, we are still acting within the power of Allah.

Allah knew what man would do even before man was created. Destiny is Allah's knowledge of the ever-existing and the endless. If Allah had no knowledge of what man would do, he could not have created the things that man has the potential to do. Man behaves by starting with the knowledge, given by Allah, he will be held responsible for what he does with his free will and choice.

Well, then, so *can* a Muslim drink? Does he really have freedom of choice?

Answer: Of course he can drink if he so chooses. There is no limit to his freedom, *but* that is not to dispute the fact that if he drinks, he sins. Sinning is error. When man does something without the approval of Allah, this necessitates a punishment in the other world for the offense he committed against his own body, against humankind, and against nature. It distances man from divine approval.

So, what about in this world?

The Holy Qur'an is a contract that offers us the promise that if we sacrifice our property and ourselves in the cause of Allah, then he will definitely grant us paradise. It invites us to be the representatives of Allah on earth—his seeing eyes, hearing ears, holding hands, calling voices. And in return, Allah will call humankind to the divine approval that will save them from hellfire. No one is obliged to sign this contract. But those who do sign it establish a law of brotherhood among themselves. According to Islamic belief, when Muslims hear the Qur'an being read, they say, "*Amenna wa saddakna,*" which means: "We believe and we confirm that it is true." This can be compared to what you do when you go to a notary and you sign a statement that says something to the effect that "I have read, understood, and accepted." Thus, an agreement exists between Allah and the Muslim who understands his rights and responsibilities. Allah offers his Qur'an, and man either accepts or rejects it. The Qur'an is a declaration of what Allah allows and what he forbids. If man accepts it and lives according to its approved principles, he is given the assurance that he will find worldly and heavenly happiness. On Judgment Day, the reality will be revealed, and all of us will have to account for what we have said or not said, and done or not done.

Man is free to accept or reject this agreement, but contrary behavior after acceptance becomes a question of morals and law. To behave contrary to how I have decided to act is not an exercise of freedom. Would it be consistent or logical for someone who claims to be a vegetarian to eat meat, or for a Hindu to declare that he loves beef?

A Muslim is not compelled to comply with judgments, commentaries, and *fatwas* (judgments and decisions of Islamic scholars or leaders) that other people issue, according to their own understanding. You may be an expert in the canon law of Islam (a *Fakih*), or you may be free to choose any version of the decision based on the Qur'an as explained by someone qualified to interpret the meaning of the Qur'anic verses. But the Qur'an itself is the absolute law. It is *Haq!* But while Qur'anic commentary is related to the truth, that commentary is still only the product of man's intelligence, and there is room for error in it. This, of course, has given rise to the variety of religious sects. There can, however, be no alternative interpretation of a subject clearly explained and fixed in the Qur'an. Contradictory or differing views are not acceptable. Anyway, commentaries are not made on what is *muhkem*, decided and clear-cut subjects, but instead on what is called *müteşabih*—that is, verses that can have different meanings according to time and place, or in the interpretation of principles and limits for their application in daily life. It is sad that our Muslim brothers are not very well informed about Allah's contract. Along with a few hectares of land and a house, they have also inherited a religion and a sect. This is not something they reject but it is not something they have chosen either. And the religion they practice is not so much true Islam as a mixture of Islam and inherited traditions. More correctly, it is the religion of their forefathers. The Qur'an says to ancient peoples in this situation: "Oh, ye who believe, believe."

The Qur'an was revealed for the living, but these people read it as though it were for the dead. As Mehmet Akif, the author of the Turkish national anthem, wrote: "The Qur'an has not descended from heaven to be read to the dead at graveside, nor for fortunetelling." It has descended for the living.

The Qur'an shows man how to reconcile the purpose of his creation, his reality, with his nature. The Qur'an reconciles man with himself. And it reconciles man with nature, for it is the life guide from Allah, the Creator, to the created. He who realizes these three reconciliations reconciles himself with his Creator. And the name of this order of peace is paradise, whereas hell is like a correctional prison where the condemned are made to taste not only the bitterness of their wrongdoing, but also the perversion and the wrong and evil that they did to their own bodies and to other living creatures, and where they will remain for as long as it takes to perfect their spirit.

My final word is that people should be free! Free so that they are not forced to fight to obtain their freedom or recover their rights. Let these be rights from birth.

Let us all work for this goal.

Make people free to explain their beliefs and thoughts, and organize themselves around these ideals. Give them a chance to protect and improve themselves.

The Assyrians and the Yezidis have been living in these lands for thousands of years. The Yezidis attach a special meaning to Satan. For the last fifteen hundred years, the Muslims of these lands have been going to Mecca to stone the devil, yet they do not stone the cairns the Yezidis put up in their villages in the name of Satan.

The reality of Andalusia[111] and Bosnia stares us in the face, as does the long history of the Assyrians and Yezidis.

Allah created men and left them free to recognize him or not. Freedom is a right given by Allah to humankind; let no one take away this gift of Allah from them.

Let people be free!

For the views of Şanar Yurdatapan on this subject, see The Red *chapters 8 and 9.*

---

111. Muslim rule in the Iberian Peninsula came to an end in 1492, but a large population continued to live under Christian kingdoms. After the Inquisition started, Muslims began to be pressured to convert or emigrate, and all were driven out by 1615.

18. WHO IS SECULAR, WHO IS DEMOCRAT, WHO IS FUNDAMENTALIST?

Who is accepting what, and why, and with what meaning? And who is rejecting what, and for what reason? Let me explain. It is possible to think like this: You can say, "If socialism means social justice, then I am a socialist." Or: "If fundamentalism means terror, then I am not a fundamentalist." But this kind of approach is not very meaningful. To put it a little more clearly, if I do not identify myself with a particular concept, it does not automatically imply that I am against that concept. Just as when I say, "I am not from Ankara," it does not mean that I am opposed to the people of Ankara. And being a member of the Hanefi sect does not necessarily mean that I am against those professing the Shafi'i[112] sect, and being a man does not make me opposed to women, and so on.

Basically, the meaning of any particular thing depends not only on what we understand about that thing, but also on what kind of a meaning we attach to it. It is not possible to answer the question of meaning without adopting an ontological, semantic, and epistemological view of it. Otherwise, although we may seem to be talking the same language, we might very well be saying different things and this distorts our communication. We must try to understand what the other is saying, and show some empathy with that point of view. At all times, the most important thing is to try to understand what the other is trying to say.

Are you a secularist?

Well, what does *secular* mean?

How many countries are there in the world whose constitutions describe them as *secular?* Would you be surprised if I said, "Only four"? And what if I were to say that Turkey's secularism is nothing like that in the other countries?

---

112. Hanefi and Shafi'i, together with Maliki and Hanbali, form the four principal schools of Islamic law.

Turkey is the only secularist country in the world where religious teaching in schools is compulsory, where the state organizes religious worship, where the *imam* (prayer leader) is a government employee, where mosques are official state offices, and the Department of Religious Affairs is under the authority of a cabinet minister.

Therefore, Turkey looks more like a Byzantinist country than a secular one. If the religious officials have sovereignty over the state, then we call it a *theocracy*. If the state is sovereign over the religious institutions, then it is called *Byzantinism*. If the church and state are independent, each with sovereignty in its own domain, then we call it *secularism*. In other words, as Jesus said in the Bible: "Render unto Caesar the things which are Caesar's; and unto God the things that are God's." So in our country, in spite of all claims to the contrary, secularism does *not* signify a separation between religion and state. Rather, it organizes the relationship between them. It is a sharing, a cooperation. Secularism in our case does not indicate a system that leaves our spiritual affairs to our discretion and material affairs to the state. Secularism should not be an imprisoning of religion within the individual conscience and, socially, within the walls of the mosque. Did you know that France is the only secular member country of the European Union?

The assertion that there cannot be a republic without secularism and that there cannot be democracy without a republic is one big fat lie. The United Kingdom, for example, has neither a republic nor secularism. The same is true of Spain and Belgium. The majority of the EU countries are not republics. A monarchic order persists in these countries, and they still have official religions or churches. Even in France, the mother of secularism, secularism does not hold sway in every province. For example, Strasbourg is not secular. Areas taken from Germany in the settlement after the Second World War are still subject to a contractual relationship between state and religion.

To repeat, secularism is not a separation of religion and state; it merely regulates their relations.

Today in France, there are still universities and social clubs affiliated with the churches. The churches collect their own religious taxes and spend the money as they choose, without interference from the state.

And in our country? The state lays its hands on the skins of the slaughtered sacrificial sheep and cattle,[113] collects religious dues from the people, organizes the pilgrims' travel to Mecca, and interferes with the wearing of the headscarf even in religious education schools.

In France, not only does the church run primary schools, but many Christian sects operate kindergartens, primary schools, and high schools or colleges where nuns give lessons wearing gown and wimple.

How can we talk about relations between the state and a religious institution, when the religion in question has no church or clergy class? We could only talk about relations between the state and the religious establishment in Muslim countries if there were indeed an establishment that either represented the religion or Allah. States may adopt secularism in response to the Catholic church, since the pope is the shadow of God on earth, but in Islam, the caliph is not a holy man; the institution is local and secular. He is only a local or regional person. The caliph does not represent Islam or Allah, but only the Muslim community. This is why it is difficult to make sense of secularism in a Muslim country.

We should stop trying to define each other, and let individuals define themselves. We should define others as they define themselves.

Of course, nobody has to believe as I believe, think as I think, or live as I live. And likewise, I don't have to be like everyone else.

I am neither a democrat nor a secularist! And I even despise such discussions.

I cannot understand those who push democracy without first understanding it. What kind of democracy? People never stop to ask themselves this. If you were to say *classical democracy*, well ... in that democracy, the women had no voting rights and there was slavery. It was not that easy to be part of the *demos*. Real democracy is a rather anarchistic idea. It considers the

---

113. According to a decision of the Council of Ministers, the pelts of animals slaughtered during the Feast of Sacrifice are collected by the Aviation Foundation, which funds institutions and activities related to Turkey's aviation industry, the Child Protection Foundation, and the Foundation for Religious Affairs. Every year this is an issue of dispute and resentment for those who would prefer to donate the skins to charities of their choice.

state nonexistent. In a Marxist democracy, the *demos* in authority can only be the working class. To that extent, democracy would be a class dictatorship.

Parliamentary democracy can turn at any time into an oligarchical bureaucracy.

He who pays the piper calls the tune. In a liberal democracy, with its laissez-faire attitude, the little fish become food for the big fish. In Britain, democracy came into existence within a monarchistic regime.

In U.S. democracy, the right of citizenship is linked to the responsibility to pay taxes because the taxpayer has the right to oversee the institution to which he pays his taxes. So in this case the *demos* is the taxpayer.

Contrary to what is commonly claimed in Turkey, secularism is not an indispensable aspect of the republic, nor is the republic an indispensable aspect of democracy.

In reality, there are fundamental differences between a republic and a democracy. A republic is a government system based on majority rule, whereas a democracy is a populist system based on rule by a pluralist majority. As for a democratic republic, it is a synthesis that tries to guarantee the sovereignty of pluralism in a majority system; the people to first use this name were the Democratic People's Republics of the Marxist regimes. Some preferred to use the term *Socialist Republic* to soften an authoritarian and disciplinarian structure.

Today Japan and the United Kingdom, as well as Holland, Belgium, and various other European countries, have neither secularism nor a republic, yet it can be said that they have democratic systems.

In Turkey we have the mistaken idea that secularism clarifies the relations between state and religion and ensures their separation. Secularism does not clarify the relationship between state and religion. After all, why do people form states other than to protect and develop their belief and identity?

In fact, secularism expresses the right of individuals not to be members of the clergy, if they so choose. The fundamental aim of secularism is to clarify the relationship between church and state, not religion and state. So, a person you refer to as secularist does not have to be a member of the clergy, but could still be someone devoutly attached to his religion. That would still fall within the meaning of secularism.

In an Islamic country, secularism has neither legal justification nor moral basis. In Turkey, secularism was brought to the National Assembly without any justification, and was made law without debate, contrary to the raison d'être of a parliament. Moreover, no legal definition was given for the idea of secularism, so the establishment shifted its interpretation of secularism depending on who was in power.

In many countries today, Catholic churches are still considered the property of the papal state, and this dual view is maintained. In the United Kingdom, on the other hand, the national church manifests a different church-state relationship with the monarch being the head of the Anglican church.

We began this subject by discussing the relationship between the state and the religion, noting that Western nations take one of three approaches: secularism, theocracy, or Byzantinism. Under secularism, the state-religion relationship is founded on basic principles. In Byzantinism, the state officials have sovereignty over the church. The situation in Turkey, to some extent, reflects this Byzantine arrangement. Further, theocracy means the church is sovereign over the state. All three approaches have non-Islamic characteristics.

I am not secular because there is no clergy class in Islam. But Turkey is not secularist either. Under no definition of secularism are religious officials government officials or the members of leading religious councils appointed by the political authorities.

When we look at the general shape of the arrangement in Turkey, we observe what can be called a "Kemalist theocracy." But the Kemalisms of İnönü, Demirel,[114] Baykal,[115] and Derviş have little in common. That is why the contemporary writer Atilla İlhan poses the question in the title of his book *Which Kemalism?* Another writer, Nadır Nadi,[116] protests the reinvention of Kemalism when he says, "I am not a Kemalist."

---

114. Süleyman Demirel, former prime minister and president, founder of the center-right True Path Party.

115. Deniz Baykal, leader of the Republican People's Party.

116. Founder and owner of the newspaper *Cumhuriyet*, generally regarded as a stoutly Kemalist.

Since the military coup of May 27, 1960, members of parliament have been required to swear an oath to a series of principles, concepts, and institutions that cannot be questioned or disputed or challenged. There is an official history and an official ideology. Can this state be called a democracy when its practices would not be found even in the most inflexible of religions? Consider this: In the early days of the Kemalist Turkish Republic—the 1920s—the following was written in the dictionaries of the Turkish Language Institute: "The religion of the Turkish people is Kemalism."

Nowadays, it is an accepted fact that Kemalism took on different forms during the political reigns of different ideological groups in Turkey. So we can say openly say that Kemalism is not the ideology of Kemal Atatürk, but the name of an ideology proposed by various interests that call themselves Kemalists in order to obtain political advantage in pressing their private goals.

Catholics believe that the pope is the shadow of God on earth. In Orthodox belief, on the other hand, the church, not the pope, is the shadow of God on earth, and the church includes the sovereign ruler. The two separate manifestations of God represent his heavenly authority and his worldly authority. The coexistence of these two authorities brings about a third dimension, which reminds us of the God–Jesus–Holy Spirit trinity.

I am not, therefore, secular—these issues are of no importance to me. But this does not mean that I am antisecular. For Christians, secularism is a fundamental problem. I understand this, and I accept it. But it is impossible to understand how a Muslim or an atheist can be secular. Perhaps they have a secular view of things, but this is something rather different.

Democracy must not be treated as a religion that everyone should be forced to accept or believe. Aside from the obvious reasons for this, so many types of democracies exist. So what democracy are we talking about, anyway? Marxist democracy? Liberal democracy? Capitalist, Christian, Socialist, Nationalist democracy? One could also cite ideologies such as fascism, capitalism, and communism that hide behind the mask of democracy, but if the intention is to say that democracy encompasses partnership, cooperation, populism, openness, transparency, honesty, and the rule of law, perhaps it would be easier to talk about those characteristics. And in order to define *democracy* correctly, we would have to define who the *demos* is, and how the *kratos* ("authority") is to be implemented.

Let us agree that the source of democracy is not divine revelation and that democracy cannot promise us paradise. Democracy is not a modern messiah. Nobody can claim that everything will always go well under democracy, and we must remember that democracy in its current form evolved over time—as we have discussed, classical democracy was a slave society in which women had no right to vote.

If the *demos* is not productive, participatory, and honest, then the *kratos* will fail and we have democratic collapse. All we are discussing is no more than a technical arrangement for authority. With that in mind, I believe that *shariah* is a more meaningful, comprehensive, and inclusive concept. If you define *shariah* correctly, you will see that it is the art of making peace between man and man, man and nature, man and his own creation, and, finally, man and Allah. *Shariah* is another name for love, peace, and freedom. You must look at whatever you are trying to understand not only from a religious point of view, but from a philosophical and a conscientious perspective as well. It is not enough simply to hide behind labels. Of course, just as you can do good things with *shariah* and democracy, so too can you oppress people in their name. What is important is to ensure harmony between the name and the content. This is true regardless of whether the source, the aim, and the method of government are right.

One more time in closing: Secularism regulates relations between *church* and state, not religion and state.

When we interfere with the efforts of any interest groups to bring their demands to the political stage, we are actually obstructing a natural process of discussing and resolving these problems in the social arena, and thereby opening the way to terror. Sometimes such obstructions are set in place by force and sometimes by law, but they are wrong in either case.

In Turkey we mistake Byzantinism for secularism. We have lost sight of the fact that official ideologies are being subverted into a political and philosophical religion of the Sacred State.

For the views of Şanar Yurdatapan on this subject, see The Red *chapter 9.*

19. CAN'T WE LIBERATE OUR MINDS?

We must adopt the morality and ethics of freedom. We must be able to think freely. With an open heart and mind, we must be able to pose questions and search for their answers. Using our brains and our feelings, benefiting from the experiences of earlier nations and civilizations and the thoughts of other peoples, we must create our own reality and awareness of our responsibilities.

We must search for truth with love and wisdom. Prejudice, anger, passion, and our ambitions may obstruct our ability to see reality and understand the truth.

Above all else, we must succeed in being free, and not become prisoners of our own or other people's passions.

People in our country also must learn to exercise the right of conscientious objection. They must be able to resist and to protect themselves from things that offend their conscience, such as military service, war, eating meat, and many others. As long as people do not harm or coerce others, they must be allowed to think differently, believe differently, and live differently...just like the Yezidis, who respect, love, and even worship Satan, but have lived an unhindered existence within a society that believes in Islam and that at every opportunity seeks refuge in Allah from the evil of Satan.

Civil disobedience has become a subject of discussion, in spite of the fact that it is not easy to debate such a matter against a cultural background based on obedience and respect, where the state is regarded as sacred. It is difficult for people to understand the concept of civil disobedience in a society that places duties before rights, and where the judicial system is set up to ensure that the populace obeys those in authority.

We need a new social order that not only asks questions, makes demands, and shows respect, but is also prepared to hold the government accountable—a social order that can say "no," supervise those in government, and that can reshape the system of law so that it serves society.

We do not want to be clones or the bionic robots of official ideology, and we do not want to be the missionaries of a government-approved religion. We want a world in which people live as they wish and can express freely whatever they think.

Just think! A country in which people live with hopes rather than fears, and where love conquers hatred. A country whose money is money, whose justice is justice, whose people are free, and whose passport is a sign of respectability. A state in which the individual is respected and the wronged can obtain justice. To be the citizen of a country where free-thinking voters live. To enjoy the respect and honor of living in the land of the Medes!

Life is sweet. The flowers, birds, and children are a source of joy. This world, this earth, this sky, all of it is ours—if we have room for it in our hearts. We must change. Before trying to change others, and telling them who we are, we should listen to others and change ourselves. We should not get bogged down in political lies and ideological slogans. Our political system was founded on lies. Those who put their own interests and personal ambitions first have cost this nation dearly, for they are the people who control wealth, armaments, and power. They pile tax upon tax, and price increase upon price increase, and still try to sell whatever they can lay their hands on. They also borrow domestically and externally. Turkey's entire budget is not enough to even pay the interest on our debts. The rulers are sucking the treasury dry, leaving the debt of bankrupted banks to the nation. Others are swindling the industrialist and the merchant.

Politics is wasting too much time, money, labor, and hope. It is destroying civic awareness and understanding; it is undermining society's confidence in itself. But we have nowhere else to go. This country is our country.

The majority of Turkey's population are Muslims, but although Islamic education is compulsory, it is an offense to live as a Muslim. It is an offense to use the title *Haji* (pilgrim), yet the government organizes the annual pilgrimage to the Holy Lands of Islam, whereby participants earn the title of *Haji*.[117] The government tries to lay its hands on religious alms like *fitre* and *zakat*, which Muslims give to the poor once a year. This is Turkey: Mosques are government buildings and *imams* are civil servants.

---

117. The pilgrimage to Mecca, which all male Muslims are expected to perform at least once in their life, is coordinated by the Department of Religious Affairs.

There are too many inconsistencies and anomalies to count. Islam forbids certain things, but many people do not obey these prohibitions, and those who do obey them are criticized. Sometimes, this even causes legal trouble. How can these people, who, as Muslims, have given their word to Allah to stand up against oppression and exploitation, remain silent in the face of such wrongs? Does Islam not say that those who remain silent in the face of injustice are tongueless devils? Indeed, our blessed prophet said so! The same people who criticize devout Muslims profess to believe that fate, destiny, daily bread, and death are all from Allah, as it is written in the Holy Qur'an.

Many people who identify themselves as Muslims are unaware of the commands and prohibitions of Islam. Those who say that they are *Alevi*, *Bektaşi*,[118] *Hanefi*, or *Shafi'i* are unaware of the virtues behind the beliefs they profess. They do not know, and they do not know that they do not know!

For example, are there no Bektaşis who drink? According to the late Hacı Bektaşi Veli (may Allah rest his soul), the founder and leader of the Bektaşi sect, "If a drop of wine were to be dropped into a well, and if they were to empty the well in order to clean it, and if they were to spread around this water removed from the well, and if they were to cut and make kebab from the meat of a lamb that ate a blade of grass grown in the soil moistened by the water removed from the well and spread in the soil, even a morsel of this meat would be abominable."

We love Hacı Bektaşi Veli very much, but we do not listen to his advice. An Islam without *shariah*, would be like a beef-eating vegetarianism or Hinduism.

Those who say they are Muslims have, on some subjects, given their word to Allah. If these members of the religion of Islam—the religion of *tevhid* (unity), which defines this world and the life after as parts of a single whole—go back on their word to Allah after they have said they believe, what can we expect from them? If they do not worship, if they hold nothing sacred, if they have no knowledge of moral values such as *namus*, honor, self-respect, then how can they claim to be Muslims? They become bestial, even monstrous, and when their minds become slaves to their mad

---

118. A dervish order that reportedly incorporates moderate drinking of alcohol in its gatherings.

desires, they can take on a lower form wilder and more dangerous than an animal.

Man is a thinking creature, not an animal. He is the most perfect and the most honored of the created. He is the seeing eye, the hearing ear, the holding hand, the calling voice of Allah on earth, and Allah wants, through man, to punish the oppressor and help the oppressed.

Without doubt, one day we shall be called to account for all we have done or not done in this world, and all we have said or not said. The world is a testing ground for us.

Every free individual who has not put his soul under the command of Satan, who is not the slave of his carnal desires, and who testifies to the reality of creation, will feel this inner truth within him.

To make a more beautiful world possible, we must defend the heart of our faith and not just its outer form. That heart consists of a state based on human rights and the rule of law.

For the views of Şanar Yurdatapan on this subject, see The Red *chapters 6 and 18.*

20. DID YOU SAY EDUCATION OR TRAINING?[119]

To train, training, trained man!

Bionic robots, men with conditioned reflexes. You can know in advance when and what kind of reaction to expect.

The Turkish Language Institute, in its Turkish Dictionary, defines *eğitim* as: "Influencing a person's logical, physical, and moral development by grafting different behavior patterns, knowledge, and opinions, to ensure his development and training in a particular direction, according to preconceived aims."

As for training animals, the same source says: "To raise them in such a way as to enable them to carry out the desired behavior."

The above description concerning the education of animals is also valid in the general sense for humans being educated in the uniform[120] education system, practiced in the schools under the monopoly of the state. It is hardly appropriate to talk about democracy in a society that receives its training from a single center, because a whole nation will then act, think, and live in the same way on subjects related to the state. And of course, anyone who does not behave in the expected manner will be threatened with punishment for contradicting the law, for being against the existing order, for causing a disturbance, and even for immorality.

Training is the enemy of democracy.

Why is everybody in Turkey Muslim, and why are most members of the Hanefi sect? In my opinion, it is because they have been coarsely trained.

---

119. The Turkish word commonly used for education is *eğitim* (*training*) rather than *öğrenim* (*learning*). Many commentators observe that the word *eğitim*, which derives from bending a plant to train it over a framework is sadly appropriate for an education system that relies heavily on rote learning and the regurgitation of officially approved ideas.

120. *Tevhid-i tedrisat* (*unified education*—a single education system under state management and control) is a principle particularly defended by those who oppose the development of religious schools. Turkey does have a large number of *Imam Hatip* schools (priests and preachers' school).

Would it not have been more realistic to teach them and leave them free to make their own choice?

There is, of course, a period for training, both in the family and in society. But training imposed under a state monopoly is a clear violation of human rights.

Up to a certain age, a child's general form of belief and behavior is influenced by his family. To a certain extent, this is natural and acceptable, but it would be better if the family gave knowledge to the child instead of forcing a form of behavior upon him. Teach him how to think, and give him training in freedom of choice. Teach him how to catch fish instead of giving him baskets full of fish every day. True education is not bending people's will, but rather opening their way and enlarging their horizons so that they act according to their natural talents. Taking away somebody's right to choose and forcing him into a particular form of behavior is pretending divine lordship over him, and should be considered a violation of his personal identity.

Training implies exerting a directing and shaping influence upon another for a specific purpose. Forcing people to go against their natural constitution prevents the development of their personality, abilities, and creativity. People with personalities shaped by others create problems in their societies because they are not where they belong. They are living the life of an exile. Once they have reached maturity, young people must be left free to choose according to their natural tendencies and preferences, as long as these choices do not cause harm to others.

If people reach maturity of intellect and spirit, they will acquire the ability to choose what is good, right, and beautiful. They will be able to think correctly, make decisions, participate, take a stand against what is wrong, and appreciate beauty. That is to say, they will enter a natural development process.

A bionic robot stands no chance of reaching genuine maturity.

Unfortunately, our society does not treat children with proper respect. The environment they grow up in does not help them develop their individuality. They pass their lives filled with suppressed feelings and unanswered questions. Childhood constitutes the first twenty years of the average lifespan of sixty years. Children are constantly forced to obey either the state or their elders, who, ignorant as they may be, still force children to accept their opinions. Then comes military service. Children are not considered adults until they have completed their military service. Montaigne said that the Turkish soldier fears his commander more than he fears the enemy. Of course, Montaigne was talking about the soldiers of the Ottoman Empire, but it is an interesting observation concerning the roots of fear in Turkish society. Once military service is over, there is a twenty-five year fight to find a job, earn daily bread, and settle into a marriage. People will witness bribery, and have to pull strings in order to get ahead, and by the time they are thirty-five, half their life will be gone. They will have children to provide for, in a small two-room house. They will attend the funerals of friends. They will retire and by then they are close to the end of the road. An encumbrance, they will be pushed around the house like unwanted furniture, just waiting for death. The elderly are no longer respected, and nobody wants to hear their advice. All that remains is regret for the errors of their youth.

Man must learn from man to be human. I can do this through reading and benefiting from the experience of yesterday, but nobody should force this on me. I must be myself. Life should not be something that somebody else orchestrates or writes like a play in which I am a mere actor.

The only training one needs is to be taught to use one's head.

Training blinds knowledge, morals, and intellect.

You can train people to make them enemies of other people and ideas. You cannot train people to consider each other brothers. What is natural is best, and the laws of nature in Allah's revelation are incomparably better than manmade laws.

I especially despise the institutions that raise slaves within and/or for the state. In our Islamic system, we do not have training; we have teaching and the proposal of ideas, providing an unthreatening invitation to knowledge. Our holy book advises us to talk rather than to argue, and the life of our prophet is a wonderful example of the power of persuasion rather than dispute.

Education is what is desirable, not training.

Training is the presumption of illegitimate authority over others. Our Lord is Allah. And in our belief, there is no slavery of man by man.

For the views of Şanar Yurdatapan on this subject, see The Red *chapters 11 and 13.*

21. SCHOLASTIC THOUGHT AND SCIENTIFIC THOUGHT

It is quite wrong to put Christianity and Islam, the church and the mosque, the Christian and the Muslim in the same category. Islam forbids us to chase after rainbows and pursue the unknown. There is no blind faith in Islam and bigotry is forbidden by Islamic law. Those who label themselves as *mutaassıb,* or zealots, do not understand the straitjacket they are voluntarily putting on.

Of course, people have the right to think freely and to seek the truth.

For this reason, they must be able to talk to other people and consult those who know. Only scholars fear Allah truly. He who knows one language is one man; he who knows two languages is like two men. For this reason, we are advised to roam the world and learn how earlier nations succeeded and failed, how they rose and how they fell.

We are commanded to appoint only the properly qualified to a particular post. We are told that we should serve for forty years whoever teaches us a single letter, and that one moment's deep insight and discernment is more precious than a one year's nonobligatory prayer. The sleep of the scholar is worth more than the useless worship of the ignorant. The first command of the Qur'an is: "Read." Opinions expressed without a basis in knowledge and that don't lead to the truth of the matter are futile and vain. Therefore, scholastic thinking cannot be compared with Islamic meditation. Can those who know be compared with the ignorant? Scholars, even if they reach incorrect conclusions, deserve merit for the effort they have made to seek the truth.

It is worth remembering that at the time of the caliph Al-Mu'min, the number of books in the *Beytül Hikme,* the house of wisdom or library of the caliph, was greater than the number of books then believed to exist elsewhere in the whole world. Muslim scholars played an important role in the transfer of ancient Greek and Egyptian knowledge to the West. The fundamentals of many sciences were discovered by Muslim scholars. The contributions of Muslim scholars, in the fields of mathematics, astronomy, medicine, history, and geography to the development of Eastern and Western civilization, are among the most outstanding.

Very few people know that Immanuel Kant was anathematized for being a Muslim and that he wrote the *Sura Fatiha*, the first chapter of the Qur'an, in his own handwriting at the front of the original edition of his book *The Critique of Pure Reason*. Also, research about the connection between the renowned German thinker, Goethe, and Islam have produced striking findings.

Even today, the West accepts that until a couple of centuries ago the highest levels of civilization, with respect to geographic discoveries, political philosophy, science, mathematics, and technology, were achieved in the Muslim world. The civilized history of the modern West does not go back very far. The French Revolution dates back only to 1789, and America was discovered only five hundred years ago.

If we were to put aside the modern West's responsibility for the two world wars, it is well-known that the rise of the West has been achieved on the blood of the Native American, the tears of the black-skinned, and the stolen sweat on the forehead of the yellow-skinned.

It can hardly be claimed that the West has actually produced a civilization, for Western civilization is one driven by selfish interests and constructed by usurping the common heritage of humankind.

The attitude of the West toward the church, religion, and knowledge does not reflect the truth. But in Turkey, great efforts are being made to produce a mosque like a church, an *imam* like a priest, a Qur'an like the Bible, and a Muslim like a Christian. This is why religious education is compulsory, which is nothing but an unjust interference by politics in religion. They talk about "political Islam," but this is the real political Islam—political manipulation to produce a government-approved form of religion. In conclusion, the criticisms aimed at scholastic thinking cannot be directed against Islam as well.

For the views of Şanar Yurdatapan on this subject, see The Red *chapters 8 and 13.*

22. THE STATE, THE LAW, THE CONSTITUTION, AND ME!

To paraphrase Montaigne, "If the laws I serve were to try to make my little finger a slave, I would go away and look for new laws."[121]

Another thinker has said, "If the color of my shirt conflicts with the fundamental principles of the constitution, what needs to be changed is the constitution."

Because I do not exist for the constitution; the constitution exists for me.

It must not be forgotten that the reason for the existence and legality of the state is to protect and improve the fundamental rights and freedoms of the people and to ensure the welfare, the happiness, and the security of the society.

Constitutions are a means through which society contains the state and prevents abuse by the legislative, executive, and judicial branches that it supports with the taxes it pays, or by the armed forces, which it equips with weapons. A further objective is to stop one group from seizing power and authority and using them to enslave others.

Often, the lawmakers, in trying to protect the state, restrict the rights of the individual, forgetting that the very reason the state exists is to protect the rights and the freedoms of the individual. When a power assumes control of wealth, arms, and authority and then attempts to strip the society of its beliefs, history, and cultural character and to impose on it what is contradictory to its will, then the result is a hell of a row.

Authority is the mirror image of society. It cannot be otherwise, because the fundamental element is the people. The laws also have a soul, and this soul is the belief, values, history, and culture of society. Nobody willingly obeys laws that are foreign to these values and treats them as ene-

---

121. "Good God! How ill should I endure the condition wherein I see so many people, nailed to a corner of the kingdom, deprived of the right to enter the principal cities and courts, and the liberty of the public roads, for having quarreled with our laws. If those under which I live should but wag a finger at me by way of menace, I would immediately go seek out others, let them be where they would." Michel Montaigne, *Denemeler* (*Essays*), translated by S. Eyüboğlu, Book 3 (İstanbul: Cem Publications, 1989), Chapter 13.

mies, because then the laws become tools of oppression. In such a country you might say that laws were enforced, but you could not say that it was a state properly under rule of law. Nobody could divide or undermine a state that has a valid currency, that is to say, where the money in your pocket is not melting away like a block of ice left in the blazing sun,[122] a state where you can protect the wages from the sweat of your brow, where you can earn money via legal channels, which has a passport respected in the outside world, where justice and peace reign, where freedom is not under threat. When everybody is trying to seek asylum in your country, nobody will want to emigrate, for the simple reason that nobody deliberately seeks out a less favorable condition.

But if your money has no value, your passport has zero international respect, your people are hungry, justice is silenced, fundamental freedoms are denied, and belief and thought are considered offenses, you cannot persuade people to stay even if you tie them up.

What is sacred is not the state; it is human beings themselves. The state should be a servant state.

One of the fundamental errors in our society is that the people in authority, even the civil servants, consider themselves the embodiment of the state. But a state is meaningless without the country and the people. You can't talk about a state without them. The government is merely the wheel that makes the state turn and the organization function.

Authority should be transparent—perhaps something like an immune system that in normal times operates unseen but that springs into action the moment a microbe enters the body. Everything that society can do with its own resources should be left to society. A clumsily functioning state and a bureaucracy that has tasted bribery will never achieve anything worthwhile.

As Antigonos said, "The man who empties my chamberpot knows that I am not the son of God."[123]

---

122. The average annual rate of inflation in Turkey during the 1990s was 75%. In 2001 it was 68.5%.

123. Former general to Alexander the Great, Antigonos II Gonatas, when Hermodotus proclaimed him "offspring of the sun, and a god," replied, "The man who empties my chamberpot has not noticed it."

No authority on earth is the shadow of God on earth.

Again, the only representative of God on earth is man himself. All the governments on earth represent not the authority of Allah on earth, but the authority that comes from the power of attorney provided by the people.

And the more laws you make, the more restricted your freedoms become. The best law is the shortest, the purest, and the most general.

So what can we say about our laws in Turkey? Every constitution we have had has been the result of a coup d'état. Most of our laws were imported from Italy, Germany, Switzerland, and France, translated and applied in a hurry, mistakes and all. Today, none of the new laws are in accord with the needs or the wishes of the people; they were enacted to conform with laws in the West and based on the West's demands and advice.

For example, isn't it astonishing that the Temporary Law on the Prosecution of Civil Servants is still in force?[124]

You cannot seriously set out to create a national system of laws by adopting and translating parts of the fascist Italian criminal law, the German commercial law, and the French civil code, but that is what we did.

Those who run the state often do not say what they think but, rather, what people want to hear. Government programs and election declarations are splendid, imposing documents, but often the reality turns out to be quite different from what is written.

For the views of Şanar Yurdatapan on this subject, see The Red *chapters 6, 16, and 17.*

---

124. This law, dating from 1913, gave local governors (who oversee police affairs) the right to block prosecutions, and was frequently used to halt actions against police and gendarmes for torture and unlawful killing. In December 1999 this law was abolished and replaced by the Law on the Prosecution of Civil Servants and other Administrative Officials, which was little better than the original. However, in January 2003, a measure was passed to ensure that local governors could not block prosecutions brought with respect to such abuses.

23. ECONOMY AND MORALITY

Allah sees and cares for everything in this world, and one day he will ask us to account for all we have done. A good Muslim is obliged to take a stand against injustice and be on the side of the oppressed, no matter from where the injustice comes and no matter against whom it is directed. If he does not, he will be, at the least, an oppressor, perhaps immoral, wicked, and even perhaps guilty of a kind of rejection of faith based on denial. If he thinks, "The guilty party is my relative or brother," then he puts himself in the presumptuous position of the arbitrator of right and wrong alongside Allah.

Allah interests himself in everything from the size of building reinforcing bars to quantities of cement because he is concerned with the details of whether one keeps one's word, fulfills a contract, or protests against fraud.[125]

Because he says, "When you promise, keep your word."

Allah demands justice.

The purpose of an economy is not only to produce or to consume. Money may be a certificate of success or a means of reward, but by using it unjustly and ensuring that it circulates exclusively among a privileged few, we can transform it into a tool of exploitation. All of us should receive the wages of our work justly and without delay. We should earn and spend legally, in a just and acceptable manner. Being wasteful is neither a right nor a freedom. Nowadays, when labor, capital, and knowledge circulate freely, we cannot consider political and economic issues as separate affairs.

Very often, possessors of great wealth use the power that wealth confers for their own dishonest ambitions, and their riches are often obtained in dishonest ways. It is not decent or acceptable to obtain unearned income from the exploitation of ownership of the land, to use politics as a tool for economic benefit, or to obtain income through interest, prostitution, gambling, and similar methods. Connections with the mafia, smuggling, fraud, and bribery are multiplying like cancer.

---

125. The negligence of construction companies was widely and passionately condemned when thousands of apartments collapsed in the August 1999 earthquake.

Charging interest on money is the worst way to earn money and is an abuse. Those who, with their bad tax and incentive policies, create an opportunity for crooked, undeserving people to get rich on unearned money, will one day, too late, realize that they have produced a Frankenstein's monster. Unrestrained inflation, unemployment, the continued sharp fall in the value of money, and the external debt burden are the first messengers of the catastrophe awaiting that nation.

Just like Sultan Murat IV once said, many years ago, those who feel that they need to borrow money today must not forget that one day in the future, they will have to obey the commands of those from whom they borrow.

The economy is one of the most important pillars of the palace of the state.

The sovereignty of a nation that succumbs to the weakness of borrowing cannot have a very long life.

In Turkey there is currently much talk of separatism and the Sèvres Treaty,[126] and is this not linked to the economic disaster in which we find ourselves?

Turkey did not enter World War II; however, even countries like Germany and Japan, which suffered utter destruction at the hands of the allies, recovered and are prospering today. What is the reason for Turkey's "privileged backwardness," particularly in view of our important geopolitical position?

Should we not think (and think hard) about the fact that although we are surrounded by three seas, we are importing fish, that although we have

---

126. The 1920 Treaty of Sèvres, one of the treaties that concluded the First World War, liquidated the Ottoman Empire, and handed much of Anatolia to Greece and Italy, as well as creating an autonomous Kurdistan. Following the War of Independence under Atatürk, the new Turkish republic concluded the Treaty of Lausanne in 1923, which established borders much as they stand today. Armed Kurdish insurgencies, as well as nonviolent political parties (regularly banned as unconstitutional), have persistently sought to reestablish an independent Kurdish state, or at least a degree of autonomy for the mainly Kurdish southeast—political demands that the Turkish establishment has refused to discuss. The emergence of a de facto autonomous Kurdish entity in northern Iraq has been viewed with suspicion by the Turkish government, which threatened to invade Iraq following the 2003 war if there were any attempt to establish a Kurdish state. The Turkish government admitted that its opposition to such a development was grounded in the fear that this might inspire Kurdish separatism within its own borders.

the most abundant freshwater supplies we are suffering from water short-ages, and that despite our great underground mineral resources and oil we are suffering serious unemployment? Should we not think about who is responsible for this catastrophe?

For the views of Şanar Yurdatapan on this subject, see The Red *chapter 14.*

24. DEMOS! CONTRADICTORY THOUGHTS CONCERNING DEMOCRACY

Who is this *demos*?

Do you know him?

Everybody is talking about democracy, but no one knows *demos*!

Many think that they themselves are *demos*. Many are so ignorant of politics that they do not know the difference between democracy and the republican system.

Demos. Cratos.

First we must discuss *cratos*.

Up to what point are you prepared to surrender rights and responsibilities to the authority, to the state? We must think seriously about the reality of authority. We must redefine the meaning of the state. Who are "the people"? What is this thing called "the nation"? What is "sovereignty"?

Then we must discuss *demos*.

The old Greek democracies were based on slavery, and they were not interested in peace. In this democratic order, the women had no right to vote or be elected. In other words, we are talking about an antifeminist democratic order of slaves and warriors.

But perhaps what you are talking about is a parliamentary democracy.

Yes, I understand you. Isn't England nowadays considered the cradle of modern democracy?

Parliamentary democracy is possible even within a constitutional monarchy, and perhaps the first and the second constitutional periods of Ottoman times[127] were more democratic, more participatory, and more pluralistic than today's Turkish democracy.

Or are they just mocking us with all this talk of Turkish democracy? In our country, the army imposes democracy with coups d'état! This is a democracy, yet it exists *in spite of* the people and it is in fact antipeople. It is not *for* the people.

---

127. The periods of the first constitution, declared under Sultan Abdul Hamid, lasted from 1876 to 1878.

Or, better stated, it is a democracy without a *demos*, without the people.

The various reforms being carried out in order to fall in line with the European Union are really not reforms demanded by the people at all. They are an arrangement developed in response to pressure and recommendations from the West.

U.S. democracy provides for a capitalist democratic structure. When the world proletariat could not unite to bring about democracy, the world capitalists united and established their own version of democracy.

In Turkey the army, the politicians, the businesspeople, the workers, the intelligentsia, and others all want democracy, but somehow it refuses to materialize.

The Kemalists, adopting the new fashion, are also talking about democracy, but they are concerned that democracy would just open the way for a fundamentalist, religious dictatorship by *mollas* (religious leaders). They say that whenever the religious conservatives take up the fight in the name of the *shariah*, they will be crushed if they hide behind the flag of democracy and attempt to achieve their goal of Islamic rule in Turkey. Turkey needs dictatorship, the kind of disciplined, authoritarian rule that Mussolini adopted in order to civilize and save the Italian population from Latin backwardness. To bring democracy to Turkey would be to take the country into an anarchistic hell. Democracy is the anarchy of the masses. Democracy brings sedition and destroys stability...

And so on!

But democracy is just the fashion of the age. And the identity of *demos* is far from clear.

What kind of a democracy *are* you in favor of?

You must make up your mind if you are calling for democracy.

Is it a Western democracy? Is there just one kind of democracy in the West? Don't forget the backyards of Western democracy, where the colonialism of Africa haunts like a ghost.

Don't forget, either, that behind the regime of Saudi Arabia, you can see the top hat and the stars and stripes of Uncle Sam. Everyone knows about the tyrannical regimes of the Gulf states, supported by the antidemocratic disciples of Western democracy. In spite of France's famous slogan, *"Liberté! Fraternité! Egalité!"* Western democracy does not rest upon universal equality, brotherhood, and freedom!

The West proposes a flawed democracy in which Westerners are the first class and our people are the second class. *Demos cratos* means "the people's government." But, if you are evil or careless, you make a Demon Cratos out of democracy, the Devil's Government.

The fame of the West is counterfeit. The West has double standards. Think of Algeria, Bosnia, Montenegro, Chechnya...

When Westerners' interests are at stake, they forget their promises and contracts. What the West finds important is not its principles or obligations but its interests. Since 1789, the West gave us two world wars. Fascism, capitalism, Marxism—their offspring. Nagasaki, Hiroshima—their works of art. They pierced the ozone layer, polluted the rivers and the seas, consumed two-thirds of the known underground energy reserves of the world. And don't think that they are satisfied or that they are about to stop!

Within the span of two lifetimes, the West has soaked the soil with blood and tears.

Of the four great races living on earth, one they wiped out, another they enslaved, and the other they colonized.

Montaigne, in his trials, related the events experienced in the discovery of America (the atrocities toward the natives) and asked why all these were committed, and he concluded, "For trivial swindling and trivial pleasures."[128]

We cannot imitate the democracy of the West and achieve the same level of affluence unless we are prepared to travel the same criminal route. If you were to restrict the Germans to live on $150 a month, you would find out pretty quickly how much they cherish their democracy. Their affluence created their democracy, not vice versa.

We must not consider democracy worse than other systems, but unless we define *demos* and *cratos*, we cannot sensibly discuss democracy.

Democracy in today's Turkey is a comedy, without a proper basis in sense or a genuine constituency. *Democracy* is just a magic word, a cosmetic used to hide and embellish the face of politics. Democracy is not the savior of modern societies. Using it like a saint's tomb, and chanting it in songs contributes nothing to the language of politics. *Demos* is important, but nowhere is it written that *demos* solves everything.

---

128. Quoted in Michel Montaigne, *Denemeler* (*Essays*), translated by Sabahaddin Eyüboğlu (İstanbul: Cem Publications, 1989), p. 94.

If you are talking about a humane democracy, then you should speak instead about tolerance, for this is something of genuine value. Without understanding how there can be poverty in abundance, the reasons for disgraceful behavior and for the collapse of morality, the spread of self-interest and bribery, fraudulent elections, the abuse of laws, the decay of order, the modern slavery of workers, the love affair between money and authority, imperial aspirations, the irresistible attraction of money, destructive ignorance, the erosion of government by immorality, the decline of social cooperation in favor of exploiting the weaknesses of others—without understanding all these, we will never truly understand how things are, and what democracy is.

Promises are nice, but reality is often bitter.

If society is not to experience bitter collapse after unrealistic dreams and hollow hopes, the individuals who make up society should strive to develop a sensible, informed, responsible, and decent character.

If the majority of the people possess these virtues, if the others have confidence in them, and if the decent people can be as brave as the indecent ones, then unrealistic dreams and hollow hopes can be avoided.

If the *demos* is moribund, then the *cratos* too is doomed. New democracy can only be born when *demos* is strong.

I want nothing to do with today's talk of democracy. Democracy as it is being talked about now will never express the utopias that I hope for.

In their speech, a fascist, a Marxist, and a capitalist can all be democrats.

But for me, none of the solutions advanced in the name of democracy promise me a paradise, nor are these solutions based on any of the divine methods I prize so highly, nor are they based on any of the premises that I value.

As source, method, and end, they are completely foreign to me.

Can I, as a member of the *demos*, turn any of these into to a political demand that I can identify with?

Because *demos* is *demos* only when it possesses all the riches I speak of. Without those riches, the *demos* is only a flock. And flocks do not have authority; they only have shepherds.

We in Turkey could reshape these ideas to produce something new, but there is no need to call it democracy. If you insist on calling it democracy, then it should be something new—not an imported system, but something built on our beliefs, history, and cultural values, and proposed as a new manifesto of virtue furnished with universal values.

For the views of Şanar Yurdatapan on this subject, see The Red *chapter 15.*

25. LA ILAHE! THERE IS NONE TO WORSHIP!

There is no *ilah*.[129]

This is the first condition on entering religion. There is no *ilah*, an entity with authority over me, who can judge me; it does not exist. I do not recognize such an entity. I am the one who decides. I am free; I am so free that I am entitled not to recognize even the Creator, if I so choose. No one can enter the domain of *iman*, belief, until he acquires this knowledge concerning freedom. In Islam, those who ascribe partners to the authority of Allah, which is equivalent to saying that there is more than one God, are called *mushrik*. Their religion is a coalition of gods, who share the sovereignty of the Creator. They have fabricated a mixed religion, one that is different from the pure one under one single authority, one ruler, one judge, one God, Allah.

Religion is a whole revealed to the created by the Creator, through the agency of the prophet. It is a whole without anything superfluous, unnecessary, and with nothing missing, a whole to which nothing can be added and from which nothing can be subtracted. And the first condition of *iman* is freedom.

When atheists say that they recognize the authority of "neither God nor king," they distance themselves from God to the same extent that they distance themselves from those who establish authority over them against their will. For that reason, their attitude is not an absolute escape, but a step somewhere between correctly asserting their independence and taking advantage of the gift of independence. Atheists are the slaves of their fancies and desires. That is to say, they have lost their freedom by bowing to the authority of the invisible devil, whose existence they deny, but who has set up a throne in the flesh of the godless.

---

129. Deity. *La ilaha illallah, Muhammad-ur-Rasul-Allah* (There is no God but Allah and Muhammad is his messenger) are the words of the confession of faith made by any person converting to Islam, the first two words meaning "There is no God..."

Freedom is the condition of being free, independent; it is returning to one's own nature and making peace with the truth of creation.

The knowledge of freedom finds expression only in an atmosphere of peace, whereas real peace is possible only with justice. If there is no justice, there is no peace. When there is no peace, people who are thirsty for each other's blood are the slaves of their anger.

This is why the Holy Qur'an tells us, "Don't let your enmity toward a people push you to be unjust to them." "Respect is mutual." The Qur'an also advises us "not to insult what others hold sacred and holy and to be above all just."

There can be no doubt that Allah is One. He was not born. "He begat not nor was he begotten." He had no beginning and he has no end. Good and bad are within his will and power. His approval defines a special area within his will. He hears, sees, knows, and is sovereign. He created the angels, jinns, and Satan, and our return is only unto him.

No doubt this explanation is the expression of a condition that tests the limits of the intellect, and rightly so. If Allah meant someone definable, measurable, with known limits, I would not believe in him. I would not call him my lord or my God. We grasp the meaning of Allah from his works. He is *kadiri mutlak*, meaning the possessor of absolute power. He is the creator of destiny, sustenance, and death. He is unique, he has no equivalent, and there is none like him. He is One and Only.

This is the reason that one enters the religion of Islam and becomes a Muslim by saying *Illa Allah*, "except Allah," after having said *La ilaha*, "There is no one to worship." And this is the complete Islamic expression of belief in Allah: *La ilaha illallah.*

Allah created man and made him "the most perfect and the most honored" of all of creation, and also the most intelligent. Allah gave him brains and taught him the names of things. He gave man the knowledge of reality and truth.

Shariah is the knowledge of truth, the sense of laws and justice, the realization of legality, the created universe, the purpose and wisdom of existence.

Reality is the knowledge of the purely material world as perceived by the intellect—what can be perceived by the five senses and analyzed in the brain.

Allah gave man intelligence and flesh and made him superior to the angels. He wanted to reward humankind with greater favors and blessings, so he granted us *freedom*. He granted us an area of free will within our power. He gave us a law—the *shariah*—that specifies goodness, beauty, honesty, justice, peace, and freedom. He gave the glad tidings of paradise to those who behave as he approved. And he threatened those who chose evil with the punishment of hell.

In the divine order of things, there is an absolute justice. Nothing done by anyone will remain hidden. There are two recording angels who write only the truth and who are continuously recording everything. Those who so much as throw a stone at a dog in the street will be made to suffer the same pain as that dog. This is what is called *cehennem azabi*, or the agony of hell. In this way, people will see the cost of the evil things they did or caused; they will taste that agony, they will repent, and after their souls have been cleansed of mischief by the fierce fire of hell, which separates gold from dirt, they will be allowed to return to paradise. Hell is a place where the dog you threw stones at on earth will come and have the right to take its revenge and bite you, or forgive you. Who knows? Perhaps the bone you gave to another dog out of the kindness of your heart will be a reason for the forgiveness of some evil that you have done. That is why our ancestors used to say, "One kind deed prevents a thousand disasters." This is true in this world and in the hereafter.

If there is a deficiency in your worship, with the permission of Allah, your bad deeds can be exchanged with your good deeds. That is to say, perhaps by forgoing some of your credits in paradise, you can have some of your punishment in hell forgiven.

Now, this explanation may be an oversimplification, but it is only meant to create a picture of the situation. Allah alone knows the reality.

Regarding your good deeds, Allah, who knows what is in your heart and in your mind, will reward even your good thoughts and intentions with a 50 percent incentive credit; he will reward your efforts to realize what is in your heart, according to the coefficient of your intention and thought, by a multiplier of ten, one hundred, and even seven hundred. Allah demands from everybody the equivalent of what he has given them, and in paradise all of us will be rewarded in proportion to the effort we have made in accordance with our gifts and advantages.

Allah created mankind and asked, "Am I not your Lord?" And there in the spirit world, at a time when the intellect had been granted but was not yet incarnate, they swore, *Bela*, which means "Surely yes." We call this period the *kalu bela* period, because it means the period in which, "They said 'surely yes.'" This was the first pledge by us, and after this promise, Allah sent us to the world in order to keep our promise and thereby merit paradise.

Every Muslim should first read the Qur'an, then understand it, and then sign in his own handwriting at the bottom of the last page, "I read, I understood, and I accepted." Remember that the first revelation starts by saying: *Iqra* ("Read"), that it continues: "Read, in the name of your Lord who created," and then, "Do not pursue what you do not know."

Nobody's belief is greater than his intellect. You can only believe to the extent that your intellect permits. For those who are without intellect, belief is not an obligation. Intellect alone is not the source of truth, nor is it its measure. Intellect, perhaps, is like a riding horse, a legendary Arabian steed. If the flesh or Satan gets control of the reins of the mind, this horse will run toward hell, but if you surrender your intellect to your belief, then it will run straight to paradise.

It is for this reason that when Allah created man and gave him shape, he placed the mind at the very top of the body.

If man, who should use his intellect according to the intention of its creation, instead entrusts it to his carnal body or Satan, the intellect that could have made him the most honored of all humankind will make him lower than an animal. Murderers, torturers, mafiosi, narcotics merchants, and those who run prostitution, gambling, and drinking parties generally are not people without intellect, but because they are unfaithful to the created purpose of their intellect, they put it right into the hands of the devil. For example, those who invented the atomic bomb and used it to massacre thousands of civilians were not without intellect. And the warmongers and the political authorities who oppress the people are not stupid either. But when their interests, their anger, their hatred, and their ambition for position, women, rank, and power take a lofty position in their eyes, they terrorize the people with the wealth, arms, and authority on which they lay their hands. They have eyes but they do not see, they have ears but they do not hear, and they have hearts but they do not feel. When they are told not to cause mischief in the world, they say, "We are only improving things." When they are with the believers, they say that they believe too. But when they are with their friends, they say, "We were joking with them, pretending." They are not at ease in their hearts. Their anger and their ambition pour out of their mouths, and the more they eat, the hungrier they feel. They are the worst of mischief makers. They are forfeiting the other world for a small price, to buy temporary pleasures. What they are doing is hardly intelligent, however; they are exchanging eternal life for a temporary one. How great is their loss!

A believer does not carry doubt or uncertainty in his belief. Allah created us as men, and sent us a book and a prophet to show us the difference between right and wrong. By giving us intellect, he gave us the chance to learn the realities of the world into which we were sent, to develop arguments, and to discover truth. He also told us that if we live a life filled with goodness, honesty, and kindness, he will reward us with paradise, but that if we misuse the opportunity granted us, then hell will be our lot.

The moment we become aware of our existence, we should realize that a far higher entity has granted us that existence. Life did not originate as a result of meaningless and pointless chance.

If not used correctly, the intellect transforms man into a monster that threatens nature. And perhaps religion is the method of turning man back to his natural self. Nothing can happen without the intellect, but intellect alone is not the source or measure of reality.

Allah exists, and he is only One. If his existence could be proven by other arguments, then man would not have to seek inside himself, in the depths of his spirit, to find the real proof. A finite intellect is incapable of understanding infinite value. That is why belief is a matter for the heart, and real belief is a reward given only to mature souls.

For the views of Şanar Yurdatapan on this subject, see The Red *chapter 9.*

26. BUILDING CIVIL SOCIETY, OR, HAVE YOU EVER SEEN A FIREFLY?

How can we know what *civil society* means? It is as difficult for Turkish citizens to picture a member of civilian society as it would be for us to describe an avocado to a shepherd in the Hakkari mountains. In fact, to be a member of civil society means not to be political or official.

We think that *civil society* is the opposite of a *militarized society*. We assume that since it is not military, then it must be civilian. We should ask, "Have you ever seen a member of civil society?" in the same spirit as one might ask, "Have you ever seen a firefly?"

Is the holding company and its managers part of civil society? The company is a nationally owned, public organization, a front company for the deep state. That man you consider a businessman is a civil servant who works for that company and acts as if he were a manager.

And this newspaper? In practice it is more or less state-owned, from its working capital down to its reporters. It is a semi-official newspaper.

And this association? That, too, was established by the deep state. This, like the front company of such-and-such a political party, this, too, is a front association. It is the party's backyard, with the president of the party providing leadership and ideology. There are also illegal political groups organizing with the aim of seizing control of the state, and they want to make their particular ideology the ideology of the state.

Which is to say that what you have around you is not a genuine civil society. If we disregard the very young and the very old, 90 percent of voters are supporters of this or that party. Their political identities are formed by the party they support, and they may be working within the party structure or working for it at the district or municipal-council level. Nobody is a genuine member of civil society, because the awareness of civil society has been destroyed.

Everybody wants to take control of the state and save the nation and the state. How can we expect to make members of civil society out of a population formed by a monolithic official ideology? One-party mentality still rules, and our docile society follows like sheep. The state is the major part-

ner in every business. Of course, against such a background we are bound
to think that *civil* means merely nonmilitary. In the press there is talk of
increasing the number of civilians in the MGK (National Security Council),
whatever that means—are they going to recruit members from Mazlum-
Der (the Society for Solidarity with Oppressed People) and the IHD (the
Turkish Human Rights Association)? I think not! We are the lucky benefici-
aries of the media that perceive "the increase in the military membership of
the MGK" as a sign of civilianization! That is hardly surprising. In our
country, many professional associations and foundations, even unions,
cannot be considered completely civilian. Since we have never seen anything civilian, mayors, members of parliament, and the rest of them consider themselves civilian. A good many people think the constitution,
which was drawn up by the military, is a civilian constitution.

I hope that one day the distinction between civilian and political is
understood, and that we no longer feel obliged to hide behind politicians to
save ourselves from those who want to seize power.

For the views of Şanar Yurdatapan on this subject, see The Red *chapter 14.*

27. IT IS TIME TO SAY SOMETHING NEW

Mevlana[130] had said so. Yesterday is the past. Now new things must be said.

We cannot express the hopes and fears of twenty-first-century people with concepts and institutions forged at the beginning of the twentieth century, following World War I. We must reexamine history. At a time when knowledge, labor, property, and wealth are freely circulating, words like *nation, state,* and *sovereignty* will not be sufficient for our discussions. Kebab-eaters and vegetarians, those who worship the cow and those who, like Muslims, sacrifice cows in their religious festivals have to live together in the same world. Warlike societies now have to shake hands with those who are against war. Civil disobedience groups and conscientious objectors take a stand against the sovereign state culture.

People no longer want to be ruled only by the sovereign laws of their own state. People have different religions, languages, traditions, sects, professions, philosophical and conscientious beliefs, political preferences, ideological views, and interests.

Nowadays, we have the Internet. You may have difficulty communicating with your neighbor, but you can play chess with a youngster in Latin America and gossip in chatrooms. One day, when I was searching on the Internet, I entered the virtual mosque on the "IslamiCity.org" site. I asked those in the mosque if there were any Turks among them. A girl from Turkey was chatting with a friend in the virtual mosque. I asked her what part of Turkey she was from. How fascinating that one can find oneself chatting with a young student from just down the road in a virtual mosque in the USA. We are living in a different world now. Surely we can build twenty-first-century Turkey without the help of Hitler and Mussolini's criminal code and defective translations of laws from France, Germany, and Switzerland, which date back to the end of World War I.

---

130. Jalal-e-Din Mohammad Mevlavi Balkhi Rumi (1207–1273), poet, religious thinker in the Sufi tradition, and founder of the Mevlevi dervish sect.

Yesterday is the past and now it is time to say something new. And what we must say is, "No more! I have had enough of this political order that brings happiness to so few. But we must be making a mistake somewhere—perhaps, as Nazım Hikmet said, it is that we are "singing the same song in many different languages." But, we are making a mistake somewhere.

We want to be happy. We want to feel secure. We want to be confident. But we are striving to gain these things by taking them away from our nearest neighbors. It is essential that we learn that we can achieve all of our desires only if we work together.

In reality, each one of us is the other. If only we were able to respect the rights of others rather than trying to force others to change. We should first try to change ourselves, sympathize with others, and ask ourselves, "Where did I go wrong? What must I do now?" rather than constantly talking about what others should do.

We must start to review some of our ideas. Instead of trying to decide what Şanar should do, and instead of him trying to dictate how I should live, we would succeed more easily if I were to think how I could help Şanar feel secure and happy. And this is a better way of thinking for Şanar if he wants to convince me to be an atheist and for me, too, if I want to persuade him to become a Muslim!

In the end, the intellect and the heart will win. To the extent that we try to understand each other, we shall benefit from each other and respect each other more. And we will not have encroached on each other's rights.

For the views of Şanar Yurdatapan on this subject, see The Red *chapter 14.*

28. WE ARE THE CHILDREN OF CONQUERORS!

For shame. Some of us boast of the Ottoman conquests, and feel pride in our conquering past, while some of us dismiss any connection with our past as mere Muslim fundamentalist reactionism. History should not be viewed merely as an allocation of praise or blame. We should learn lessons from the past. History is society's collective memory and awareness, our knowledge of society. The fundamental truths have not changed since Cain slew Abel. Today, also, will become history, and a new page about the conflict between the good and the bad will have been written.

Who is good? Who is bad? The terms *good* and *bad*, as applied to history, will continue to serve no purpose except as a means for individuals and groups to subjectively describe each other. And third parties, instead of investigating an event in light of independent principles, will either turn their backs on reality or twist the truth in order to legitimize their own actions and ideas.

The actual facts of history get lost amid this manipulation, and then history is no longer a reliable store of our knowledge and experience.

Let's examine the *Fetih*, the conquest of İstanbul by the Ottoman Turks. Was it, as some say, "a brute invasion of the weak by the mighty"? Or was it an event in which one group of people seized the legal rights of another group, permissible because Islamic belief asserts that the prophet Muhammed had predicted the conquest of İstanbul centuries earlier?

In fact, of course, the prophet did not give his permission for any type of injustice, but nor was the conquest simply a "brute invasion..."

By way of comparison, consider this example: Jerusalem was conquered in the time of the caliph Omar by three living things: Omar, his servant, and his camel.[131] They had neither protectors nor armies behind them.

---

131. The Arab conquest of Jerusalem was allegedly bloodless. Tradition has it that the patriarch Sophronios surrendered the city to Omar, the commander of the Arab forces, renowned for his habit of ascetic simplicity and humility. In return the patriarch was granted a writ of privileges that guaranteed the right of Christians to maintain their holy places and practice their customs unhindered.

At the gates of Jerusalem the camel was tired and could not carry both men. The caliph Omar had forgone his turn and made his slave ride on the camel. Those who heard about their impending arrival and met them at the city gates (don't forget there was no TV in those days, so they did not know what Omar looked like) started to show respect to the slave, but the slave tried to explain that he was not the caliph Omar.

Now you may wonder: Why did the slave not try to escape while the caliph Omar slept?

I must confess that in Islam there is a master-slave order. Some prejudiced people will hear this with some glee, but let me also tell you that Islam regulated the liberation of slaves. Islam took precautions to ensure that prisoners of war were treated like human beings, that animosities between the warring sides ended, and that enemies were reconciled. The enslaving of the blacks would never have been acceptable according to Islamic principles.

People who speak about history often have no idea of the real meaning of the institutions they are talking about, how they originated, how they developed, and how corrupt practices emerged. Many people are not aware of the Mameluke state.[132] Yes, those who were prisoners one day came and took over the government! Sokollu Mehmet Paşa, who became a *vezir*, a prime minister, in the Ottoman Empire, was a *devşirme*, a Christian son taken as tribute, converted to Islam, and set to work in the Ottoman civil service.[133] Many people may not be aware that a slave was appointed as the successor of Khalid ibn Walid, the famous Sword of Islam, as commander of the Muslim armies in the seventh century. In addition, the famous Islamic mystic Rabiyyetül Adeviyye was also once a *jariye*, a female slave or concubine.

When one says *conquest*, I wonder how many people think of freedom! The Islamic word for conquest is *fetih*, which means to open the doors and to make free, to liberate. Sultan Mehmet, the conqueror of İstanbul,

---

132. The sultans of the Mameluke state of Egypt (1257–1517) were soldier slaves, mainly Caucasian Circassians, Turks, and Tatars. The sons of these rulers were not allowed to join the army or become rulers, and native Egyptians were excluded from the government. Following the defeat of the Mameluke, Egypt was finally defeated by the Ottomans at Aleppo, and their territory was subsumed into the Ottoman Empire.

133. See page 74 in the section written by Yurdatapan concerning the recruitment of the Janissaries.

was given the title *fatih*, the Liberator. Remember that the Ottomans were in Bosnia and the Ottoman flag was flying in Sancak fifty years before the conquest of İstanbul.

You say invasion, war, occupation, but the number of Fatih's troops at the time was more than the total population of Byzantium. With all of his guns and soldiers, he could have leveled Byzantium flat if he wanted. But the capture of İstanbul happened as follows: The emperor of Byzantium murdered a number of Muslim Arab traders, confiscated their property, and destroyed their places of worship. Then a number of Greek students who had accepted Islam were thrown into jails for demanding more freedom. Sultan Mehmet demanded the release of the Greek students and insisted that the murderers of the Muslim merchants be brought to justice.

Here is the point of my argument: We have a different view of the conquest of İstanbul than, for example, Greeks may have. As defenders of human rights, the Fetih is a matter of pride and honor for us. We are proud that for days and weeks, plans were made so that no civilian Byzantine who did not take part in the war should come to harm, and that huge siege guns suitable for pinpoint target firing were specially developed so as to inflict the minimum of casualties on Byzantine soldiers, and minimal damage to the city. The Fetih is not something we should be ashamed of; it is one of the golden chapters of our history and we feel proud of it. It is the legend of a struggle for human rights and freedom.

One of the first things that Sultan Fatih Mehmet did when he captured İstanbul was to declare himself Emperor of Byzantium, thus giving himself this title in addition to the Khan of the Turks, the Caliph of the Muslims, and the Sultan of the Persians. What Fatih did can also be considered the overthrow of an oppressive regime with the help of the people, because the conquest of İstanbul was hardly a proper war, as we know it. This is analagous to the conquest of Jerusalem, where the swords were only carried as a precaution against wild animals and attacks by brigands.

As for the prophet's good tidings, he does not mention only İstanbul. He also gives good tidings that miraculously help the poor and helpless in their most difficult hours—promises that the palaces and the castles of oppression in India, China, Iran, Egypt, and İstanbul will be destroyed; promises that the people will become free and that they will enter Islam; and promises that Islam will spread across the world. Islam advises people to follow their own religion, to become brothers with the people in oppressed countries, and to support their struggle for freedom. Yes, Ayyub al-Ansari[134] did indeed come to İstanbul—his tomb is there—but he came in order to invite people to his religion, Islam, and to be brothers with the people of Byzantium, not for the purpose of conquest. Unfortunately, the Byzantine administration of that day forced al-Ansari's group, which had come to explain the new religion, to leave Byzantium, and in the conflict that ensued, they were martyred. In reality, *these* were the first conquerors.

Islam is a religion of peace, and it spells out a way of life aimed at saving humankind from slavery to Satan; it wants to make people free to live according to the intentions of the Creator. Conquest, in this sense, is the conquest of the soul. This sincerity of belief was the source of self-confidence that enabled Ayyub al-Ansari, an eighty-year-old man, to take his sons and go from Medina to İstanbul to liberate the city.

According to Islamic belief, a Muslim cannot ignore what is happening in the world, for he is the seeing eye, the hearing ear, the holding hand, and the calling voice of the Just One, Allah. "If a wolf were to steal a sheep on the shores of the Tigris River, divine justice comes and asks the caliph Omar about it." Allah wants to punish the oppressors and help the oppressed through the agency of the Muslims. That is why every Muslim is obliged to join the struggle for justice, peace, freedom, and the environment. What we call *kul hakkı*—a man's right, a servant's right, a slave's right—is a sacred trust that the Creator revealed and granted mankind. In our book, there is no servitude of man to man. Muslims have always struggled and will always struggle for freedom against those *mushriks* who declare themselves gods and lords by presumptuously putting themselves on an equal footing will Allah, and by making men their servants.

We shall sing songs of conquest and liberation that give joy to our hearts, so that in the name of all humankind oppression shall be ended and the oppressed made free.

---

134. Eyüp Sultan Mosque was the first mosque to be built in Constantinople (İstanbul) after the city's conquest by the Ottoman Turks on May 29, 1453. It is built on the grave of Ayyub al-Ansari, a companion of the prophet and his standardbearer, who died during the first Islamic siege of Constantinople in 668 C.E.

History is not a catalogue of happy events, of course. Like us, the Ottomans had their faults and made mistakes; otherwise, the empire would not have collapsed. As I said before, history is not simply a process of allocating praise or blame. The whole of humankind has a common history; it is our common homeland, and we can only reach it with an intelligent view of the past, and sensitivity about what is to come.

For the views of Şanar Yurdatapan on this subject, see The Red *chapters 5, 6, and 15.*

29. WHAT IS REALITY? WHAT IS TRUTH?

Well, are you asking what reality is?

Reality is understood by the five senses. The mind, which synthesizes it, tries to understand it and interpret it through a framework of value judgments, belief, tradition, ideology, biases, and political or personal interests. Often, the ontological nature of a thing (the science of existence or the purpose of creation) does not even interest us at all; we are trying to find a meaning we can understand. That is to say, we try to approach something semantically and epistemologically.

Truth, on the other hand, expresses the wisdom that reflects the purpose of the Creator in creation. If you start with reality, you reach wisdom and knowledge, but if you start with truth, you reach enlightenment. The wise (aydın)[138] man, starting with the perception in his own senses, continuously focuses on material questions. The enlightened (münevver) man, starting with an inherent knowledge of truth, strives, using his intelligence and belief; he aims at understanding the beginning and the end of this world, and evolves in this process. He tries to contribute to morals, ethics, and laws (shariah). He looks upon the objects outside him as independent. He regards them as sacred. He feels that as an intelligent being he has a responsibility toward each object. He knows that even when he is carrying out his ablutions by the vast ocean, he must still not be wasteful with water, for one day he will be called to account for his actions. Using his intuition, he perceives things in an abstract, aesthetic way. He sees the meanings

---

135. Throughout this chapter, Dilipak contrasts the Turkish-rooted word for wise (aydın) with the Arabic-rooted word (münevver). Both are normally translated as "enlightened," but the author is attempting to contrast worldly enlightenment with spiritual enlightenment. Here aydın is translated as "wise," and münevveri is translated as "enlightened." At the conclusion of the chapter, Dilipak also contrasts the French-rooted burjuva with its Arabic-rooted equivalent havas. Devout Turks often prefer to use the Arabic-rooted vocabulary associated with Ottoman times rather than the neologisms devised or rediscovered from Central Asian Turkish during the republican period. To any Turkish reader, the vocabulary used by Yurdatapan and Dilipak instantly identify their political and cultural leanings.

beyond the visible in everything around him, endowing everything with spiritual character. He has a spiritual nature, and Revelation will always be a guide, a compass showing him the way.

Without intellect, man cannot be man. That which is able to understand and interpret Revelation is intellect, and man can only believe to the extent that he has intellect. For this reason, a person's religion cannot be greater than the extent of his intellect. But intellect alone cannot be the source or the measure of reality. If intellect alone were sufficient, we would have achieved something a little more concrete in all these thousands of years of history. As intellect grows, conflict increases. Intellect is imprisoned in time, place, and the senses, a crazy thing that by itself is incapable of action. Without belief, intellect cannot be a vehicle for peace, because intellect without belief is a prisoner of the flesh. Undisciplined by belief, the flesh serves Satan, who incites carnal passions. That is why the ancients say, "The road to hell is paved with good intentions." Certain types of intelligent people are not destructive, though, and this indicates that they possess a secret set of beliefs called *morality*. Morality: This is a conception of life at peace with the purpose of creation, in harmony with the order present in nature from creation. That is to say, morality can be achieved through our determination to live in harmony with our nature, using our intellect, and we come to the end of the process of finding belief through intellect.

Wisdom is centered around man and intellect. Prometheus steals fire from the gods, Pandora opens her box, and hell is let loose. The fire is both a burning force and a truth that gives off light. With it, one both understands and subdues matter. The enlightened, however, doe not reject the light. The unconsuming, smokeless fire within the enlightened person reveals the spiritual nature of matter and the purpose of creation in a piercing, X-ray image.

Enlightened ones can distinguish between intellect and flesh. They control their animal and sensual inclinations and desires. Their knowledge of the beginning and end of the world encourage them not merely to dominate but also to know, to liberate, and to order the environment around them in a way that is pure and in harmony with the truth of creation.

Mafia bosses and junta generals are intelligent enough, but they have no love or faith.

To lack intellect is seriously dangerous, yet a person endowed with intellect but deprived of belief is infinitely more dangerous. How dangerous can an animal be? Can it make an atomic bomb? Can it bomb Nagasaki? These are the acts of the intelligent, faithless human. That is why it has been said that a person who has intellect but no faith may come to a point when he will be lower than an animal; he will be the person who has access to faith but puts it aside, choosing instead to become a slave to his flesh, the most dangerous of paths.

I do not count myself a wise man, but an enlightened one.

For the views of Şanar Yurdatapan on this subject, see The Red *chapter 7.*

30. MAN HAS ALWAYS BEEN MAN!

They say that man originally was an animal and later became a man.

They even say that he was once a single-celled thing that lived in water.

Man was created as man.

Plant, animal, man.

We all come from the same place. Our Creator is One. Our purpose of creation One. The world does not consist only of animals and plants, the single-celled creatures and other living things between animal and plant.

We are living in a mixed world of living things made up of man, angels, jinns, and devils, and before man even existed, there were other thinking, living creatures in this world.

But Allah was always there, without beginning and without end, existing from time immemorial to eternity!

Some people have difficulty understanding this, but remember: If Allah could be understood, he would have to be an entity that we could add, subtract, divide, and multiply. And then Allah would not be Allah the Creator.

The finite cannot possibly understand the infinite. As a result, the intelligence of man has difficulty understanding an Allah without beginning or end, and is inclined to deny what it cannot comprehend.

Well, then, where did we come from? How far back do you think you can go? If we say that we came from monkeys and that monkeys came from single-celled living things via mitotic division, well, there must have been water before that! And there was gas before the water. And before that there was matter. And before that, matter was in the form of energy. Well, where did that come from? Intelligence in the end comes up against a brick wall. We Muslims know all about that insurmountable wall, and the secret behind that wall has been given to us by our prophet.

There are angels who cross that wall in both directions, as well as other living creatures who travel among times and realms that are beyond our reach.

There is our soul, beyond matter.

That is why they call those imprisoned in the physical world *material-ists*. The final destination of the ship of intellect is known, but that sea has a farther shore. Those who do not accept that Satan is circulating in their own veins and that angels are waiting over their shoulders reject the very order that shapes life.

But the day will come when everything we are discussing will be laid out before us. But by then, the bill will already be made out for payment by those who deny religion. For them, it will be too late. They will learn the cost of their actions, and their souls will be brought to heel as they are made to taste the bitter result of what they have done. Man was created as man.

Those studying fossils ought to be aware that there was a group of men who fell into sexually perverted ways, and Allah transformed them into monkeys. The transformation was not monkeys into humans but humans into monkeys. They and their lineage died out. So if one day the skull of one of these is found, what would this show? When Darwin went to Australia and witnessed the genocide started by the British against the natives of that land, he provided an excuse for the British government's uncivilized and murderous policy, saying, these are animals that have not completed their process of humanization—that is to say, they have not fully evolved. By presenting this *fatwa* of genocide as a scientific document, both Darwin and the British government were trying to present a scientific pre-text for ethnic cleansing. This example shows us that some people are pre-pared to present atheism as if it were a scientific fact, hiding truths and twisting reality in order to legitimize and justify crimes against humanity.

Man is a thinking being, not a thinking animal. Man's evolution is a linear progression of his intellectual powers. In fact, the word *evolution* cannot properly be used for this process. His adaptation to fit changing conditions over time is actually an emergence of traits present at birth, a biological response to nature.

Man has always been man.

We are all the children of Adam. Adam, in his turn, was created from the earth. We came from Allah, and ultimately we shall be returned to him.

For the views of Şanar Yurdatapan on this subject, see The Red *chapters 9 and 12.*

31. I LOVE A REACTIONARY WITH A SEASONING OF TERROR!

Terrorism is over; the threat of fundamentalism continues.[136]

Irtica is the century-long product of deep state forces, particularly the army. They say that Islam amounts to reactionism, that the Muslim is necessarily a reactionary Islamic fundamentalist. According to this analysis, the supposed backwardness of the Muslims is explained by the fact that Muslim women cover their heads and Muslim men grow their beards.

Irtica was devised by certain forces who deemed it a necessary and useful tool, just as they did with terror and terrorism. Both were used as an excuse for carrying out coups d'états. The Alevis were expected to be a cheap supply of votes for the left; the Sunnis, on the other hand, were to be the cheap votes for the right. The Alevis were expected to send their children to the village institute;[137] the Sunnis, to the *Imam Hatip* school. And, of course, the village *imam*, a graduate of the Imam Hatip school, was set against the village teacher. While the *imam* explained how we came from Adam, the village teacher would expound on Darwin's theory.

It really is not credible that devout Muslims are trying to bring back the Sultanate a century after its demise. Quite apart from other considerations, back then the devout were directing plenty of criticisms at the Sultanate. What we now call the reforms of Atatürk were being discussed long before the republic came along. So we got rid of the Sultanate and established the republic. What more do you want?

---

136. By 1997 the threat posed by the PKK and other illegal armed organizations was receding. However, in response to increasing electoral success on the part of Necmettin Erbakan's Welfare Party, military leaders began to warn of the threat of *irtica*, code for radical political Islam. In 1996 Erbakan became prime minister but was forced out of office under pressure from the military following the February 28, 1997, ultimatum. (See note 30 on page 38 in *Red*.)

137. A brief experiment in bringing education to rural areas and teacher training in 1940–1946 that was strongly criticized and eventually shut down by right-wing politicians, who viewed it as a maneuver to radicalize the peasant population. The village institutes are frequently referred to by the left as an example of Kemalist-inspired reform at its best.

Some self-serving people in the state bureaucracy are behind all the whispered fears of *irtica* and its links with terrorism. We Muslims are being used as cheap stage extras and fall guys for the interests of those dark forces. In the end, they have always made us the losers.

It is now time to put a stop to this dark and dirty game.

No matter from which side oppression comes, and no matter who it oppresses, we must stand on the side of the oppressed and against the oppressor.

There is no other way out.

For the views of Şanar Yurdatapan on this subject, see The Red *chapter 4.*

32. WHAT ARE DİLİPAK AND YURDATAPAN COOKING UP TOGETHER?

One of them is devoutly religious, the other an atheist.

I do not think that the religion Şanar is rejecting is actually Islam. The religion he is rejecting is one that he formulated around his groundless fears, which are unfortunately corroborated by the practice in the general population. For that reason, his rejection does not distance him from Islam, but rather from an illusion of Islam.

As I mentioned earlier, the first steps on the road to faith are the words *la ilahe*, "There is none that I should worship." This establishes a condition of absolute freedom. And then, with your own free will, you restrict your freedom in accordance with the divine will. Don't forget for a moment that Satan, too, is under Allah's command.

When a Muslim places a limit on his freedom, he has deliberately chosen to confine himself within the area that is the most lawful and the most cognizant of the divine warning, as well as the most in harmony with his own nature. Outside this area, there is no real freedom; outside, there is only servitude and slavery to the devil and the flesh in the name of freedom.

When the assertion that "There is none that I should worship" has been made, it is a claim that rejects all claims to divinity, but the Muslim follows this with the condition *illallah*: "...except Allah." How strange! That some Muslims should first say, "There is none to worship except Allah," and then surrender themselves to oppressive regimes. You go on to say *Iyyaka na'abudu wa iyyaka nastain*, meaning, "Only You do we worship and only from You do we ask sustenance," emphasizing that you believe in an Allah who possesses absolute authority, who gives everyone the sustenance he needs, and who has authority over destiny and death. And even after having confirmed the power and providence of Allah, some Muslims are afraid of people who hold earthly power?! Even though they are only demanding what is right, their knees shake!

Oh, ye who believe, believe fully.

Well, then, you might ask, what am I, Abdurrahman Dilipak, doing with a nonbeliever, an atheist like Şanar Yurdatapan? Well, I am uniting with him against injustice; that is to say, we are uniting on principles. We are doing something together that we classify as morally exemplary, virtuous, and upright. I am doing this for the sake of Allah; Şanar is easing his conscience.

I hope Şanar believes one day. But even if he does not, all of his good deeds on earth will afford him some cool respite when he is in the suffocating heat of hell, because there is a recompense for every deed that everybody does, be it as small as an atom. Şanar gets part of his recompense here on earth and part of it in the hereafter. Only Allah knows what is to come.

When Şanar dies, if he dies without faith, I shall not attend his funeral, and I hope that his family will not impose upon Muslims by asking such a thing. Also, I cannot eat any meat that he slaughters, for it is not *helal*, lawful in Islam. Still, we are together in the fight against the criminalization of thought. The religion, race, or gender of my fellows in this fight is not a consideration for me. I, like Şanar, am simply against oppression and on the side of the oppressed, no matter whence the oppression comes from and no matter against whom it is directed.

This is a union of the virtuous. *Hılfül fudul*. It is a union aimed at the coexistence of people who are different but, like all human beings, wish to live in peace, with freedom and happiness. We are doing this in the name of our future, in the name of our children, and in the name of peace, freedom, and justice. I, for the sake of Allah, and Şanar, to ease his conscience!

For the views of Şanar Yurdatapan on this subject, see The Red *chapter 15.*

33. THE LAST WORD—EPILOGUE

These texts, written, perhaps in haste, in the manner of speech, are like notes from a scrapbook.

I wanted a text to come out as natural as possible, without weighing every word. I used simple, unadorned, and straightforward expressions.

I did not fill the page with references (Qur'anic or otherwise), footnotes, or numbers. I want what I wrote to stay in your mind; I want you to look at the world this way too. [Footnotes were added by the publisher for an English-language audience.]

Natural, plain, simple, and ordinary.

I say that this work was prepared in a hurry, but in fact it has been in the making for years.

Allah must have not have meant it to be published until now.

That this work finally reaches you is due largely to Şanar's insistent follow-up.

I believe in Allah; he does not.

Perhaps he teases me with such remarks: "Who created Allah?" or "Can he destroy himself?" But I know he is looking for an excuse not to believe; perhaps this makes it easier for him.

To me, denial of the faith is a profound denial, treating as nonexistent something that exists.

Şanar can deny all he wants; even his denial is proof of the existence of Allah. (The existence of Allah is quite different from the existence of matter.)

I know that every proof dismisses a doubt; it means you have as many doubts as proofs.

I do not find it necessary to indulge in speculative games about the universe, asking if the world were so close to the sun . . . if this were like that, then this would happen, and so on. If Allah had willed it, he could have given us life at the center of the sun! This is the kind of Allah he is.

No matter how much or how little Şanar believes, he is to some extent a natural believer. In my view, even lack of religion is a religion, since reli-

gion is the knowledge of truth. People need something to hold on to, something by which they can weigh, measure, and put things in their place.

He too is a searcher for truth. Perhaps what Ṣanar actually rejects is the
kind of Muslims with whom he is familiar.

In my mind, the secret might possibly be in the great Muslim scholar
Iqbal's paradox: "Keep away from the Muslims, and take refuge in Islam."
Denial means knowingly rejecting. The heat of politics, the condition of the
Muslim world and society are so degraded that it is quite possible that
what nonbelievers are actually rejecting is the deficient and erroneous
information in their own consciousness. And perhaps Satan and their own
carnal nature are drawing a curtain before their eyes. But in the end, they
have their religion, and we have ours.

*   *   *

Yes, Ṣanar's message and my message are different, and yes, our styles are
different.

But we prepared this work together. We talked together, and worked
together.

Our differences did not get in the way of our joint project; perhaps it
even encouraged us.

What appeared impossible, we made possible.

Dilipak did not become a Marxist, nor did Ṣanar become a fundamentalist Muslim. But we benefited from each other, nonetheless, and we
wanted you to benefit too.

You do not have to applaud us or support us. It is enough if you do not
curse us or make fun of us. We ask no more than that. But if you show some
reaction, we will be pleased. Criticize what we have said. Write and tell us
how it could have been better, what should or should not have been included.

We can make corrections in later editions based on your recommendations.

We hope that our effort will contribute positively to our need to live
together.

We wanted to show that it is possible for us all to live together, with all
our differences, indeed, embracing them.

We wanted this book to be a small example of what can be achieved.

We wanted to avoid building walls between us, and to protect against people becoming deaf to one another.

We wanted that people in the same country would not be strangers to one another.

We wanted to do something to stop the way people were being shut down inside themselves, shut down into ghettos in inner cities.

We think that we can achieve a lot together by cooperating to transform life into a joy.

We think that building our own existence on the extinction of the other is a form of social suicide.

If we are to open up, grow, evolve, and develop, we must explain ourselves to others instead of fomenting enmity in our hearts toward others.

We have poured out what is in our hearts and in our minds, hiding nothing. Take what pleases you; push aside what you don't like. Perhaps, you can take something out of this and combine it with your own store of experience to create new and richer values for yourself, and so renew yourself.

This book is an invitation for those who feel a responsibility to seek such development.

*　　*　　*

It is time to say farewell. None of my books or writings have stayed so long on my desk, and none were so difficult. This was a text that was both long overdue, but also prepared in haste. There was not time to review or make corrections. If Şanar had not been chasing me, this book might never have seen the light of day.

We are two different people—our faith, our world, our ways of life, our thoughts, all different. But we never argued or lied to each other; we did not deceive each other. At times we told each other the truth about ourselves, but at no time did we behave like missionaries. If one day Şanar becomes a Muslim, I shall surely be very happy for him and on my own account, because then I will be with him in the hereafter. But he has no such expectation, because he believes after death comes annihilation. I, myself, cannot understand how he can bear the thought of such a terrifying end.

I applaud his determination with his thankless efforts, and I feel good knowing that everybody, no matter how small his deed, even if it be the size of an atom, will be compensated some day. There are gradations in both paradise and hell. The difficulties he has had to endure in his struggle for human rights will be a source of benefit for him, as well as for others who, like him, deny Allah but work for the common good. All of these acts will be a solace for him in the hereafter in which he does not believe. In hell, these good deeds will provide him with shade and comfort.

While believers drift toward hell with all the evil that they do, the non-believers come closer to paradise with all the good that they do. No doubt faith and denial are two separate zones, and people will be tested not only on what they do but also on why they do what they do, how they do it, together with what passes in their hearts and minds.

I know this: Şanar rejects the religion that is practiced widely in Turkey today. But because he does not know true Islam, and because he does not try to understand it (accursed Satan, that Şanar also does not believe in, is entertaining him with things that appear pleasant to his flesh), he only *thinks* he is rejecting Islam.

In spite of everything, Şanar and I are good friends. In spite of our differences, in the name of living in peace together, we have signed this work. We consider our differences to be the treasure of our culture. My distance from him is equal to his distance from me. To the same extent that my thoughts appear strange to him, sometimes his thoughts appear strange to me too. With united intelligence, we meet each other at a common word: *adalet,* justice. We are calling for peace. We are calling for freedom. We are saying that our differences are not grounds for animosity. Şanar and I never quarreled or fought. We did not seek our own existence in the annihilation of the other, and we did not look for our own happiness in the other's sorrow. We know that happiness multiplies as it is shared, and sorrow decreases as it is shared.

We struggled together against those groups that are creating authority and wealth for themselves on the blood, sweat, and tears of society that they are keeping divided into different religious, ethnic, cultural, and ideological groups. These groups do not need to be in conflict, and it should not have been necessary for Şanar and me to meet in prison.

He never pretended to be a Muslim, and I did not behave as if I were on his side.

This work is a result of this mutual respect, and it is our contribution to society's longing for tolerance. I pray for forgiveness if I made any mistakes or blunders, or if I used any words that harmed another's heart in these writings. I do not wish to go into the presence of Allah in a state of material or spiritual debt to any member of humankind.

Finally, let those who wish to believe, do so, and those who wish to deny Allah, do so. With selam and prayer.

Abdurrahman Dilipak
February 2002

AFTERWORD

"I have attempted with the red and the green to express the terrible passion of man.

—*Vincent van Gogh in a letter to his brother*

Red and green clash, and news reports encourage us to believe that Islamic green is conflicting with just about every political color around the globe. Political commentators on the "clash of cultures" are debating whether Islam and Western liberal democracy are so irredeemably opposed that the only solution is to pave over Muslim passions with heavy secularist concrete, or if some synthesis can be achieved to develop a domesticated, docile species of Islam.

For years, Turkey has been touted as the prototype of democracy in a Muslim nation. Said James Woolsey, former directory of the U.S. Central Intelligence Agency (CIA), "Turkey is a wonderful model that indicates how the Middle East should be."[138] But Abdurrahman Dilipak and Şanar Yurdatapan denounce the Turkish model as deeply repressive. Yurdatapan wants to live his leftism and his atheism publicly and unashamed. Dilipak wants the freedom to preach and practice his own trenchant and peppery Islamism. Both refuse to give a single inch, and in their intransigence they propose a more constructive clash of cultures in which both are permitted to exist in full flower side by side.

Turkey does offer a "wonderful model" for democracy and Islam in the Middle East, but not the state-manipulated religion currently being sold as secularism. As Dilipak points out, Turkey can hardly be described as secular, since it has what amounts to an established church. The state runs an overblown Religious Affairs Directorate that prescribes the content of the Friday sermon, shuts down any political party that tries to represent the devout sector of society, and imprisons people who choose to practice their

---

138. James Woolsey, quoted in "Not accepting Turkey's membership is crazy," *Turkish Daily News*, June 6, 2002.

own independent form of Islam in public. The really valuable model of Islam and democracy is what is being worked out by people like Yurdatapan and Dilipak, who show that the blunt atheist and the stringent Islamist can bring their clashing lives to a shared platform. Yurdatapan goes to the university gates and stands up for the young devout Muslim women who are barred from education because they cover their heads. Dilipak was a founder of Mazlum-Der, an organization that approaches human rights from a Muslim perspective. In 2002 Mazlum-Der orchestrated a campaign for an amendment to the law that would protect the property rights of foundations belonging to Armenian, Greek, and Jewish foundations. These are grassroots developments that deserve very close attention from the Christian world currently in the grip of nation-building hubris.

The question almost any Turk on the left would ask is, "What would happen if the Islamists took full control? Would they give us a chance to speak then?" No doubt devout Turks were asking the same question in reverse when they pondered the possibility of the left seizing power in the late 1960s, but the question of whether the religious right is prepared to protect freedom of expression is currently a serious one. Full control by the Islamists is a conceivable proposition, notwithstanding military intervention, which such a move would almost certainly provoke. The government of Turkey is presently in the hands of the center-right religious Justice and Development Party that includes Islamists but can probably be fairly described as Islamic Democrat (as an analogue to the Christian Democrats of Europe). Devout Muslim politicians' reassurances that they are committed to safeguarding freedom of expression on the matter are frequently dismissed as *taqiya* (a tactical lie, permissible in the path of true religion [see note in *Red* section]), an allegation that brings the debate to a frustrating deadlock.

Dilipak and Yurdatapan's solution is not to attempt the impossible task of arguing matters of principle and theory to a conclusion, but to work together on a shared project in order to see if trust and understanding can be built up in the course of the work. Yurdatapan often uses the analogy of a neighborhood threatened by natural disaster: If you've just been struck by an avalanche, you don't ask your neighbor's party affiliation before you give him a spade. The analogy is not an abstract one. Turkey and Greece have come to the brink of war several times in the past few decades, and all diplomatic attempts at resolving intricate disputes such as ownership of the Aegean seabed have failed. But in August 1999 Turkey suffered a terrible earthquake, and Greek volunteer rescue teams responded promptly to assist in rescue operations. Less than a month later, another large earthquake struck Greece, and Turkish volunteers were there to help within hours. The joint tragedy and joint efforts to combat the destruction (now referred to as "Earthquake Diplomacy") opened a new age of trust between the two countries that broke down the principal barriers to Turkey's candidacy for EU membership. The Aegean seabed question is as tricky as ever, but it will now be discussed within a context that has been completely transformed.

The tolerance urged in *Red* and *Green* is not a sentimental one. The political and cultural divisions in Turkey are not going to be charmed away by a few verses of *Kumbayah*. In the past three decades, competition between rival political paradigms has cost many lives and inflicted terrible misery on hundreds of thousands of people. In the late 1970s, left and right were killing each other at the rate of one murder a day. Adherents of the Alevi sect of Shia Islam, who make up nearly a third of the population, have been the victims of discrimination and periodic massacres. Both Yurdatapan and Dilipak refer to the long and wretched conflict between the illegal armed Kurdish PKK and state forces that broke out in 1984 and is not yet fully resolved. More than 30,000 people have died on both sides, including civilians. The violence in the Southeast dominated the course of politics over the past two decades and created a state of emergency marked by censorship, brutal round-ups, torture, the murder of suspected Kurdish sympathizers, and the forced displacement of a million or more Kurdish peasants from their homes.

In 1923, the borders of Kemal Atatürk's new Turkish republic were racially, religiously, and politically extremely diverse, and that diversity was seen as a threat. The diversity of the Ottoman Empire had contributed to its disintegration and dissolution throughout the nineteenth century. Diversity nearly brought about the complete dismemberment of the Anatolian heartland in the initial settlement following the First World War, as tracts of Asia Minor were severed and allocated to Greece, to an independent Kurdistan, and to an enlarged Armenia. Atatürk overturned that arrangement by force of arms, but still had to contend with the centrifugal potential of the territory that expressed itself in ethnic and religious-based uprisings throughout the 1920s and 1930s. Atatürk and his successors used highly authoritarian means to control the areas of life that were fertile ground for disruptive forces. In order to exclude religion from politics and public life, he enacted a battery of revolutionary laws that abolished the caliphate and Islamic law, outlawed clothing that advertised Islamic piety (such as the turban or fez), and enacted a legal code that severely punished actions or advocacy of theocracy. The army and Independence Courts ruthlessly suppressed ethnic uprisings and sought to undermine tribal structures with internal exile. The new citizenship was exclusively Turkish, and the legal code severely punished any attempt to conduct any ethnic discourse in politics other than that based on Turkishness. Atatürk's authoritarianism was rather less draconian than that being imposed elsewhere in the mid-twentieth century—it controlled religion rather than outlawing it, and members of ethnic minorities were able to rise to high positions provided that they fully subscribed to the monolithic program of national unity. But the state has consistently persecuted groups attempting to organize their religion outside state control, and has attempted methodically to expunge whatever is non-Turkish—renaming thousands of Kurdish villages with Turkish names, outlawing Kurdish personal names, and, finally, in 1981, outlawing the Kurdish language altogether. The law was repealed in 1991 but language issues rumble on. Socialist ideas that might challenge the Atatürkist state were also punishable, and from 1970 until the end of the Cold War, hundreds of thousands of leftists were tortured or imprisoned.

Many Turkish people believe that this highly intrusive and controlling state is still needed in order to suppress potentially destructive forces. Arguments for liberalization based on human rights and self-determination are viewed with great suspicion, because these were exactly the arguments used by the European powers to break off parts of the empire and claim large chunks of Anatolia before the First World War. Added to this, almost everyone has some personal memory of the cost of the internal conflict of recent years. Diplomats express regret about the restrictions on freedom of expression, but point to the bloodshed in the Balkans, Azerbaijan, and North Africa as examples of what can happen when religion and race get mixed up in politics.

The host of long-standing restrictions on alternative ideas, organizations, or expression has encouraged the Turkish state to become domineering, untransparent, unresponsive, and intolerant. In order to survive, it has
perpetuated its own climate of fear through torture, disappearance, and
political murder. When Yurdatapan and Dilipak talk about the state, the
deep state, or the state within the state, they are not talking about government and parliament, but a self-perpetuating *nomenklatura* that includes
officials of key ministries, the police, the prosecutors, the judiciary, local
governors, press barons, tribal leaders in the Southeast, and, most important, the armed forces. It is quite common to hear politicians and governors
describe the state as "sacred," and criticism of the army or a ministry
deemed to be "insulting" is punishable by imprisonment. Yurdatapan has
been tried and convicted for presenting evidence that the gendarmerie executed eleven Kurds in 1996. The conviction was subsequently overturned.
In practice the army remains senior partner to the elected government. It
has seized power openly on three occasions since 1960, executed a prime
minister, and in 1997 bullied Necmettin Erbakan's government out of
power for "reactionism," the code word for Islamism. Generals frequently
speak out about issues such as the constitution, law, and education, and
periodically scold politicians. The armed forces have secured a degree of
financial independence from the elected authorities with a network of
supermarkets, biscuit factories, and car-manufacturing deals. Is it a pre-
dictable consequence of the army's dominant position or a paradox that, in
opinion polls, the public consistently names the army as their most trusted
institution?

Those who espouse ideas that the state brands as beyond the pale—
Kurdish nationalists and Islamists in particular—are denied a place in legitimate politics. The courts have closed down twenty-five political parties in
the past twenty years. Some disenfranchised groups have resorted to violence, which merely worked to legitimize the overbearing state. In other
cases, groups unable to conduct conventional party politics focused on creating free spaces in which to organize by conquering liberated zones. If
they could not capture the state, they might be able to take over a ministry,
a university, a city district, a community organization, or even just a tea-
house. This tendency ran riot in the 1970s when wearing a "leftist" mous-
tache in a rightist district of Ankara could be a fatal mistake, but even today

it is common to hear that a campus or a coffee shop has been taken over by a particular group or faction.

Turkish politics tends to view ethnicity or religion as a zero sum game in which you cannot afford to grant more freedom for your political opponent because that would mean less freedom for you. The headscarf debate is typical. No woman wearing a headscarf for religious reasons can attend school or university, work as a doctor or lawyer, teach or join the civil service. She cannot even take up a seat in parliament. Those who defend the headscarf ban say that if the right were to be granted, then before long no woman could attend school or work as a doctor *unless* she were wearing a headscarf. (I have spoken to many women who wear the headscarf who say that they would as strongly defend their sisters' right to go bareheaded as they themselves assert their right to cover their heads. Many on the other side of the argument dismiss such words as insincere, but a journalist recently denied a press card because she submitted a headscarfed photograph expressed exasperation: "There is no way out of it when they say that you are practicing *taqiya*. I cannot open up my heart and show it to them.")

The Freedom of Expression Initiative, coordinated by Yurdatapan and strongly supported by Dilipak, is a bold departure from the zero sum game. This informal group's activities, described in detail by Yurdatapan in *Red*, are inspired by the Voltairean principle that we should protect the freedom to express even those ideas that we find offensive or wrong. The participants believe that by empowering their social opposites, they empower themselves. The Initiative members have been very energetic in building their campaign across ideological and party lines, opposing limits to freedom of expression imposed on the left, the right, the religious, the atheistic, and various ethnic groups. Whenever people are convicted for the expression of their nonviolent opinions, Yurdatapan and Dilipak find prominent journalists, actors, and artists who will republish these statements under a Voltairean protocol that they are defending the authors' right to express their views, not the views themselves. The republications are just cheap photocopies, but even this is sufficient to trigger a prosecution under Turkish law. Prosecutors have been reluctant to bring actions against so many prominent people, knowing that such prosecutions are a photo opportunity (celebrities forced to sit on each others' knees in order to fit onto the defendant's bench) which only serves to bring ridicule on bad laws. But where the prosecutor has attempted to ignore the republications, then the Initiative has warned that they will prosecute the prosecutor for dereliction of judicial duty.

Members of the judiciary do all they can to rid themselves of these excruciatingly embarrassing cases. But getting rid of the Initiative is like getting rid of a sticky candy wrapper. In one case, Yurdatapan repeated a conscientious objector's offense of "criticizing the institution of military service." He should have received a prison sentence, but the court acquitted him. Yurdatapan appealed the acquittal, stating that the law unambiguously required the court to imprison him, since they had imprisoned the first offender. They must convict the second "offender" or repeal the law, he said. The Supreme Court acquitted again. Yurdatapan set out to complain to the European Court of Human Rights. Yurdatapan's lawyers were doubtful, saying that only the victim of a violation could make such a petition, and since he had been acquitted, he could hardly call himself a victim. Yurdatapan replied that if he had been imprisoned, it would have been lawful, though unjust. But the acquittal imposed a much harsher punishment by condemning him to live under an arbitrary state. Yurdatapan's petition is currently before the European Court.

The Freedom of Expression movement is effective because it challenges the state's brand of Atatürkism in creative, nimble-footed, and often very amusing ways. The movement is using the armored weight of its adversary to bring it down. This innovative approach is not just a rejection of violence, but a rejection of the whole idea of defeating the social and political opposite in favor of finding a way for incompatible ideas to be accommodated in the same society. In this connection, I am eager and curious one day to hear Dilipak and Yurdatapan discuss the issue of blasphemy. It is one thing to share space with people who reject your ideas, but more challenging to permit them to insult what you believe in. Of course, many countries with a strong tradition of freedom of expression have unresolved issues over blasphemous statements and insults to public figures or institutions—in the United States, for example, there is persistent pressure to criminalize flag burning—but in Turkey the need to be careful what you say is underpinned by a persistent fear of the state or mob. Relatedly, I look forward to reading further frank dialogue on *namus*—the honor that can only be held by men and stained by women—an issue that Dilipak and

Yurdatapan both treat in their own ways. Whereas Yurdatapan criticizes *namus* with an anthropological crash course and an emphasis on sexual conduct as a personal and individual affair, Dilipak would just as surely condemn "honor crimes," but approaches this from a completely different direction with the argument that the *namus* system is propped up by chastity, and that, as such, it is one of the fundamental forms of security that hold society together and is endorsed by God.

"We wanted to make it so that people in the same country would not be strangers to one another," says Dilipak. And he is right that the devout Turkish family and the Turkish family that share a bottle of wine on a Saturday night have drifted very far apart. In *Green* and his writings elsewhere, Dilipak espouses a set of ideas that would seem conventional to the average reader in Konya, but probably outlandish and repugnant to many readers in Ankara (or in New Jersey, for that matter). In *Red* Yurdatapan does the reverse, particularly in his approach to sexual morality. What comes across strongly in Yurdatapan's *Red* is a flavor of the indignation of offended reason that many modern Turks feel in the face of religion, traditional ideas, and prejudices that they feel are holding their society back. Dilipak's section expresses the indignation of offended honor. *Green* is a Blakean rage against sterile rationalism, but it is also the expression of a disregarded culture's pain, for Atatürk's new republic very deliberately dismissed the five hundred years of Ottoman heritage that led up to it. The year 1923 was not just goodbye to the fez and hello to the new alphabet. It was a drastic, year-zero break with the past, in which all language, ideas, poetic and musical forms, and social organizations dating from before that date were condemned as backward, corrupt, and fatally associated with the capitulation and collaboration at the end of the First World War. This may be one explanation of why the divide between traditional and modernist, the devout and the secular, has been particularly sharp in Turkey. The two social groups are distinct and instantly recognizable by dress, habit, and language, and move in largely separate universes. Dilipak has commented that when he goes to a meeting with Yurdatapan's circle, people are polite but find it difficult to talk because it seems "They just do not know what to say" to somebody from that background; similarly, Yurdatapan has described the same phenomenon when he is in a gathering of the devout. These separations give rise to all manner of misunderstandings and invite us to exercise some humility whenever we are thinking about "the other." For a Western reader, Dilipak's account of the story of religion and state in Europe is not altogether recognizable, and it is plain that he is describing something out of his world. We can be sure that any account we give of religion and state in Muslim countries is likely to be just as off target.

The Freedom of Expression movement is going to succeed because Turkey is changing fast. The dramatic dynamism of the place will forcefully strike any visitor making the briefest visit. The state has held the lid down for decades, but the boiling media and the luxuriant growth of civil society are constantly pushing the envelope, and inexorably outwitting the slow-footed state. The State Security Court prosecutors are supposed to scan the media output for separatism, insults to the institutions of state, and "incitement to religious hatred" (code for Islamism), but their task becomes less realistic every day because there is just too much going on.

In fact, Dilipak reminds us that Turkey's history goes back long before 1923, to Ottoman society that, for all its many faults, pioneered ideas of tolerance, was a refuge for Jews expelled from Spain, and provided a secure home for the Yezidis, regarded as worshippers of Lucifer. The signs are good for tolerance in Turkey; despite all the bitter fighting in the Southeast, the propaganda, and the body bags, intercommunal violence between Turk and Kurd is more or less unheard of. In August 2002 the government recognized the right to broadcast and educate in minority languages. Those rights are still circumscribed by so many pettifogging limitations as to make them practically impossible to exercise. The newspapers are still full of absurdities. To cite one example, the local registrar of Mersin who in April 2003 refused to register the Kurdish name Berçem because it was "contrary to national culture and moral rules." Another is the fourteen-year-old currently on trial in Diyarbakır State Security Court charged with "incitement to racial violence" because he said, "Happy is he who says I am a Kurd" at morning assembly instead of the prescribed formula, "How happy he is who calls himself a Turk." But the principle that Turkey is multiethnic has finally been conceded. There are Turks in Turkey, and there are also Kurds, as well as Arabs and Laz and Roma and many others. Outraged politicians of the extreme right warned that the August 2002 legislation would provoke racial disharmony that would tear the country apart, but the Turkish public phlegmatically shrugged its shoulders—it always knew that the country was a rich ethnic and cultural mosaic.

It is a journalistic commonplace that the Turkish government is going to have to clean up its human rights performance in order to join the European Union. The European Union's requirement that Turkey must demonstrate "stability of institutions guaranteeing democracy, rule of law, human rights, and respect for minorities" has been a positive force, and recent Turkish governments have made some praiseworthy steps in that direction. But a careful look at the past decade shows that the really effective pressure for change has come not from Brussels but from Turkish teachers, doctors, lawyers, journalists, and ordinary citizens who do not want their children to be tortured or imprisoned, their government manipulated by ruthless criminal elements, or to be embarrassed by scandals like the prosecution of Yaşar Kemal, the grand old man of Turkish letters. Turkish society is establishing its own de facto pluralism that is a worthy model for imitation, not just by the Muslim world. This book is part of that process.

Jonathan Sugden
Human Rights Watch
London Office

BIOGRAPHIES

ŞANAR YURDATAPAN

The musician and human rights defender Şanar Yurdatapan was born in 1941 in Susurluk. His life in music began in 1958 when he and some friends studying at the Science Faculty of İstanbul University formed a band, the Comet Vocal Group. In 1965 he enrolled in the Turkish Workers Party (TIP) headed by M. Ali Aybar and took an active role until its dissolution in the 1971 military coup. In 1971 Şanar Yurdatapan, together with Attila Özdemiroğlu, established Turkey's first music production company, ŞAT Productions, in İstanbul. In this productive period of about eight years, Yurdatapan became known as a composer, lyricist, and arranger.

In 1974 he married Melike Demirağ, the lead actress in the film *Arkadaş* (*Friend*), for which Yurdatapan composed the music. Together they took part in the Turkish, Greek, and Cypriot Film Friendship Festival held in Cyprus in 1981. For this they received a summons from the military junta that had taken power again in Turkey in 1980. When they refused to return, the couple was stripped of their Turkish citizenship. Their involuntary exile lasted twelve years. They filled these long years by struggling for Turkish democracy. The husband and wife traveled around the world, from New York to Moscow and Mexico City to Sydney, giving concerts and attending political meetings.

After the 1991 elections there was a change in government that opened the way for the couple to return to Turkey. But as soon as Yurdatapan returned to Turkey, he was in trouble again—for shaving his head at a press conference he had organized as a gesture to expose and condemn a case of torture he had discovered.

In January 1995 the indictment of Yaşar Kemal by the State Security Court appalled thinking people in Turkey, and Yurdatapan became the spokesperson and coordinator of the Freedom of Expression Initiative, a civil disobedience movement that continues today.

In January 1996 Yurdatapan also became the spokesperson of the Unite for Peace Initiative, formed with the aim of putting an end to the undeclared war then going on in the Southeast of the country. The initiative sent many delegations to the war zone to monitor human rights violations and inform the public. Yurdatapan was arrested twice in the course of these activities, in the autumn of 1997 and in April 1998. On each occasion he was released at the first hearing and acquitted. However, when in 2002 he was sentenced to two months' imprisonment for a "thought crime," he volunteered to serve his sentence in one of the much-debated isolation cells in Kartal Special Type Prison. As the end of 2002 drew near, close to 80,000 people were taking part in the Freedom of Thought movement.

The most familiar of Yurdatapan's compositions are *Arkadaş* (*Friend*) and *İstanbul'da olmak* (*To Be in İstanbul*). His *Anatolia*, the first time a full symphony orchestra was set to accompany a *saz*, was first performed in 1985 in the Köln WDR Radio Hall, and then two years later in the famous Philharmonia Hall, with the Köln Philharmonic Orchestra, and recorded in the WDR studios.

Besides receiving Freedom of Thought awards from Mazlum-Der and the Contemporary Journalists' Association, in 2001 Yurdatapan received the Human Rights Watch's Hellman-Hammett Award and the Best Circumvention of Censorship Award from the Index on Censorship in 2002.

As well as his contributions to the *Freedom of Thought* series, he also wrote a book of humorous stories titled *Fatoş's Diary*.

ABDURRAHMAN DİLİPAK

Abdurrahman Dilipak was born in Haruniye, near Adana, in 1949. After graduating from İmam Hatip Okulu School, which specializes in religious education, first he registered in Arabic and Farsi philology classes, and then graduated from the Journalism High School. He has worked as a truck driver's assistant, an agricultural worker, an agricultural products trader, an electrical surveyor, a judo instructor, a publisher, an advertising copywriter, a journalist and a writer. He founded the Fetih Publishing House. He published or was on the administrative board of the *Adım, Hicret, Seriyye, Cuma, Cıngar,* and *Yeni Sanat* magazines. He was among the first members of the writing and publishing staff of the *Milli Gazette, Yeni Devir, Akit, Vakit,* and *Yeni Şefak* newspapers. He paints and produces TV programs. He has prepared and presented discussion and news commentary programs on TV channels Kanal D, Kanal 6, and Kanal 7. He is the director of the Copyrights Agency, a member of the selection board of *Who's Who in Turkey*, recipient of the Tolerance Medal (an award given by the Turkish Journalists and Writers' Trust), and a recipient of the Hellman-Hammett human rights award administered by Human Rights Watch. He was a founding member of Mazlum-Der (the Association for Solidarity with Oppressed People), a member of the Journalists' Association, the Press Council and Independent Consumers' Association, and a press consultant for MUSIAD (the Association for Muslim Employers and Industrialists) and other institutions. From 1978 to 1980 he served as a press consultant for the National Salvation Party. As a speaker, he has given hundreds of talks in Turkey and abroad. More than a hundred court actions have been brought against him for his writings and speeches. He is a unique entrepreneur who, together with Şanar Yurdatapan, participated in the Freedom of Thought Initiative. He has forty-three published works to his credit.

He is married and the father of four children.

ARON AJI

Born in İzmir, Turkey, Aron R. Aji is a professor of literature at Butler University in Indianapolis. His translations of works by Turkish authors Elif Shafak, Bilge Karasu, Latife Tekin, and Murathan Mungan have appeared in *Grand Street*. He has completed translations of two of Bilge Karasu's books: a novel, *Death in Troy*, which was published by City Lights in 2002, and a collection of short fiction, *The Garden of Migrant Cats*, for New Directions in 2003.

JONATHAN SUGDEN

Jonathan Sugden was born in 1954. He worked as a technical writer on industrial equipment and as a journalist writing on science and society before working to support communities of single homeless people in Coventry. He also set up a construction cooperative. In 1988, Sugden graduated from the School of Oriental and African Studies at London University and worked as a translator. From 1990 to 1999, he worked as Amnesty International's researcher on Turkey, Greece, and Cyprus. Since 1999, he has worked as Human Rights Watch's researcher on Turkey. Sugden works in London and lives in Hastings, England.